THE BEST MOVIE TRIVIA
AND
QUIZ BOOK EVER

THE BEST MOVIE TRIVIA AND QUIZ BOOK EVER

Malcolm Vance

Bonanza Books
New York

Designed and packaged by Tribeca Communications, Inc.

Copyright © 1982 by Tribeca Communications, Inc.

This 1982 edition is published by Bonanza Books,
distributed by Crown Publishers, Inc.

Manufactured in the United States of America

Library of Congress Cataloging in Publication Data

Vance, Malcolm.
  The best movie trivia and quiz book ever.

  1. Moving–pictures—Miscellanea.   I. Title.
PN1993.85.V29   791.43   82-1349
ISBN 0–517–364115   AACR2

h g f e d c b a

Dedicated to the ladies of my life:
Ethel, Randy, and Tracy.

Acknowledgments

The Best Movie Trivia and Quiz Book Ever, like its companion, *The Best TV Trivia and Quiz Book Ever*, was designed primarily for enjoyment. The author and his editors had fun planning the quizzes and in reminiscing throughout the trivia section. If a particular favorite film or star is missing, blame it on the author. *His* favorites are here and, in the words of that TV series, it's "Diff'rent Strokes" for diff'rent folks.

Grateful acknowledgment for their help goes to: Judie Annino, Bob Armour, David Cohn, Hal Haskell, Noreen Kremer, Jim Mann, my editors, Rowena McDade and Chuck Adams, and of course, my agent, Lewis Chambers.

Contents

Photo Quiz

There are 96 photos scattered throughout this book. Here you'll find pictures of many popular movie stars in addition to some less well-known actors and actresses. Test your knowledge of the movies by identifying the performers and answering the questions listed below. Answers to this photo quiz will be found at the back of the book, at the beginning of the answer section. Enjoy this quiz and the 111 others you'll find in the book.

1. Name this actress's 1977 movie which was nominated for 11 Academy Awards but failed to win a single Oscar.
2. For what 1954 movie did this performer do the singing for Edmund Purdom?
3. For what 1962 movie did this actress win the best actress award at the Cannes Film Festival?
4. What was this actress's first movie?
5. What was the surname of the Chicago physician who raised this star after the death of his parents? (It is the same name as the manager of the newspaper chain in his most famous movie.)
6. What was this actress's last movie?
7. What was this actress's last completed movie?
8. How many movies did this star make with Fred Astaire?
9. What famous lawyer did this actor portray in a 1960 movie? (Orson Welles had played the same man in a movie the preceding year.)
10. What animated 1968 movie featured the voices and music of these men?
11. Name the tough cop this actor has frequently portrayed in the movies.
12. Who is the actress daughter of these performers?
13. Name the movie.
14. What was this actor's role in *Gone With the Wind?*

15. In what famous 1939 movie did this actor have a comic role?
16. In what 1954 movie did this actor co-star with Kim Novak?
17. What was this actor's last movie?
18. In the 1948 screen production of what Shakespearean play did this actress appear; in what role?
19. What was this actor's first movie?
20. What was this actor's last movie?
21. Name the movie.
22. Name the movie.
23. In which movies did this actress co-star with John Wayne?
24. In what 1948 movie did this actress portray a waitress strangled by Ronald Colman?
25. Name the movie.
26. In what 1943 movie did this performer appear in his first acting role?
27. Name the movie.
28. Who was the first screen Tarzan?
29. Who was this performer's co-star in *Daddy Long Legs*?
30. In what 1938 Frank Capra movie did this actor have a featured role?
31. What Swedish director was this actress's mentor early in her career?
32. What was this actress's first movie?
33. What was the name of the character this actress played in *The Blue Angel*?
34. In what 1936 movie did this actress portray Florence Nightingale?
35. In what 1935 movie did this performer appear with W. C. Fields?
36. With what movie did this actor-director make his directorial debut?
37. Whose wife did this actress portray in the 1968 movie *Petulia*?
38. Name the movie.
39. Name the movie.
40. In what 1947 MGM musical comedy did this actor appear with June Allyson?
41. Who was this actress's male co-star in *The Stratton Story*?
42. What was this actor's first movie?
43. What was this actress's first movie?
44. Who directed the 1954 version of *A Star is Born*?

45. Who is the photographer-secret service agent this actor portrays on the screen?
46. In what 1976 movie did this actress make a cameo appearance?
47. In what 1941 movie did this actress appear with Sonja Henie?
48. What was the name of the character this actress played in *All About Eve*?
49. What Shakespearean character has this actor played in the movies?
50. What was this actress's first movie?
51. Who directed the 1936 movie *Sylvia Scarlett* in which this actor co-starred with Katharine Hepburn?
52. What was the name of the character this actress played in *Casablanca*?
53. Name the movie and the author of the book on which it is based.
54. In what 1935 film rendition of a Shakespearean play was this actor a featured player?
55. In what 1958 Orson Welles movie did this actress make a cameo appearance?
56. In what 1958 Anthony Mann adult western did this actor star?
57. For what movie did this performer receive an Academy Award nomination?
58. Who wrote the novel on which this movie is based?
59. In what 1929 Ronald Colman movie did this actress establish herself as a screen talent?
60. What was this actress's Oscar winning role?
61. In what 1942 movie did this actress play a character named Randy Monaghan? (Her co-star was Ronald Reagan.)
62. Name the movie.
63. Name the movie.
64. What 1959 Howard Hawks western featured this actor, John Wayne, Dean Martin, and Ricky Nelson?
65. Name the movie.
66. How many Academy Awards has this actor won?
67. Who played this performer's playwright wife in *Critic's Choice*?
68. What director did Victor Fleming replace on this movie?
69. Name the movie.
70. Name the movie.

13

71. Name the movie.
72. Name the movie.
73. Name the movie.
74. What Jules Verne character did this actor portray in a 1956 movie?
75. Who was the title character this actress played in a ten movie series of comedy adventures from 1939 to 1947?
76. Name the movie.
77. Name the movie.
78. To what President of the United States was this actor-director an advisor?
79. What is this actress's real name? (In 1939 she used it in her first two movies.)
80. What 1950 Alfred Hitchcock movie did this actor appear in with Jane Wyman, Marlene Dietrich, and Michael Wilding?
81. Name the movie.
82. Name the movie.
83. What was the name of the character this actress played in a 1951 movie version of a Tennessee Williams's play?
84. What was this actress's first movie?
85. Name the movie.
86. In what 1964 movie did this actor play a character named Alfred Doolittle?
87. Name the movie.
88. In what movie did this actor-director make his acting debut?
89. What was this actor's first movie?
90. Name the movie.
91. What was the first movie of the actor on the left?
92. What was this actress's role in a 1974 Richard Lester movie that she re-created in another film the following year? Name the movies.
93. What was the role of the actor on the right in *The Spirit of St. Louis*?
94. Name the movies in which this actor starred.
95. In the screen version of which Tennessee Williams play did this actor star?
96. For what 1957 movie was this actress nominated for an Oscar?

THE BEST MOVIE TRIVIA
AND
QUIZ BOOK EVER

Photo 1

NAME DROPPERS (1)

Listed below on the left are stars whose real names are listed on the right. Match the stars with their names.

1.	Rita Hayworth	A.	Lucille Langhanke
2.	Al Jolson	B.	Lucille LeSueur
3.	Merle Oberon	C.	Lucille Collier
4.	Cary Grant	D.	Reginald Truscott-Jones
5.	Lauren Bacall	E.	Archibald Leach
6.	Joan Crawford	F.	Margarita Cansino
7.	Ginger Rogers	G.	Merle Johnson, Jr.
8.	Mary Astor	H.	Estelle Thompson
9.	Edward G. Robinson	I.	William Henry Pratt
10.	Jean Arthur	J.	Betty Perske
11.	Ray Milland	K.	Marjorie Reed
12.	Richard Burton	L.	Virginia McMath
13.	Boris Karloff	M.	Emmanuel Goldenberg
14.	Ann Miller	N.	Gladys Greene
15.	Anne Bancroft	O.	Asa Yoelson
16.	William Holden	P.	Joe Yule, Jr.
17.	Troy Donahue	Q.	Jane Peters
18.	Martha Raye	R.	Anna Italiano
19.	Carole Lombard	S.	William Beedle
20.	Mickey Rooney	T.	Richard Jenkins, Jr.

NAME DROPPERS (2)

Listed below on the left are stars whose real names are listed on the right. Match the stars with their real names.

1. Joan Fontaine	A. James Stewart
2. Vera Miles	B. Maria von Losch
3. Roy Rogers	C. Tula Finklea
4. Mario Lanza	D. Roy Scherer, Jr.
5. Shirley Booth	E. David Kominski
6. Judy Garland	F. Benjamin Kubelsky
7. Stewart Granger	G. Eunice Quedens
8. George Burns	H. Joan de Havilland
9. Jack Benny	I. Gwyllyn Ford
10. Kay Francis	J. Thelma Ford
11. Marlene Dietrich	K. Alexandra Zuck
12. Rock Hudson	L. Frances Gumm
13. Eve Arden	M. Francesca Gerber
14. Glenn Ford	N. Alfred Cocozza
15. Cyd Charisse	O. Jeanette Morrison
16. Mitzi Gaynor	P. Marion Morrison
17. Danny Kaye	Q. Vera Ralston
18. Sandra Dee	R. Katherine Gibbs
19. John Wayne	S. Nathan Birnbaum
20. Janet Leigh	T. Leonard Slye

Photo 2

MALE CALL

Identify the actors who played the title roles in the following films.

1. Johnny Eager
2. For Pete's Sake
3. Fitzwilly
4. Along Came Jones
5. Anthony Adverse
6. Marty
7. Tony Rome
8. Cool Hand Luke
9. Gunga Din
10. The Eddy Duchin Story
11. Popi
12. Birdman of Alcatraz
13. Arthur
14. Luther (1974)
15. Butley
16. The Lemon Drop Kid
17. Gunn
18. The Godfather
19. The Cardinal
20. The Graduate

WHO WAS THAT LADY? (1)

Identify the actresses who played the title roles in the following films.

1. Rosie
2. Myra Breckenridge
3. Lady Caroline Lamb
4. Vicki
5. Penelope
6. Claudine
7. Jessica
8. Judith
9. Modesty Blaise
10. Foxy Brown
11. Mame
12. Rachel, Rachel
13. Georgy Girl
14. Irma La Douce
15. That Lady
16. Gypsy
17. Ada
18. Buona Sera, Mrs. Campbell
19. Roxie Hart
20. That Forsyte Woman

19

WHO WAS THAT LADY? (2)

Identify the actresses who played the title roles in the following films.

1. Two Mules for Sister Sara
2. The Singing Nun
3. Tell Me That You Love Me, Junie Moon
4. Little Miss Marker
5. Baby Doll
6. The Lieutenant Wore Skirts
7. The Miracle Worker
8. From the Mixed-up Files of Mrs. Basil E. Frankweiler
9. All About Eve
10. The Romantic Englishwoman
11. Diary of a Mad Housewife
12. A Countess from Hong Kong
13. Lady in the Dark
14. A Big Hand for the Little Lady
15. The Bride Wore Black
16. The Bride Wore Red
17. The Bride Wore Boots
18. Lady from Shanghai
19. Lady of Burlesque
20. The Americanization of Emily

ROYAL TREATMENT (1)

Identify the stars who played royalty in the following films.

1. Elizabeth I in *Mary, Queen of Scots*
2. Henry VIII in *The Private Life of Henry VIII*
3. Richard III in *Richard III*
4. Richard the Lion-Hearted in *The Crusades*
5. Elizabeth I in *Young Bess*
6. Eleanor of Aquitane in *A Lion in Winter*
7. Eleanor of Aquitane in *Becket*
8. Elizabeth I in *The Virgin Queen*
9. Henry V in *Henry V*
10. Richard III in *Tower of London*
11. Elizabeth I in *Fire Over England*
12. Henry VIII in *Anne of the Thousand Days*
13. Anne Boleyn in *Anne of the Thousand Days*
14. Anne Boleyn in *The Private Life of Henry VIII*
15. Henry II in *Becket*
16. Henry II in *A Lion in Winter*
17. Henry VIII in *A Man for All Seasons*
18. Elizabeth I in *The Sea Hawk*
19. Elizabeth I in *The Private Lives of Elizabeth and Essex*
20. Henry VIII in *Young Bess*

ROYAL TREATMENT (2)

Identify the stars who played royalty in the following films.

1. Queen Christina in *The Abdication*
2. Mary of Scotland in *Mary, Queen of Scots*
3. Louis IV in *Becket*
4. Louis XV in *Marie Antoinette*
5. Alexandra in *Rasputin and the Empress*
6. Queen Christina in *Queen Christina*
7. Catherine the Great in *The Scarlet Empress*
8. Catherine the Great in *A Royal Scandal*
9. Caesar in *Caesar and Cleopatra*
10. Alexander the Great in *Alexander the Great*
11. George III in *Beau Brummell*
12. Marie Antoinette in *Marie Antoinette*
13. Louis XVI in *Marie Antoinette*
14. Caesar in *Julius Caesar*
15. Mary of Scotland in *Mary of Scotland*
16. Alexandra in *Nicholas and Alexandra*
17. Napoleon in *Desiree*
18. Napoleon in *Conquest*
19. King Herod in *Salome*
20. Empress Josephine in *Desiree*

KATE

Listed below are plots of Katharine Hepburn films. Identify them.

1. Small-town girl falls in love with wealthy man and tries to impress him. Directed by George Stevens.
2. Midwestern spinster falls in love with a traveling con-man. Directed by Joseph Anthony.
3. Teacher on vacation in Europe falls in love with a married Italian. Directed by David Lean.
4. Oldest sister sacrifices young love and wealth to a younger one, finally finds success as writer and love of an older man. Directed by George Cukor.
5. Young aspiring actress falls for philandering producer, finally realizes earnest playwright is the true love. Directed by Lowell Sherman.
6. Spirited Scottish lass falls in love with a man of the cloth and pretends to be a gypsy. Directed by Richard Wallace.
7. Group of ne'er-do-well trouping actors encounters romance and troubles on the road, with Hepburn disguised as a boy. Directed by George Cukor.
8. Anthropologist gets involved with dizzy heiress and her pet leopard, loses his self-aplomb but finds love. Directed by Howard Hawks.
9. Non-conformist runs headlong into stuffy New York society family, but finds his match in spirited younger daughter. Directed by George Cukor.
10. Newly released from a mental institution, a father finally gets to know his grown daughter. Directed by John Farrow.
11. Missionary spinster in the Congo is forced to seek refuge with gin-guzzling riverboat captain during World War I. Directed by John Huston.
12. Female journalist and leading sports writer marry and parry a battle of wits and pride. Directed by George Stevens.
13. Inventor and Washington widow marry for convenience during World War II and fall in love. Directed by Harold S. Buquet.
14. Wealthy Southern matriarch wants neurosurgeon to perform lobotomy on her niece to suppress details of son's death. Directed by Joseph L. Mankiewicz.
15. Eccentric Parisienne and her off-beat friends offer bizarre solutions to world problems. Directed by Bryan Forbes.
16. An English king, who has imprisoned his wife, deliberates over his successor on a fateful Christmas Eve. Directed by Anthony Harvey.

Photo 3

17. Detailed portrait of 1910 family: dope-addicted mother, pompous father, alcoholic older son, and tubercular younger son. Directed by Sidney Lumet.
18. TV researcher almost loses her job because of efficiency expert and his computer. Directed by Walter Lang.
19. Socialite is beset with troubles from her first husband on the eve of her second marriage. Directed by George Cukor.
20. Judge and wife face problems when daughter announces her engagement to a black doctor. Directed by Stanley Kramer.

BETTE

Listed below are the plots of Bette Davis films. Identify them.

1. Two sisters, both former actresses, one is a cripple at the mercy of her demented sister. Directed by Robert Aldrich.
2. Twin sisters bear a long-time grudge over a man; the evil one is murdered by the good one who tries to take over the other's life. Directed by Paul Henreid.
3. Twin sisters, in love with same man; evil one is drowned after marrying the man and good one tries to lead her life. Directed by Curtis Bernhardt.
4. Widow teams up with ex-thief to rob bank that dispossessed her to "liberate money for worthwhile causes." Directed by Gerd Oswald.
5. Aged and demented recluse is forced by sinister cousin to relive past horrors that brought on her dementia. Directed by Robert Aldrich.
6. Devoted schoolmistress in Welsh mining town sponsors young miner who shows sparks of genius. Directed by Irving Rapper.
7. Ugly duckling spinster blossoms in hands of psychiatrist, falls in love with married man, and helps his ugly duckling daughter. Directed by Irving Rapper.
8. Southern matriarch joins her greedy brothers in shady business deal, allowing her husband to die of a heart attack for his money. Directed by William Wyler.
9. Southern belle who goes too far to make her fiancé jealous, later atones when he contracts yellow fever. Directed by William Wyler.
10. Two female novelists in a love/hate friendship over many years. Directed by Vincent Sherman.
11. Unwed mother gives up daughter to married cousin, lives in the shadow of daughter's life as spinster aunt. Directed by Edmund Goulding.
12. Society belle marries Jewish financier for his money, later spurns him and grows old trying to retain her youth and beauty. Directed by Vincent Sherman.
13. Heiress is kidnapped by flier (hired by her father) on the eve of her elopement to a band leader. Directed by William Keighley.
14. Evil woman steals her sister's husband, drives him to suicide, then accidentally kills a child with her car and blames it on black servant. Directed by John Huston.
15. Famous stage star helps a young unknown who sets out to usurp her roles and her lover. Directed by Joseph L. Mankiewicz.
16. Oscar-winning has-been is helped from alcoholism by former co-star. Directed by Stuart Heisler.

Photo 4

17. Bored wife of small-town doctor commits adultery and murder in her attempt to escape her environs. Directed by King Vidor.
18. Bronx housewife and husband battle continuously over daughter's upcoming wedding plans. Directed by Richard Brooks.
19. Head-strong heiress, dying of a brain tumor, falls in love with and marries her doctor. Directed by Edmund Goulding.
20. Plantation owner's wife shoots her lover, then contrives with her lawyer to prove her "innocence." Directed by William Wyler.

ORSON

Listed below are the plots of Orson Welles films. Identify them.

1. Spy drama of World War II about the smuggling of munitions into Turkey, with Welles as Colonel Haki, chief of police in Istanbul. Directed by Welles.
2. Escaped Nazi war criminal settles as a college professor in small Connecticut town. Directed by Welles.
3. Man listed as dead in war returns with a new face to find his wife remarried with a family. Directed by Irving Pichel.
4. A woman hires an unemployed sailor to abet her in a plot to murder her crippled husband. Directed by Welles.
5. Pulp-writer undertakes a personal manhunt in post-war Vienna for mystery man. Directed by Carol Reed.
6. Mexican-American narcotics detective and his new bride get involved in a murder frame-up. Directed by Welles.
7. Charlatan Cagliostro seeks to rise in power in 18th-century Italy. Directed by Phil Rosen.
8. Young governess falls in love with moody owner of mansion whose secret is an insane wife. Directed by Robert Stevenson.
9. Young adventurer in 13th-century Italy defies the all-powerful Cesare Borgia. Directed by Henry King.
10. Eccentric European financier hires a young American to find out about people from his own past. Directed by Welles.
11. Domineering Southern father matches wits with a wandering handy-man who wants to marry his daughter. Directed by Martin Ritt.
12. A group of adventurers, opportunists, and exploiters join an idealist in his efforts to provide a sanctuary for elephants in Africa. Directed by John Huston.
13. Fictionalized version of the Loeb-Leopold murder case, with Welles as a Clarence Darrow-ish character. Directed by Richard Fleisher.
14. Rancher responsible for a helper's death is undone by earnest sheriff probing the murder. Directed by Jack Arnold.
15. Newspaper tycoon's rise to unprecedented power. Directed by Welles.
16. Straightlaced skipper of ferry boat parries wits with a drunken Austrian on a trip to Macao. Directed by Lewis Gilbert.
17. Puzzling tale of young man in a nameless country who is arrested for a crime that is never explained to him. Directed by Welles.
18. Grand Hotel-ish plot set in London airport of passengers about to embark on a flight. Directed by Anthony Asquith.

19. Boxer/adventurer, hired to tutor rich widow's son, becomes a pawn of Fascist millionaire intent on retaking Europe. Directed by John Guillerman.

20. Episodic film recounting events in the life of Marco Polo. Directed by Denys De La Patelliere.

Photo 5

JOAN

Listed below are plots of Joan Crawford films. Identify them.

1. Middle-aged woman marries younger man and discovers he is mentally ill and already married. Directed by Robert Aldrich.
2. Petty thief with scarred face is nearly involved in murder plot but is redeemed when she undergoes plastic surgery. Directed by George Cukor.
3. Southern matriarch dominates the lives of all around her while illicitly involved with estate foreman. Directed by Ranald MacDougall.
4. Waitress builds chain of restaurants but loses control of her ungrateful daughter. Directed by Michael Curtiz.
5. Woman in love with married man finally settles for returning veteran who loves her. Directed by Otto Preminger.
6. Woman adopts new religion, nearly loses her husband and daughter by her short-sightedness. Directed by George Cukor.
7. Perfume salesgirl steals society matron's husband, but her philandering proves her undoing. Directed by George Cukor.
8. Western gambling house owner matches wits with rancher-woman to gain control of town. Directed by Nicholas Ray.
9. Carnival dancer in small town finds love and gets mixed up in local dirty politics. Directed by Michael Curtiz.
10. Society woman becomes patron of gifted violinist, falls in love with him, but kills herself rather than stand in his way. Directed by Jean Negulesco.
11. Wife's mania for cleanliness and perfection drives away her family and friends. Directed by Vincent Sherman.
12. Escapees from Devil's Island, with one woman, are strangely touched by Christ-like man in their midst. Directed by Frank Borzage.
13. Ruthless Broadway musical comedy star falls in love with blind pianist-accompanist. Directed by Charles Walters.
14. Ex-burlesque beauty becomes top Broadway musical comedy star and is loved by millionaire playboy and her director. Directed by Robert Z. Leonard.
15. Prostitute finds redemption through evangelist, who then seduces her and commits suicide. Directed by Lewis Milestone.
16. Wealthy American in Nazi Germany aids downed flier by having him pose as her chauffeur. Directed by Jules Dassin.
17. American couple on honeymoon in Europe at outbreak of World War II become Allied spies. Directed by Richard Thorpe.
18. Famous playwright marries man who then plots to kill her. Directed by David Miller.

19. Woman authoress who loves married man is forced to meet his wife. Directed by Robert Z. Leonard.
20. Hotel stenographer gets involved with German industrialist and a dying man. Directed by Edmund Goulding.

29   Photo 6

MARILYN

Listed below are plots of Marilyn Monroe films. Identify them.

1. Two musicians who witness gangland killing join an all-girl orchestra to elude pursuers. Directed by Billy Wilder.
2. American entertainer in London has romance with foreign nobleman, heir to his country's throne. Directed by Laurence Olivier.
3. Millionaire wants to stop a show that is spoofing him until he meets the leading lady. Directed by George Cukor.
4. Divorcee in Reno falls in love with aging cowboy involved in capturing wild mustangs for dog food factory. Directed by John Huston.
5. Night club singer is romanced by youngest son of famed vaudevillian family. Directed by Walter Lang.
6. Saloon singer hires Western farmer to help her track down her husband who has deserted her. Directed by Otto Preminger.
7. Three New York gals pool resources to capture wealthy husbands. Directed by Jean Negulesco.
8. Two girls from Midwest have a fling in Paris and find romance. Directed by Howard Hawks.
9. Faithless wife plots to kill husband, but is murdered by him instead. Directed by Henry Hathaway.
10. Episodic film, with Monroe as a streetwalker accosted by a derelict in her episode. Directed by Henry Koster.
11. Scientist discovers rejuvenation serum, injects himself, his wife, his secretary, and his boss. Directed by Howard Hawks.
12. Singer is relentlessly pursued by enamored, brash cowboy till she succumbs to his charms. Directed by Joshua Logan.
13. Summer-bachelor is tempted by girl upstairs and fantasizes a romance. Directed by Billy Wilder.
14. Mistress of crooked lawyer betrays him in well-laid plans for grand robbery. Directed by John Huston.
15. Ex-G.I. and wife buy an apartment building; wife is jealous of ex-WAC friend of husband. Directed by Joseph Newman.
16. Psychotic baby-sitter is saved from killing herself and her ward by boyfriend of singer. Directed by Roy Baker.
17. Episodic film about wedded couples who discover their nuptials were illegal due to a technicality. Directed by Edmund Goulding.
18. Bored wife of good-natured fisherman has affair with his best friend. Directed by Fritz Lang.
19. Married couple, planning a friendly divorce, try other partners first, but are reconciled. Directed by Richard Sale.
20. Daughter of burlesque queen pursues same career, marries rich admirer. Directed by Phil Karlson.

Photo 7

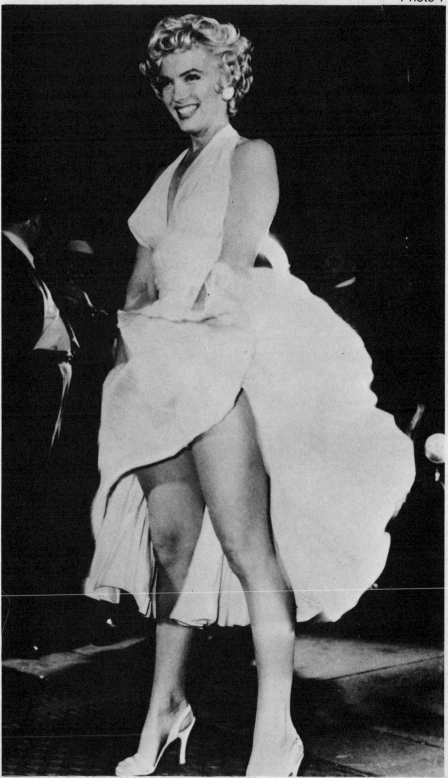

GINGER

Listed below are plots of Ginger Rogers films. Identify them.

1. Famed psychiatrist tries to straighten out the lives of his patients and gets in trouble with his own affairs. Directed by Nunnally Johnson.
2. Divorcee, on second marriage, tries to reestablish an understanding with her resentful daughter of first marriage. Directed by Edmund Goulding.
3. Adventures of two lady corset-sellers in the old West. Directed by Arthur Lubin.
4. Ex-convict is used by police as bait to trap a crooked cop. Directed by Phil Karlson.
5. Remake of *Grand Hotel*, with Ginger in the Garbo role, playing a Hollywood movie star. Directed by Robert Z. Leonard.
6. Fictionalized version of Dolly Madison's life, including a romance with Aaron Burr. Directed by Frank Borzage.
7. Fashion magazine editor undergoes psychoanalysis in order to straighten out her unhappy life. Directed by Mitchell Leisen.
8. Convict on Christmas leave falls in love with a mentally disturbed soldier. Directed by William Dieterle.
9. Young girl jilts several men at the altar until her dream lover, a fireman, finally materializes. Directed by Don Hartman.
10. Older Broadway star finally realizes she is too old to play ingenue roles, allows writer to cast young girl. Directed by Irving Rapper.
11. Female attorney marries, then divorces Western cowboy star, but comes to his defense in a criminal case. Directed by Richard Whorf.
12. Show business couple spat, split, she flops as a dramatic actress, and they reunite. Directed by Charles Walters.
13. Two members of a jury, both married to others, fall in love during a murder trial. Directed by Bretaigne Windust.
14. Two sisters in the South; one witnesses a Klan killing and is terrorized by her brother-in-law, a member. Directed by Stuart Heisler.
15. Silent-screen star tries to get former co-star, now a sedate college professor, to cash in on their old films, now on TV. Directed by Claude Binyon.
16. Wealthy heiress shares room with dancer in a rooming house for aspiring actresses. Directed by Gregory La Cava.
17. Secretary marries Philadelphia socialite, marriage is annulled, she bears his child and eventually settles for earnest young doctor. Directed by Sam Wood.

Photo 8

18. Flapper dancer confesses to a killing to gain publicity for her career. Directed by William Wellman.
19. Working girl disguises herself as twelve year old to save train fare, gets involved with a boys' military school. Directed by Billy Wilder.
20. Clerk in store discovers abandoned baby, is mistaken for the mother, with son of store-owner suspected as father. Directed by Garson Kanin.

SPENCER

Listed below are the plots of Spencer Tracy films. Identify them.

1. Group of unrelated people try to find hidden money of dead gangster under the watchful eye of detective. Directed by Stanley Kramer.
2. Judge and wife are confronted with problems when daughter announces her engagement to a black doctor. Directed by Stanley Kramer.
3. U. S. judge presides over German war-criminal trials in post-W. W. II Berlin. Directed by Stanley Kramer.
4. Fictionalized version of famous Scopes "Monkey Trial." Directed by Stanley Kramer.
5. Fictionalized version of life of Irish Boston mayor, based loosely on Mayor James Curley. Directed by John Ford.
6. Aging fisherman's daily battle with the elements. Directed by John Sturges.
7. One-armed veteran uncovers shady dealings in Western town. Directed by John Sturges.
8. Western patriarch fights to control his cattle empire and hold his family together. Directed by Edward Dmytryk.
9. Farmer-rancher's wife has illegitimate son by family lawyer. Directed by Ella Kazan.
10. Aging judge tries to keep pace with young wife in small town. Directed by George Sidney.
11. Presidential candidate is helped by his estranged wife and fights for his integrity in world of cut-throat politicians. Directed by Frank Capra.
12. British businessman and alcoholic wife discover they drove their son to suicide. Directed by George Cukor.
13. Husband-wife lawyers in a battle of the sexes find themselves on opposite sides of same "crime of passion" case. Directed by George Cukor.
14. Dead flier returns to earth to help former fiancée and her new love, an inexperienced flier. Directed by Victor Fleming.
15. Irascible father in Massachusetts small town is convinced to allow daughter to pursue an acting career. Directed by George Cukor.
16. Aggravated father goes through the familiar pangs of his daughter's wedding. Directed by Vincente Minnelli.
17. California fishing community is led by a happy-go-lucky Mexican-American. Directed by Victor Fleming.
18. Reporter investigating death of a beloved politician unveils Fascist plot by same. Directed by George Cukor.

19. Working girl becomes fashion model, marries wealthy man, but is haunted by her past. Directed by Frank Borzage.
20. Innocent bystander is almost lynched by mob, makes his brother and his sweetheart avenge his "death." Directed by Fritz Lang.

Photo 9

GOOD TIMING

Listed below are the stars of films whose titles contain the words "night" and/or "day." Identify the films.

1. Peter O'Toole, Omar Sharif, Tom Courtenay, Donald Pleasance, Joanna Pettet.
2. Jacqueline Bisset, Jean-Pierre Leaud, Francois Truffaut, Jean-Pierre Aumont.
3. Robert Mitchum, Shelley Winters, Lillian Gish, Peter Graves.
4. Spencer Tracy, Robert Ryan, Anne Francis.
5. John Lennon, Paul McCartney, George Harrison, Ringo Starr.
6. Cary Grant, Alexis Smith, Monty Woolley, Jane Wyman, Mary Martin.
7. Robert Mitchum, Anne Heywood, Dan O'Herlihy, Richard Harris.
8. Katharine Hepburn, Ralph Richardson, Dean Stockwell.
9. Albert Finney, Susan Hampshire, Mona Washbourne, Sheila Hancock.
10. Al Pacino, John Cazale, James Broderick, Charles Durning, Chris Sarandon.
11. Jason Robards, Britt Ekland, Norman Wisdom, Forrest Tucker, Bert Lahr.
12. Jack Lemmon, Lee Remick, Charles Bickford, Jack Klugman.
13. Tyrone Power, Joan Blondell, Colleen Gray, Helen Walker, Mike Mazurki.
14. Marx Brothers, Allan Jones, Maureen O'Sullivan, Margaret Dumont.
15. Marx Brothers, Allan Jones, Kitty Carlisle, Margaret Dumont.
16. Richard Burton, Ava Gardner, Deborah Kerr, Sue Lyon, Grayson Hall.
17. Dirk Bogarde, Charlotte Rampling, Isa Miranda.
18. Barbara Stanwyck, Robert Taylor, Lloyd Bochner, Rochelle Hudson.
19. Grace Moore, Tullio Carminati, Lyle Talbot.
20. Michael Rennie, Patricia Neal, Hugh Marlowe, Sam Jaffe.

Photo 10

VERBATIM

Listed below are some memorable lines from movies. Identify the films.

1. "Mother of God, is this the end of Rico?"
2. "Do me a favor, Harry—drop dead!"
3. "My mother thanks you, my father thanks you, my sister thanks you, and I thank you."
4. "Kill! Kill for the love of Kali!"
5. ". . . et ceterah, et ceterah, et ceterah!"
6. "Can't wipe us out. Can't lick us. We'll go on forever. 'Cause we're the people."
7. "How do you live? How do you get by?" "I steal!"
8. "I'll live to see you—all of you—hang from the highest yard arm in the British fleet!"
9. "Fred C. Dobbs don't say nothin' he don't mean."
10. "I'm still big. It's the pictures that got small."
11. "Hello, gorgeous!"
12. "Behold the walls of Jericho! Maybe not as thick as the ones Joshua blew down with his trumpet, but a lot safer."
13. "Is that a gun you've got in your pants pocket or are you really glad to see me?"
14. "Randy, Randy—where's the rest of me . . .?"
15. "I'm in trouble, George—bad trouble."
16. "If you want anything, just whistle. You know how to whistle, don't you, Steve? You just pucker up your lips and blow."
17. "Why should I cry? It was Claude Daigle got killed, not me!"
18. "Nurse, will you take your clammy hands off my chair. You have the touch of a love-starved cobra!"
19. "I could have had class. I could have been a contender."
20. "It was Beauty killed the Beast."

BORN AGAIN

The films listed below on the left are remakes, sequels, or spin-offs of the films on the right. Match the films.

1. *The Black Bird*	A.	*Our Man Flint*
2. *The Slipper and the Rose*	B.	*Grand Hotel*
3. *You Can't Run Away from It*	C.	*Harper*
4. *What's Up, Doc?*	D.	*A Fistful of Dollars*
5. *Ten Little Indians*	E.	*Lady for a Day*
6. *The Heretic*	F.	*The Glass Slipper*
7. *Lady in Cement*	G.	*Auntie Mame*
8. *Weekend at the Waldorf*	H.	*The Exorcist*
9. *A Shot in the Dark*	I.	*The Maltese Falcon*
10. *Farewell, My Lovely*	J.	*Bringing Up Baby*
11. *Stolen Hours*	K.	*And Then There Were None*
12. *In Like Flint*	L.	*The Silencers*
13. *The Drowning Pool*	M.	*It Happened One Night*
14. *A Pocketful of Miracles*	N.	*The Women*
15. *Magnum Force*	O.	*Murder, My Sweet*
16. *The Front Page*	P.	*Dark Victory*
17. *The Opposite Sex*	Q.	*Dirty Harry*
18. *For a Few Dollars More*	R.	*Tony Rome*
19. *The Ambushers*	S.	*His Girl Friday*
20. *Mame*	T.	*The Pink Panther*

Photo 11

Photo 12

MIXED DOUBLES

The stars of the films listed below had personal, as well as professional connections. Identify the couples.

1. The Taming of the Shrew
2. Sierra
3. Houdini
4. The Reformer and the Redhead
5. I Want a Divorce
6. The Illustrated Man
7. The Savage Is Loose
8. Breakout
9. All the Fine Young Cannibals
10. From the Terrace
11. The Tiger Makes Out
12. Bundle of Joy
13. Room for One More
14. Faces
15. A Distant Trumpet
16. Ladies in Retirement
17. Women's Prison
18. Homecoming
19. The Bride Wore Red
20. Footsteps in the Fog

COUNT DOWN

Listed below are the stars of films whose titles contain a number. Identify the films.

1. Barbara Barrie, Bernie Hamilton, Rich Mulligan.
2. Walter Matthau, Robert Shaw, Martin Balsam, Tony Roberts.
3. Rosalind Russell, Jack Hawkins, Maximilian Schell.
4. Oliver Reed, Raquel Welch, Richard Chamberlain, Michael York, Frank Finlay.
5. James Cagney, Arline Francis, Horst Buchholz, Pamela Tiffin.
6. Patricia Neal, Ruth Roman, Eleanor Parker.
7. Charlton Heston, Yul Brynner, Edward G. Robinson, Anne Baxter.
8. Shirley MacLaine, Robert Mitchum.
9. Roy Scheider, Tony Lo Bianco, Larry Haines.
10. Burt Lancaster, Kirk Douglas, Fredric March, Ava Gardner, Edmond O'Brien.
11. Jack Nicholson, Karen Black, Susan Anspach.
12. Audrey Hepburn, Albert Finney.
13. Robert Redford, Faye Dunaway.
14. Elizabeth Taylor, Laurence Harvey, Eddie Fisher, Dina Merrill.
15. Jane Powell, Ricardo Montalban, Debbie Reynolds, Carleton Carpenter.
16. Clifton Webb, Myrna Loy, Jeanne Crain.
17. Jack Nicholson, Louise Fletcher, William Redfield.
18. Nichol Williamson, Alan Arkin, Robert Duvall, Vanessa Redgrave, Laurence Olivier.
19. James Cagney, Annabella, Richard Conte, Sam Jaffe.
20. Cissy Spacek, Shelley Duvall, Janice Rule, Robert Forster.

41   Photo 13

TO BE CONTINUED . . .

The stars listed on the left have played the serial heroes and heroines listed on the right. Match the stars with the serials.

1.	Buster Crabbe	A.	*Perils of Pauline* (1914)
2.	Ruth Roman	B.	*Perils of Pauline* (1934)
3.	Phyllis Coates	C.	*The Phantom*
4.	Kane Richmond	D.	*The Tiger Woman*
5.	Ralph Byrd	E.	*Flash Gordon*
6.	Kay Aldridge	F.	*Jungle Girl*
7.	George Reeves	G.	*Jungle Queen*
8.	Joan Woodbury	H.	*Mandrake the Magician*
9.	Tom Tyler	I.	*Captain America*
10.	Pearl White	J.	*Adventures of Red Ryder*
11.	Warren Hull	K.	*Perils of Nyoka*
12.	Adrian Booth	L.	*Panther Girl of the Congo*
13.	Allan Lane	M.	*The Shadow*
14.	Evalyn Knapp	N.	*Brick Bradford*
15.	Dick Purcell	O.	*Brenda Starr, Reporter*
16.	Ruth Roland	P.	*Superman* in *Atom Man vs. Superman*
17.	Victor Jory	Q.	*King of the Royal Mounted*
18.	Linda Stirling	R.	*Ruth of the Rockies*
19.	Don "Red" Barry	S.	*Daughter of Don Q*
20.	Frances Gifford	T.	*Dick Tracy*

Photo 14

HAIR RAISERS

Listed below are the stars of well-known horror films. Identify the films.

1. Boris Karloff, Colin Clive, Mae Clarke, John Boles, Dwight Frye.
2. Lon Chaney, Jr., Claude Rains, Ralph Bellamy, Warren William, Maria Ouspenskaya.
3. Lionel Barrymore, Jean Hersholt, Bela Lugosi.
4. Bela Lugosi, David Manners, Helen Chandler, Dwight Frye.
5. Boris Karloff, Lon Chaney, Jr., John Carradine, J. Carroll Naish, Lionel Atwill.
6. Bela Lugosi, Sidney Fox, Leon Ames.
7. Lon Chaney, Jr., Bela Lugosi, Patric Knowles, Ilona Massey, Maria Ouspenskaya.
8. Richard Carlson, Julie Adams, Richard Denning, Antonio Moreno.
9. Kenneth Tobey, Margaret Sheridan, James Arness.
10. Boris Karloff, Elsa Lanchester, Colin Clive, Valerie Hobson, Ernest Thesiger.
11. Michael Landon, Yvonne Lime, Whit Brissell, Guy Williams.
12. Claude Rains, Susannah Foster, Nelson Eddy, Edgar Barrier, Jane Farrar.
13. Fredric March, Miriam Hopkins, Rose Hobart, Holmes Herbert.
14. Vincent Price, David Hedison, Patricia Owens, Herbert Marshall.
15. Boris Karloff, Zita Johann, David Manners, Bramwell Fletcher.
16. Burt Lancaster, Michael York, Barbara Carrera, Richard Basehart.
17. Vincent Price, Frank Lovejoy, Phyllis Kirk, Carolyn Jones, Charles Bronson.
18. Boris Karloff, Ellen Drew, Marc Cramer, Kathleen Emery, Helene Thimig.
19. Vincent Price, Mark Damon, Myrna Fahey, Harry Ellerbe.
20. Boris Karloff, Bela Lugosi, David Manners, Jacqueline Wells, Henry Armetta.

Photo 15

43

S.O.S.

Listed below are the stars of "disaster" films. Identify the films.

1. Charlton Heston, Ava Gardner, Genevieve Bujold, Lorne Greene, George Kennedy.
2. Paul Newman, Steve McQueen, William Holden, Faye Dunaway, Fred Astaire.
3. Gene Hackman, Ernest Borgnine, Shelley Winters, Red Buttons, Carol Lynley.
4. Clark Gable, Jeanette MacDonald, Spencer Tracy, Jack Holt, Jessie Ralph.
5. Tyrone Power, Alice Faye, Don Ameche, Alice Brady, Brian Donlevy.
6. Dorothy Lamour, Jon Hall, Raymond Massey, Mary Astor, Thomas Mitchell.
7. Dorothy Lamour, Robert Preston, Lynne Overman, J. Carroll Naish.
8. George C. Scott, Anne Bancroft.
9. Barbara Stanwyck, Clifton Webb, Robert Wagner, Audrey Dalton, Brian Aherne.
10. Preston Foster, Basil Rathbone, Alan Hale, Dorothy Wilson, David Holt.
11. Richard Widmark, Sidney Poitier, James MacArthur, Martin Balsam, Wally Cox.
12. Peter Sellers, Sterling Hayden, Slim Pickens, Keenan Wynn.
13. Tyrone Power, Myrna Loy, George Brent, Brenda Joyce, Maria Ouspenskaya.
14. Bette Davis, Errol Flynn, Anita Louise, Jane Bryant, Donald Crisp, Beulah Bondi.
15. Kenneth More, Ronald Allen, Robert Ayres, Honor Blackman.
16. Fred MacMurray, Paulette Goddard, Susan Hayward, Rod Cameron, Albert Dekker.
17. Edward Judd, Janet Munro, Leo McKern.
18. Harry Belafonte, Inger Stevens, Mel Ferrer.
19. Robert Shaw, Marthe Keller, Bruce Dern.
20. Tallulah Bankhead, John Hodiak, William Bendix, Walter Slezak, Mary Anderson.

Photo 16

OVER THE RAINBOW (1)

Listed below are the stars of films of the '20s whose titles contain the name of a color. Identify the films.

1. George Arliss, Alice Joyce, David Powell, Harry Morey.
2. Nancy Carroll, Charles "Buddy" Rogers, Jean Hersholt.
3. Lillian Gish, Lars Hanson, Henry B. Walthall.
4. Monte Blue, Raquel Torres.
5. Douglas Fairbanks, Billie Dove, Donald Crisp.
6. Ann Pennington, Winnie Lightner, Nick Lucas, Lilyan Tashman.
7. Colleen Moore, Gary Cooper, Arthur Lake, Kathryn McGuire.
8. Jetta Goudal, Kenneth Thomson, George Bancroft.
9. Edward Everett Horton, Louise Dresser, Ernest Torrance, William Austin.
10. Gloria Swanson, Huntley Gordon.
11. Barbara LaMarr, Ben Lyon, Conway Tearle.
12. Ramon Novarro, Enid Bennett, Frank Currier.
13. Anita Stewart, Oscar Shaw, Tom Wise.
14. Charles Chaplin, Georgia Hale, Mack Swain.
15. William Haines, Jack Pickford, Mary Brian.
16. Lillian Rich, Henry B. Walthall, Vera Reynolds, Rod LaRocque, Warner Baxter.
17. Richard Barthelmess, Patsy Ruth Miller, William H. Tooker.
18. James Pierce, Edna Murphy, Boris Karloff.
19. Alma Rubens, John Charles Thomas, Mary McLaren, William Powell.
20. Richard Barthelmess, Betty Compson, Loretta Young.

OVER THE RAINBOW (2)

Listed below are the stars of films of the '30s whose titles contain the name of a color. Identify the films.

1. Marlene Dietrich, Emile Jannings, Kurt Gerron.
2. Jean Harlow, Chester Morris, Lewis Stone, Una Merkel, Charles Boyer.
3. Claudette Colbert, Gary Cooper, David Niven.
4. Marlene Dietrich, Sam Jaffe, Louise Dresser, John Lodge.
5. Barbara Stanwyck, Robert Young, Hardie Albright.
6. Warner Oland, Sally Eilers, Robert Young, Bela Lugosi.
7. Leslie Howard, Merle Oberon, Anthony Bushell.

8. Kay Francis, Ian Hunter, Donald Woods, Nigel Bruce, Donald Crisp.
9. Jean Harlow, Clark Gable, Mary Astor, Gene Raymond.
10. Boris Karloff, Bela Lugosi, David Manners, Jacqueline Wells.
11. Fay Bainter, Claude Rains, Jackie Cooper, Bonita Granville, Henry O'Neill.
12. Robert Montgomery, Virginia Bruce, Lewis Stone, Henry Hull, Andy Devine.
13. Paul Muni, Karen Morley, William Gargan, Barton MacLane, Mae Marsh.
14. Helen Hayes, Clark Gable, Lewis Stone, May Robson, Louise Closser Hale.
15. Joan Crawford, Franchot Tone, Robert Young, Billie Burke, Reginald Owen.
16. Anne Shirley, Tom Brown, Helen Westley, O. P. Heggie.
17. Margaret Sullavan, Randolph Scott, Robert Cummings, Clarence Muse.
18. Barbara Stanwyck, William Holden, Adolphe Menjou, Lee J. Cobb.
19. Edward G. Robinson, Bebe Daniels, Aline MacMahon.
20. Rex Ingram, Oscar Polk, Eddie Anderson, Frank Wilson.

Photo 17

OVER THE RAINBOW (3)

Listed below are the stars of films of the '40s whose titles contain the name of a color. Identify the films.

1. Shirley Temple, Spring Byington, Gale Sondergaard, Nigel Bruce, Sybil Jason.
2. Walter Pidgeon, Janet Leigh, Angela Lansbury, Peter Lawford, Ethel Barrymore.
3. James Cagney, Virginia Mayo, Edmond O'Brien, Steve Cochran, Margaret Wycherly.
4. Gregory Peck, Anne Baxter, Richard Widmark, John Russell, Robert Arthur.
5. Lana Turner, Van Heflin, Donna Reed, Richard Hart.
6. Dan Duryea, Ella Raines, William Bendix.
7. June Haver, Vivian Blaine, Vera-Ellen, Celeste Holm, George Montgomery.
8. Deborah Kerr, Jean Simmons, David Farrar, Flora Robson.
9. Bing Crosby, Fred Astaire, Joan Caulfield, Billy de Wolfe, Olga San Juan.
10. Errol Flynn, Ann Sheridan, Thomas Mitchell, Bruce Bennett.
11. Edward G. Robinson, Joan Bennett, Dan Duryea, Margaret Lindsay, Rosalind Ivan.
12. John Wayne, Montgomery Clift, Joanne Dru, Coleen Gray, John Ireland.
13. Veronica Lake, Alan Ladd, William Bendix, Doris Dowling.
14. George Raft, Virginia Mayo, Gene Lockhart, Barton MacLane.
15. Irene Dunne, Alan Marshal, Peter Lawford, Roddy McDowall, Van Johnson.
16. Douglas Fairbanks, Jr., Joan Bennett, George Sanders, John Howard, Vincent Price.
17. Orson Welles, Nancy Guild, Akim Tamiroff, Raymond Burr.
18. Marlene Dietrich, Ray Milland, Murvyn Vye, Dennis Hoey.
19. Moira Shearer, Anton Walbrook, Marius Goring, Robert Helpmann.
20. Robert Montgomery, Wanda Hendrix, Thomas Gomez, Andrea King, Fred Clark.

Photo 18

Photo 19

OVER THE RAINBOW (4)

Listed below are the stars of films of the '50s whose titles contain the name of a color. Identify the films.

1. Sophia Loren, Anthony Quinn, Ina Balin, Mark Richman.
2. May Britt, Curt Jurgens, Theodore Bikel, John Banner.
3. Audie Murphy, Bill Mauldin, John Dierkes, Royal Dano, Andy Devine.
4. Cornel Wilde, Michael Wilding, Anne Francis, George Sanders, Bobby Driscoll.
5. Anna Magnani, Burt Lancaster, Marisa Pavan, Ben Cooper, Virginia Grey.
6. Bing Crosby, Danny Kaye, Rosemary Clooney, Vera-Ellen.
7. Red Skelton, Gloria de Haven, Walter Slezak, Edward Arnold, Polly Moran.
8. Dale Robertson, Rory Calhoun, Robert Wagner, Kathleen Crowley, Lola Albright.
9. Rock Hudson, Piper Laurie, Gene Evans, Kathleen Hughes.
10. Tony Curtis, Gene Barry, Angela Lansbury, Colleen Miller, Dan O'Herlihy.
11. Grace Kelly, Stewart Granger, Paul Douglas, John Ericson, Murvyn Vye.
12. Jane Wyman, Charles Laughton, Joan Blondell, Richard Carlson.
13. Tyrone Power, Orson Welles, Jack Hawkins, Michael Rennie, Cecile Aubry.
14. Carol Lynley, Brandon de Wilde, Macdonald Carey, Marsha Hunt.
15. Rosemary Clooney, Guy Mitchell, Jack Carson, Gene Barry, Pat Crowley.
16. Robert Mitchum, Susan Hayward, Walter Slezak, Timothy Carey.
17. Rory Calhoun, Peggie Castle, Noah Beery, Jr., Warner Anderson.
18. Gregory Peck, Bernard Lee, Win Min Than, Maurice Denham.
19. Mitzi Gaynor, Dale Robertson, Dennis Day, Una Merkel.
20. Audrey Hepburn, Anthony Perkins, Lee J. Cobb, Sessue Hayakawa, Henry Silva.

OVER THE RAINBOW (5)

Listed below are the stars of films of the '60s whose titles contain the name of a color. Identify the films.

1. John Wayne, David Janssen, Jim Hutton, Aldo Ray, Bruce Cabot.
2. Sidney Poitier, Elizabeth Hartman, Shelley Winters.
3. Lana Turner, Anthony Quinn, Richard Basehart, Sandra Dee.
4. Jack Lemmon, Lee Remick, Charles Bickford, Jack Klugman.
5. Vincent Price, Fred Clark, Frankie Avalon, Dwayne Hickman.
6. Peter Finch, Rita Tushingham, Lynn Redgrave.
7. Cary Grant, Deborah Kerr, Robert Mitchum, Jean Simmons.
8. Sophia Loren, Anthony Quinn, Steve Forrest, Ramon Novarro.
9. Terence Stamp, Joanna Pettet, Karl Malden, Ricardo Montalban.
10. Rex Harrison, Jeanne Moreau, George C. Scott, Ingrid Bergman.
11. Elvis Presley, Roland Winters, Angela Lansbury, Joan Blackman.
12. Pat Boone, Barbara Eden, Jack Klugman, Steve Forrest.
13. James Caan, Laura Devon, Charlene Holt.
14. George Peppard, James Mason, Ursula Andress.
15. Peter Ustinov, Dean Jones, Suzanne Pleshette, Elsa Lanchester.
16. Clint Walker, Roger Moore, Robert Middleton, Chill Wills.
17. Sean Connery, Honor Blackman, Gert Frobe, Shirley Eaton.
18. Ava Gardner, Dirk Bogarde, Joseph Cotten.
19. Capucine, Claudia Cardinale, Robert Wagner, Peter Sellers.
20. Marlon Brando, Elizabeth Taylor, Brian Keith, Julie Harris.

Photo 20

Photo 21

OVER THE RAINBOW (6)

Listed below are the stars of films of the '70s whose titles contain the name of a color. Identify the films.

1. Malcolm McDowell, Patrick Magee, Adrienne Corri, Aubrey Morris.
2. Peter Sellers, Herbert Lom, Lesley Anne Down.
3. Robert Shaw, Marthe Keller, Bruce Dern.
4. Jan-Michael Vincent, Glynnis O'Connor, Katherine Helmond.
5. George Segal, Stephane Audran, Lionel Stander, Elisha Cook, Jr.
6. Candice Bergen, Peter Strauss, Donald Pleasance.
7. Dennis Hopper, Warren Oates, Peter Boyle, Janice Rule.
8. Diana Ross, Billy Dee Williams, Richard Pryor.
9. Alan Arkin, Paula Prentiss, Sally Kellerman.
10. Roger Moore, Christopher Lee, Britt Ekland, Herve Villechaize.
11. Donald Sutherland, Jane Fonda, Peter Boyle, Howard Hesseman.
12. Charlton Heston, Edward G. Robinson, Leigh Taylor-Young, Chuck Connors.
13. Dack Rambo, Ray Milland, Suzanne Pleshette.
14. William Marshall, Vonetta McGee, Denise Nicholas.
15. Michael Caine, Janet Suzman, Donald Pleasance.
16. Roger Moore, Susannah York, Ray Milland, John Gielgud.
17. Joe Don Baker, Elizabeth Ashley, Burgess Meredith, Ann Sothern.
18. Claire Bloom, Richard Crenna, Richard Thomas, Harry Guardino.
19. James Earl Jones, Hal Holbrook, Jane Alexander.
20. Mark Lester, Walter Slezak, Patrick Mower.

UNFORGETTABLES (1)

Listed below are the principal performers in films which are regarded as screen classics. Identify the films.

1. Olivia de Havilland, Montgomery Clift, Ralph Richardson, Miriam Hopkins.
2. Fay Wray, Bruce Cabot, Robert Armstrong.
3. Victor McLaglen, Preston Foster, Wallace Ford, Margot Grahame, Una O'Connor.
4. Bette Davis, George Brent, Geraldine Fitzgerald, Ronald Reagan, Humphrey Bogart.
5. Ginger Rogers, Fred Astaire, Edward Everett Horton, Alice Brady, Eric Blore.
6. John Wayne, Claire Trevor, Thomas Mitchell, John Carradine, Tim Holt.
7. Barbara Stanwyck, John Boles, Anne Shirley, Alan Hale, Barbara O'Neil.
8. Edward G. Robinson, Douglas Fairbanks, Jr., Glenda Farrell, George E. Stone.
9. Judy Garland, Fred Astaire, Ann Miller, Peter Lawford.
10. Gary Cooper, Grace Kelly, Katy Jurado, Thomas Mitchell, Lloyd Bridges.
11. Dorothy Lamour, Jon Hall, Raymond Massey, Thomas Mitchell, Mary Astor.
12. Spencer Tracy, Mickey Rooney, Henry Hull, Gene Reynolds.
13. Joan Crawford, Zachary Scott, Jack Carson, Ann Blyth, Eve Arden.
14. John Wayne, Montgomery Clift, Joanne Dru, Colleen Gray, John Ireland.
15. James Cagney, Jean Harlow, Joan Blondell, Mae Clarke, Edward Woods.

Photo 22

16. Orson Welles, Joseph Cotten, Dorothy Comingore, Ruth Warrick, Agnes Moorehead.
17. Jeanne Crain, Linda Darnell, Ann Sothern, Paul Douglas, Kirk Douglas.
18. Judy Garland, James Mason, Jack Carson, Charles Bickford.
19. Barbara Stanwyck, Fred MacMurray, Edward G. Robinson
20. Sylvia Sidney, Joel McCrea, Humphrey Bogart, Claire Trevor, Billy Halop.

UNFORGETTABLES (2)

Listed below are the principal performers in films which are regarded as screen classics. Identify the films.

1. Burt Lancaster, Montgomery Clift, Deborah Kerr, Frank Sinatra, Donna Reed.
2. John Wayne, Maureen O'Hara, Victor McLaglen, Barry Fitzgerald, Mildred Natwick.
3. Bette Davis, Leslie Howard, Frances Dee, Reginald Denny.
4. Charles Chaplin, Jack Oakie, Paulette Goddard, Billy Gilbert.
5. Katharine Hepburn, Douglass Montgomery, Paul Lukas, Joan Bennett, Jean Parker.
6. Katharine Hepburn, Cary Grant, James Stewart, Ruth Hussey, John Howard.
7. Paul Muni, Luise Rainer, Tilly Losch, Walter Connolly, Charley Grapewin.
8. William Powell, Myrna Loy, Maureen O'Sullivan, Nat Pendleton, Cesar Romero.
9. Lew Ayres, Louis Wolheim, Russell Gleason, Ben Alexander, Beryl Mercer.
10. Greta Garbo, Melvyn Douglas, Ina Claire, Bela Lugosi, Sig Rumann.
11. Boris Karloff, Colin Clive, Mae Clarke, John Boles, Dwight Frye.
12. Henry Fonda, Dana Andrews, Anthony Quinn, Jane Darwell, Mary Beth Hughes.
13. Freddie Bartholomew, W. C. Fields, Frank Lawton, Roland Young, Madge Evans.
14. Greta Garbo, John and Lionel Barrymore, Joan Crawford, Wallace Beery.
15. Bela Lugosi, David Manners, Helen Chandler, Dwight Frye.

Photo 23

16. Clark Gable, Charles Laughton, Franchot Tone, Herbert Mundin, Eddie Quillan.
17. Charlton Heston, Stephen Boyd, Jack Hawkins, Haya Harareet, Hugh Griffith.
18. Ronald Colman, Jane Wyatt, Margo, Sam Jaffe, H. B. Warner, John Howard.
19. Gary Cooper, Jean Arthur, George Bancroft, Lionel Stander.
20. James Stewart, Jean Arthur, Thomas Mitchell, Claude Rains, Edward Arnold.

UNFORGETTABLES (3)

Listed below are the principal performers in films which are regarded as screen classics. Identify the films.

1. W. C. Fields, Mae West, Joseph Callela, Dick Foran, Ruth Donnelly.
2. Marlene Dietrich, James Stewart, Brian Donlevy, Una Merkel.
3. Spencer Tracy, Freddie Bartholomew, Lionel Barrymore, Mickey Rooney.
4. Gary Cooper, Barbara Stanwyck, Edward Arnold, Walter Brennan, James Gleason.
5. Greta Garbo, John Gilbert, Ian Keith, Lewis Stone, C. Aubrey Smith.
6. Jeanette MacDonald, Nelson Eddy, Frank Morgan, Elsa Lanchester.
7. Mae West, Cary Grant, Gilbert Roland, Noah Beery, Rochelle Hudson.
8. Bette Davis, Herbert Marshall, James Stephenson, Freida Inescort, Gale Sondergaard.
9. Anthony Perkins, Janet Leigh, Vera Miles, John Gavin, Martin Balsam.
10. John and Lionel Barrymore, Marie Dressler, Jean Harlow, Wallace Beery, Billie Burke.
11. Montgomery Clift, Elizabeth Taylor, Shelley Winters, Keefe Brasselle, Raymond Burr.
12. Brian Donlevy, Muriel Angelus, Akim Tamiroff, Louis Jean Heydt.
13. Paul Newman, Patricia Neal, Melvyn Douglas, Brandon de Wilde.
14. Katharine Hepburn, Ginger Rogers, Gail Patrick, Adolphe Menjou, Lucille Ball.
15. John Wayne, Thomas Mitchell, Ian Hunter, John Qualen, Barry Fitzgerald.
16. Barbara Stanwyck, Henry Fonda, Charles Coburn, William Demarest.
17. Tim Holt, Joseph Cotten, Agnes Moorehead, Dolores Costello, Anne Baxter.
18. Judy Garland, Margaret O'Brien, Tom Drake, Mary Astor, Lucille Bremer.
19. Eddie Bracken, Ella Raines, Raymond Walburn, William Demarest.
20. W. C. Fields, Cora Witherspoon, Una Merkel, Grady Sutton, Franklin Pangborn.

Photo 24

THE BRITISH ARE COMING

Listed below are the stars of British films which are regarded as screen classics. Identify the films.

1. John Mills, Valerie Hobson, Anthony Wager, Jean Simmons, Martita Hunt.
2. Celia Johnson, Trevor Howard, Stanley Holloway, Joyce Carey.
3. Laurence Olivier, Renee Asherton, Robert Newton, Leslie Banks.
4. Robert Donat, Greer Garson, Terry Kilburn, Paul Henried.
5. Ralph Richardson, Michelle Morgan, Bobby Henrey.
6. Robert Donat, Madeleine Carroll, Mucie Mannheim, Godfrey Tearle.
7. Orson Welles, Joseph Cotten, Valli, Trevor Howard.
8. Noel Coward, John Mills, Bernard Miles, Celia Johnson, Kay Walsh.
9. Albert Finney, Susannah York, Hugh Griffith, Joyce Redman, Edith Evans.
10. Julie Christie, Dirk Bogarde, Laurence Harvey.
11. Alec Guinness, Stanley Holloway, Sidney James, Alfie Bass.
12. Leslie Howard, Wendy Hiller, Wilfred Lawson, Marie Lohr, David Tree.
13. Laurence Olivier, Jean Simmons, Eileen Herlie, Basil Sydney.
14. Moira Shearer, Anton Walbrook, Marius Goring, Robert Helpmann.
15. Anna Neagle, Anton Walbrook, Mary Morris, H. B. Warner.
16. Raymond Massey, Cedric Hardwicke, Ralph Richardson, Ann Todd.
17. James Mason, Kathleen Ryan, Robert Newton, Dan O'Herlihy, Cyril Cusack.
18. Alec Guinness, Dennis Price, Valerie Hobson, Joan Greenwood.
19. Wendy Hiller, Rex Harrison, Robert Morley, Robert Newton, Emlyn Williams.
20. Charles Laughton, Merle Oberon, Elsa Lanchester, Binnie Barnes, Robert Donat.

FOREIGN LEGION

Listed below are the stars of foreign language screen classics. Identify the films.

1. Jean Gabin, Pierre Fresnay, Erich von Stroheim, Dalio (1937, France).
2. Lamberto Maggiorani, Enzo Staiola, Lianello Carrell (1948, Italy).
3. Jeanne Moreau, Oskar Werner, Henri Serre (1962, France).

Photo 25

4. Max von Sydow, Brigitta Valberg, Gunnar Lindblom, Brigitta Pattersson (1960, Sweden).
5. Toshiro Mifune, Masayuki Morl, Takashi Shimura (1950, Japan).
6. Charles Boyer, Danielle Darrieux, Suzy Prim, Jean Dax (1937, France).
7. Marlene Dietrich, Emil Jannings, Hans Alber (1930, Germany).
8. Carmela Sazlo, Robert Vanhoon, Gar Moore, Dots M. Johnson (1946, Italy).
9. Antonov Alexandrov, Vladimir Barsky (1925, Russia).
10. Werner Krauss, Conrad Veidt, Lil Dagover (1920, Germany).
11. Max von Sydow, Gunnar Bjornstrand, Bibi Anderssen, Nils Poppe (1957, Sweden).
12. Anthony Quinn, Giulietta Masina, Richard Basehart, Aldo Silvani (1956, Italy).
13. Marcello Mastroianni, Anita Ekberg, Lex Barker, Anouk Aimee, Nadia Gray (1961, Italy).
14. Peter Lorre, Otto Wernicke, Guitav Grandgens (1931, Germany).
15. Anna Magnani, Aldo Fabrizi, Marcello Pagliero, Harry Feist (1945, Italy).
16. Jean Serais, Carl Mohner, Magali Noel, Robert Manuel (1946, France).
17. Breno Mello, Marpessa Dawn, Lourdes De Oliviera (1960, Brazil).
18. Arletty, Jean-Louis Barrault, Pierre Brasseur (1945, France).
19. Marcello Mastroianni, Daniela Rocca, Stefania Sandrelli (1962, Italy).
20. Rinaldo Smordoni, Franco Interienghi, Aniello Mele (1946, Italy).

REGARDS TO BROADWAY

Listed below are stars of films of the '30s which were based on well-known stage plays. Identify the films.

1. Leslie Howard, Bette Davis, Humphrey Bogart, Dick Foran.
2. Norma Shearer, Leslie Howard, John Barrymore, Basil Rathbone.
3. Rex Ingram, Oscar Polk, Eddie Anderson, Frank Wilson.
4. James Cagney, Olivia de Havilland, Dick Powell, Joe E. Brown, Mickey Rooney.
5. Greta Garbo, Charles Bickford, Marie Dressler, George Marion.
6. Barbara Stanwyck, William Holden, Adolphe Menjou, Lee J. Cobb.
7. Norma Shearer, Joan Crawford, Rosalind Russell, Joan Fontaine.
8. James Cagney, Pat O'Brien, Marie Wilson, Dick Foran.
9. James Stewart, Jean Arthur, Lionel Barrymore, Edward Arnold.
10. Katharine Hepburn, Ginger Rogers, Adolphe Menjou, Gail Patrick.
11. Mickey Rooney, Judy Garland, June Preisser, Douglas MacPhail.
12. Wayne Morris, Eddie Albert, Priscilla Lane, Jane Bryan, Ronald Reagan.
13. Bette Davis, Henry Fonda, George Brent, Fay Bainter, Richard Cromwell.
14. Fredric March, Evelyn Venable, Guy Standing, Gail Patrick.
15. Joan Crawford, Margaret Sullavan, Melvyn Douglas, Robert Young.
16. Merle Oberon, Miriam Hopkins, Joel McCrea, Bonita Granville.
17. John and Lionel Barrymore, Marie Dressler, Jean Harlow, Wallace Beery.
18. Norma Shearer, Fredric March, Charles Laughton, Maureen O'Sullivan.
19. Miriam Hopkins, Gary Cooper, Fredric March, Edward Everett Horton.
20. Norma Shearer, Robert Montgomery, Una Merkel.

SOBRIQUETS

The stars listed on the left were known by the nicknames listed on the right. Match the stars with the nicknames.

1. Bing Crosby		A.	"Ski-Nose"
2. Clara Bow		B.	"The Shnazz"
3. Frank Sinatra		C.	"The Sweater Girl"
4. Betty Grable		D.	"The Sheik"
5. Jimmy Durante		E.	"The King"
6. Rita Hayworth		F.	"The Little Tramp"
7. Bob Hope		G.	"The Sarong Girl"
8. Carole Landis		H.	"The Groaner"
9. John Wayne		I.	"The Platinum Blonde"
10. Lupe Velez		J.	"The Body"
11. Clark Gable		K.	"The Voice"
12. Veronica Lake		L.	"Duke"
13. Charlie Chaplin		M.	"The Sphinx"
14. Lana Turner		N.	"The Mexican Spitfire"
15. Dorothy Lamour		O.	"The Brazilian Bombshell"
16. Carmen Miranda		P.	"The Love Goddess"
17. Jean Harlow		Q.	"The It Girl"
18. Marie McDonald		R.	"The Pin-Up Girl"
19. Greta Garbo		S.	"The Ping Girl"
20. Rudolph Valentino		T.	"The Peek-a-boo Girl"

Photo 26

MUSICAL LIVES

The stars listed on the left portrayed the life of a musician or composer in the films listed on the right. Match the stars with the films.

1. Robert Walker   A. *The Benny Goodman Story*
2. Clifton Webb   B. *The Great Waltz (Johann Strauss)*
3. Robert Alda   C. *The Great Victor Herbert*
4. Tom Drake   D. *Night and Day (Cole Porter)*
5. Danny Thomas   E. *The Glenn Miller Story*
6. Larry Parks   F. *Till the Clouds Roll By (Jerome Kern)*
7. Mickey Rooney   G. *The Gene Krupa Story*
8. Tyrone Power   H. *Stars and Stripes Forever (John Phillip Sousa)*
9. Tommy and Jimmy Dorsey   I. *The Jolson Story*
10. Steve Allen   J. *The Five Pennies (Red Nichols)*
11. Nat King Cole   K. *Rhapsody in Blue (George Gershwin)*
12. Cornel Wilde   L. *The Eddy Duchin Story*
13. James Cagney   M. *Words and Music (Richard Rodgers)*
14. Fernand Gravet   N. *Words and Music (Lorenz Hart)*
15. Jose Ferrer   O. *The Fabulous Dorseys*
16. Cary Grant   P. *A Song to Remember (Frederick Chopin)*
17. Sal Mineo   Q. *I'll See You in My Dreams (Gus Kahn)*
18. Walter Connolly   R. *St. Louis Blues (W. C. Handy)*
19. Danny Kaye   S. *Yankee Doodle Dandy (George M. Cohan)*
20. James Stewart   T. *Deep in My Heart (Sigmund Romberg)*

Photo 27

Photo 28

ME TARZAN

Name the stars who played Tarzan in the following films.

1. Tarzan's Hidden Treasure (1955)
2. The Romance of Tarzan (1918)
3. Tarzan's Jungle Rebellion (1970)
4. Tarzan's New York Adventure (1942)
5. Tarzan the Magnificent (1960)
6. Tarzan the Ape Man (1959)
7. Tarzan and the Slave Girl (1950)
8. Tarzan Goes to India (1962)
9. Tarzan and the Valley of Gold (1966)
10. Tarzan's Magic Fountain (1949)
11. Tarzan and the Golden Lion (1927)
12. Tarzan the Mighty (1928)
13. Tarzan the Fearless (1933)
14. Tarzan and the Green Goddess (1938)
15. Tarzan's Revenge (1938)
16. Tarzan Finds a Son (1939)
17. Tarzan's Deadly Silence (1970)
18. The Revenge of Tarzan (1920)
19. Tarzan, the Ape Man (1981)
20. Tarzan and the Jungle Boy (1968)

AT THE BOX OFFICE

On May 3, 1938, Manhattan's Independent Theatre Owners Association, Inc., ran a full-page advertisement in the *Hollywood Reporter* with the headline: "WAKE UP! HOLLYWOOD PRODUCERS." The ad then declared that independent theater owners were tired of losing money on top salaried stars whose box office appeal was limited. They declared that the following stars were "poison" at the box office: Joan Crawford, Fred Astaire, Edward Arnold, Greta Garbo, Katharine Hepburn, Mae West, Marlene Dietrich, and Kay Francis.

The ad stated in part: "Practically all of the major studios are burdened with stars—whose public appeal is negligible—receiving tremendous salaries . . . Garbo, for instance . . . does not help theater owners in the U.S . . . Kay Francis, still receiving many thousands a week, is now making B pictures . . . Dietrich, too, is poison. . . ."

The ad was signed by Harry Brandt, then president of the association, and he drew the wrath and ire of those mentioned. Said Mae West: "Why, every time Harry Brandt was losing money, he reran *She Done Him Wrong* and got on his feet again." Hepburn commented: "If I weren't laughing so hard, I might cry. . . . " (She had just bought up her contract with RKO, to leave herself free in hopes that she might land the role of Scarlett O'Hara in *Gone With the Wind*.) Joan Crawford had just signed a new five-year MGM contract at a reputed total of $1,500,000, so she merely shrugged, "Box office poison?" Mae West further added: "The box office business in the entire industry has dropped off 30%. . . . The only picture to make real money was *Snow White and the Seven Dwarfs*, and that would have made twice as much if they'd had me play Snow White."

At the time, Brandt said the association represented 240 theaters in New York, Connecticut, and New Jersey, which included urban, suburban, and rural theaters, thereby covering a cross-section. When pinned down, he claimed that the stars who did the most business for his theaters were Clark Gable, Myrna Loy, Sonja Henie, Deanna Durbin, Spencer Tracy, Shirley Temple, Paul Muni, Ginger Rogers, Gary Cooper, and Jeanette MacDonald (though not necessarily in that order). Brandt also claimed that a "draw" star in a bad film could be disastrous, such as Spencer Tracy in *Big City*. He also stated that, "Robert Taylor was in that same class as Joan Crawford . . . he's a star whom people want if they can see him in the right vehicles. . . . At present Joan Crawford is no draw for us, but I think her career can be resuscitated if they put her into the right roles."

He went on to elaborate: "We find that we can get more people to the box office with pictures like the Jones family, the Moto series, the Charlie Chan series, Judge Hardy's family, and other pictures which have no big stars, and that people are more satisfied when they leave than when we show a picture with Mae West or Katharine Hepburn. . . . Some of the stars are such poor draws that we've had to put Bango and Bingo in our theaters to make up for it. First we started giving dishes away; then we gave them Lucky and Bingo to get people to come in and take the dishes; then we started giving money away. Now, with so many high-salaried stars who have no drawing power at all, we can't even get them to come in and take our money."

In retrospect, the list is laughable, considering the longevity of the careers of those involved, but at the time there was some validity to Brandt's claims. All of those mentioned had had a run of not-so-successful pictures. Crawford's *The Bride Wore Red* (MGM, 1937) with leading men Franchot Tone and Robert Young, was very badly received by the public and critics alike because of a very silly and unbelievable plot, whereas her *Mannequin* (MGM, 1938) had a good story and an excellent performance by Spencer Tracy. Her career for the balance of her five-year contract with MGM vascillated in a like manner. *The Shining Hour* (1938) and *Ice Follies of 1939* were "minuses," but her next, *The Women*, was a "plus" in her favor. *Strange Cargo* (1940) and *Susan and God* (1940) were successful because of strong casting, and her next, *A Woman's Face* (1941), was her last great MGM role. *When Ladies Meet* (1941) was an old-hat remake; *They All Kissed the Bride* (on loan-out to Columbia, 1942), was only so-so, as were her remaining two MGM films, *Reunion in France* (1942) and *Above Suspicion* (1943). After her departure from MGM, she emerged as a super star at Warner Brothers with *Mildred Pierce* (1945), for which she received an Oscar. Crawford triumphed again in the 1960s, after being written off as a has-been by many, in the box office hit *What Ever Happened to Baby Jane?*

The team of Fred Astaire and Ginger Rogers enjoyed great popularity during the mid-thirties and Ginger solo had no problems (her *Stage Door* with Hepburn was one of the hits of 1937), but Fred's attempt to break away from the mold in *A Damsel in Distress* with Joan Fontaine (RKO, 1937) was a dismal flop, even abetted by the comedy team of George Burns and Gracie Allen. The 1938 Astaire-Rogers film, *Carefree*, was not as successful as their previous ones, but their final one (for the next ten years), *The Story of Vernon and Irene Castle* (RKO, 1939), was a hit, as was his next effort, *Broadway Melody of 1940* (MGM), with a new dancing partner, Eleanor Powell. Success on television has not evaded Mr. Astaire; he won Emmy Awards in 1959 and in 1961.

The apex of Edward Arnold's career was the 1935 Universal hit, *Diamond Jim*, in which he portrayed James Brady, New York tycoon. He had two near-hits after that, Goldwyn's 1936 *Come and Get It*, based on Edna

Photo 29

Ferber's tale of the early logging industry, and RKO's 1937 *The Toast of New York*, in which he portrayed another financier, James Fiske. But his other 1937 films, *John Meade's Woman* and *Blossoms on Broadway*, both for Paramount, were dismal flops. Only *Easy Living* (Paramount) enjoyed any measure of success, bolstered by the performances of Jean Arthur and Ray Milland. By 1938, Mr. Arnold was forty-eight years old, and, reading the writing on the wall, resigned himself to strong supporting roles, some of the more notable being *You Can't Take It With You* (Columbia, 1938); *Idiot's Delight* (MGM, 1939); *Lillian Russell* (Twentieth Century Fox, 1940), repeating his James Brady role; *Meet John Doe* (Warner Bros., 1941); and *All That Money Can Buy* (RKO, 1941), in which he played Daniel Webster pitted against Walter Huston's Devil. He continued working until his death in 1956.

The great Greta Garbo's career faltered considerably following her first talkie, *Anna Christie* (MGM, 1930). Only *Mata Hari* (MGM, 1931) and *Grand Hotel* (MGM, 1932) could be termed "popular." *Inspiration* (MGM, 1931), *Susan Lennox: Her Fall and Rise* (MGM, 1931), *As You Desire Me* (MGM, 1932) and *The Painted Veil* (MGM, 1934) all presented her as a fallen, world-weary woman in the same mold as some of her earlier silent successes. Turning to historical drama, MGM cast her in *Queen Christina* (1933), *Anna Karenina* (1935), *Camille* (1936), and *Conquest* (1937). All were huge *critical* successes—she won her second Oscar nomination for *Camille*—and were financial hits abroad, where her films had always enjoyed good "box office." But the American public had tired of the spate of historical "costumers," and *Conquest*, depicting the love of Napoleon for Polish beauty, Marie Walewsky, did very badly financially. Garbo wisely stayed off the screen for two years, making a triumphant comeback as a comedienne in the enchanting *Ninotchka*, receiving her third Oscar nomination in 1939. Two years after that, she appeared in the ill-fated *Two-Faced Woman* (MGM, 1941), after which she permanently retired.

Photo 30

Photo 31

Katharine Hepburn's career at RKO during the 1930s was checkered (and stormy, given the fiery redhead's temperament). From her screen debut in late 1932 to her last film in 1938, she made a total of fifteen pictures. Of this total, five could be considered unqualified successes: her first, *A Bill of Divorcement*, in which her vibrant personality and undisputed talent captured everyone; her third, *Morning Glory*, which won her the 1933 best actress Oscar: her fourth film (and biggest hit), *Little Women*; her eighth film, *Alice Adams*, which won her an Oscar nomination in 1935; and her thirteenth film, *Stage Door*, in 1937. Four films could have been considered qualified hits: The *Little Minister* in 1934; *Sylvia Scarlett* in 1935; and two which were released after Brandt's scathing article, *Bringing Up Baby* in 1938 and *Holiday for Columbia* (1938), her only film away from RKO. It was her string of flops, particularly the three preceding *Stage Door*, that landed her on the poison list. These three were *Mary of Scotland* (1936), *A Woman Rebels* (1936), and *Quality Street* (1937), all ponderous (for the '30s) costumers. Three others that failed to make money were *Christopher Strong* (1933), about an adventurous woman aviator; *Spitfire* (1934), in which Hepburn was miscast as a tomboy-mountaineer; and *Break of Hearts* (1935), a romantic drama in which she and Charles Boyer failed to make sparks. After failing to win the Scarlett O'Hara sweepstakes (Selznick claimed she lacked the proper amount of sex appeal), she hied herself to Broadway, was a hit in *The Philadelphia Story*, repeated its success in the

1940 MGM film and was off on the second phase of her long career, capturing two more Oscars (making her the only actress with three) for *Guess Who's Coming to Dinner* (Columbia, 1967) and *The Lion in Winter* (Avco, 1968). As if in defiance of Mr. Brandt, she even made the Top Ten Money Making Stars in 1969 (for the first and only time) at the age of 60, no mean feat in a youth-oriented age.

The film career of Mae West (and indeed, the woman herself) is phenomenal even though she has only twelve pictures to her credit and only four could be considered hits at the time of their release. These were *She Done Him Wrong* and *I'm No Angel* (Paramount, 1933); *Belle of the Nineties* (Paramount, 1934), and *My Little Chickadee* (Universal, 1940). A victim of the '30s censorship rulings, the public found "watered-down" West not to their liking and three "bombs" in a row, *Goin' to Town* (Paramount, 1935); *Klondike Annie* (Paramount, 1936), and *Go West, Young Man* (Paramount, 1936), combined to place her on Brandt's list. Her one 1938 release (and her last for Paramount), *Every Day's a Holiday*, was equally disastrous. So, too, was her 1943 fiasco, *The Heat's On* (Columbia), and nearly everyone connected with *Myra Breckenridge* (Twentieth Century Fox, 1970) would like to forget it. Her last film was *Sextette* in 1978, two years before her death. Yet Miss West remains a legend, thanks to various film festivals, some on TV, which made her the high priestess of "camp."

Photo 32

Photo 33

Like Katharine Hepburn, Marlene Dietrich's inclusion on the poison list of Harry Brandt stemmed largely (though not entirely) from her three films prior to May of 1938. These were *Garden of Allah* (United Artists, 1936), *Knight Without Armour* (United Artists, 1937) and *Angel* (Paramount, 1937), all of which were poorly received by critics and the public alike. That she was as beautiful as ever was no question; in fact, *Garden of Allah* was her first Technicolor film. But all three suffered from the same stiffness that most of her earlier films, under the tutelage of Josef von Sternberg, had acquired. Only *Desire* (Paramount, 1936), with Gary Cooper, had any life-like quality, being a delightful, tongue-in-cheek comedy of international jewel thieves (a common '30s plot gimmick). Prior to that, Dietrich audiences had been dulled to death by four of her worst: *Blonde Venus* (1932); *Song of Songs* (1933); *Scarlet Empress* (1934); and *The Devil Is a Woman* (1935)—all for Paramount. Indeed, one had to go back to her first three American films to find any life: *Morocco* (1930); *Dishonored* (1931), and *Shanghai Express* (1932)—all for Paramount. She remained off the screen for two years and made a successful comeback in 1939, doing a complete switch in character and scoring with one of her biggest and best blockbusters, Universal's *Destry Rides Again*. Her hair-pulling, knock-down, drag-out fight scene with Una Merkel remains a screen classic today. Equally successful in nightclubs and one-woman concerts, her last major screen role was in Stanley Kramer's *Judgment at Nuremberg* (United Artists, 1961), Dietrich made a guest appearance in *Paris When It Sizzles* (Paramount, 1964). Oddly enough, two of her biggest personal screen triumphs in her "second career" were both for the original studio that had let her go in 1937—Paramount. They were *Golden Earrings* (1947) and *A Foreign Affair* (1948).

Last on the list was the beautiful and impeccably groomed Kay Francis, one of Hollywood's leading "clothes-horses" of the '30s. Known as a "woman's" star and noted for "four-hankie" tear-jerkers, it is true that her films, so alike in their plots of either suffering or suffragettism, were by 1938 no longer box office draws. Lured to Hollywood from Broadway in 1929 by Paramount, she had had three successful years with that studio when Warner Brothers offered her more money in 1932 and she appeared in one of that year's finest love stories, *One Way Passage*, with William Powell. She graced many Warner Brothers films for the next five years. Of her four 1937 releases for Warner Brothers; *Stolen Holiday*, with Claude Rains, *Confession*, with Basil Rathbone, *Another Dawn*, with Errol Flynn; and *First Lady*, with Preston Foster, only the latter, a successful Broadway play adapted to the screen, had any originality, wit or spontaneity. Warner's hoped she would buy out of her contract, but she went on collecting

Photo 34

her handsome salary while appearing in little more than B pictures until her term expired in 1939. Former Paramount pal Carole Lombard insisted on Kay to play the bitchy wife in RKO's *In Name Only* (1939), which opened a brief success for her in the early '40s, but she had reached a low point in her career in 1945 and 1946 when she appeared in three Monogram quickies. She then retired, a wealthy woman, and, on her death in 1968, left her estate of over a million dollars to the seeing-eye dog foundation.

There were other stars who suffered personal setbacks during the 1937/1938 season, but subsequent films restored their box office appeal. William Powell, co-starred with Annabella, had a "dog" on his hands with *The Baroness and the Butler,* (1938) a very unfunny take-off on *My Man Godfrey.* His previous film, *Double Wedding* (MGM, 1937) and his next film, *Another Thin Man* (MGM, 1939) both co-starred him with Myrna Loy, a team which the public thoroughly enjoyed.

Bing Crosby's *Waikiki Wedding* (Paramount, 1937), was highly success-ful, but *Double or Nothing* (Paramount, 1937), and *Dr. Rhythm* (Paramount, 1938) were duds, even with Bea Lillie in the latter. Fortunately his next film was a hit, the sprightly *Sing You Sinners* (Paramount, 1938) with Fred MacMurray, Donald O'Connor, and Ellen Drew. Of course, the success or

Photo 35

failure of a Crosby film (like that of Dick Powell) depended a great deal on musical scores. *Waikiki Wedding* was blessed with "Blue Hawaii" and "Sweet Leilani," and *Sing You Sinners* had "Small Fry" and "Pocketful of Dreams." "The Moon Got in My Eyes" (from *Double or Nothing*) and "My Heart Is Taking Lessons" (from *Dr. Rhythm*) were minor song hits.

Dick Powell, who ranked number seven in popularity in 1935 and num-ber six in 1936 had slipped to number fourteen in 1937 and wasn't even in the top twenty-five in 1938, due to a spate of poor films and poor songs. His best film of 1937 was, oddly enough, a loan-out to Twentieth Century Fox, *On the Avenue*, with co-stars Alice Faye and Madeleine Carroll, and featured a musical score by Irving Berlin, which included "I've Got My Love to Keep Me Warm," "This Year's Kisses," and "Slumming on Park Avenue." The three films he made for his home studio, Warner Brothers, that year were all minor league: *Gold Diggers of 1937* (the poorest of that series until its follow-up, *Gold Diggers of Paris*, with Rudy Vallee); *The Singing Marine;* and *Varsity Show*. Powell's 1938 films were more of the same Warner Brothers lackluster variety: *Hollywood Hotel, Cowboy from Brooklyn, Hard to Get,* and *Going Places,* with only one song, "Jeepers Creepers," from the latter film, to redeem the quartet. Dick did not recover from his slump until he changed his screen image from romantic crooner to tough detective in *Murder, My Sweet* (RKO, 1944). He enjoyed later success as a television producer and director until his death in 1963.

On the distaff side, opera stars Grace Moore (Columbia) and Lily Pons (RKO) were on a downward trend and Paramount's hope in that genre, Gladys Swarthout, failed to capture the public's liking in films such as *Rose of the Rancho* and *Champagne Waltz,* finally ending in a minor B film called *Ambush* (Paramount, 1939) with Lloyd Nolan.

Established stars Irene Dunne and Barbara Stanwyck both suffered one-picture slumps in 1937. Miss Dunne's Paramount musical, *High, Wide and Handsome,* with Randolph Scott and music by Jerome Kern, failed to register at the box office, as did Miss Stanwyck's *Breakfast for Two,* one of the last of the screwball comedies. However, each starred in one of the year's biggest hits and as a result didn't suffer any career setbacks. Miss Dunne's hit was *The Awful Truth,* one of the best of the screwball series, and Miss Stanwyck was nominated for her first Oscar for *Stella Dallas.*

ANNUAL TOP TEN BOX OFFICE MOVIE STARS
(1915–1980)

Each year, from 1932 to the present, the *Motion Picture Herald,* a Quigley Publishing trade magazine, has conducted a poll of motion picture exhibitors and other subscribers connected with the film industry to determine the top ten box office attractions—the stars whose films grossed the most profits within a given year.

The lists for 1925–1931 were obtained by means of a questionnaire form which was abandoned in 1932. The lists for 1915–1924 were compiled by analyses from box office receipts for those years.

An interesting note is that in the teens, '20s and '30s, women stars held their own, but the '40s saw more male stars dominating the polls, and in the '50s, '60s, and '70s the lists were composed primarily of men. In fact, there were no women at all in the 1957 top ten list. But in 1980, four of the top ten box office draws were women. Perhaps if roles for women continue to improve, female stars will dominate the lists in years to come.

1915
William S. Hart
Mary Pickford
Tom Mix
Blanche Sweet
William Farnum
J. Warren Kerrigan
Dorothy Gish
Anita Stewart
Kathlyn Williams
Francis X. Bushman/Beverly Bayne

1916
William S. Hart
Mary Pickford
J. Warren Kerrigan
Anita Stewart
Tom Mix
William Farnum
Francis X. Bushman/Beverly Bayne
Douglas Fairbanks
Wallace Reid
Frank Keenan

1917
Douglas Fairbanks
William S. Hart
Anita Stewart
Mary Pickford
Bessie Barriscale
J. Warren Kerrigan
Wallace Reid
Charles Ray
Frank Keenan
Dorothy Dalton

1918
Douglas Fairbanks
Mary Pickford
Wallace Reid
William S. Hart
Mary Miles Minter
Clara Kimball Young
Dorothy Dalton
Charles Ray
Marguerite Clark
Anita Stewart

1919
Wallace Reid
Douglas Fairbanks
Mary Pickford
Charles Ray
William S. Hart
Marguerite Clark
Jane and Katherine Lee ("Lee Kids")
Mary Miles Minter
Clara Kimball Young
Dorothy Dalton

1920
Wallace Reid
Marguerite Clark
Charles Ray
Douglas Fairbanks
Mary Miles Minter
Mary Pickford
Clara Kimball Young
William S. Hart
Norma Talmadge
Theda Bara

75

1921

Mary Pickford
Douglas Fairbanks
Wallace Reid
Charles Ray
Gloria Swanson
Mary Miles Minter
Marion Davies
Norma Talmadge
Clara Kimball Young
William S. Hart

1922

Mary Pickford
Douglas Fairbanks
Anita Stewart
Thomas Meighan
Rudolph Valentino
Pola Negri
Mae Murray
Harold Lloyd
Lon Chaney
Douglas MacLean

1923

Thomas Meighan
Norma Talmadge
Douglas Fairbanks
Mary Pickford
Marion Davies
Lon Chaney
Rudolph Valentino
Harold Lloyd
Gloria Swanson
Colleen Moore

1924

Norma Talmadge
Marion Davies
Rudolph Valentino
Douglas Fairbanks
Thomas Meighan
Gloria Swanson
Mary Pickford
Lon Chaney
Harold Lloyd
Ramon Novarro

1925

Rudolph Valentino
Norma Talmadge
Marion Davies
Mary Pickford
Douglas Fairbanks
Fred Thomson
Harold Lloyd
Colleen Moore
Gloria Swanson
Thomas Meighan

1926

Colleen Moore
Tom Mix
Fred Thomson
Harold Lloyd
Hoot Gibson
Norma Talmadge
Mary Pickford
Douglas Fairbanks
Thomas Meighan
Reginald Denny

1927

Tom Mix
Colleen Moore
Clara Bow
Fred Thomson
Lon Chaney
Richard Dix
Hoot Gibson
Harold Lloyd
John Gilbert
Bebe Daniels

1928

Clara Bow
Lon Chaney
Colleen Moore
Tom Mix
John Gilbert
Harold Lloyd
William Haines
Richard Barthelmess
Billie Dove
Bebe Daniels

1929

Clara Bow
Lon Chaney
William Haines
Hoot Gibson
Colleen Moore
Buddy Rogers
Richard Barthelmess
Ken Maynard
Tom Mix
Nancy Carroll

1930

Joan Crawford
Clara Bow
William Haines
Janet Gaynor
Colleen Moore
Greta Garbo
Al Jolson
Richard Barthelmess
Rin Tin Tin
Tom Mix

1931

Janet Gaynor
Charles Farrell
Joan Crawford
Norma Shearer
Marie Dressler
Wallace Beery
Clara Bow
Al Jolson
Colleen Moore
Greta Garbo

1932

Marie Dressler
Janet Gaynor
Joan Crawford
Charles Farrell
Greta Garbo
Norma Shearer
Wallace Beery
Clark Gable
Will Rogers
Joe E. Brown

1933

Marie Dressler
Will Rogers
Janet Gaynor
Eddie Cantor
Wallace Beery
Jean Harlow
Clark Gable
Mae West
Norma Shearer
Joan Crawford

1934

Will Rogers
Clark Gable
Janet Gaynor
Wallace Beery
Mae West
Joan Crawford
Bing Crosby
Shirley Temple
Marie Dressler
Norma Shearer

1935

Shirley Temple
Will Rogers
Clark Gable
Fred Astaire/Ginger Rogers
Joan Crawford
Claudette Colbert
Dick Powell
Wallace Beery
Joe E. Brown
James Cagney

1936

Shirley Temple
Clark Gable
Fred Astaire/Ginger Rogers
Robert Taylor
Joe E. Brown
Dick Powell
Joan Crawford
Claudette Colbert
Jeanette MacDonald
Gary Cooper

77

1937

Shirley Temple
Clark Gable
Robert Taylor
Bing Crosby
William Powell
Jane Withers
Fred Astaire/Ginger Rogers
Sonja Henie
Gary Cooper
Myrna Loy

1938

Shirley Temple
Clark Gable
Sonja Henie
Mickey Rooney
Spencer Tracy
Robert Taylor
Myrna Loy
Jane Withers
Alice Faye
Tyrone Power

1939

Mickey Rooney
Tyrone Power
Spencer Tracy
Clark Gable
Shirley Temple
Bette Davis
Alice Faye
Errol Flynn
James Cagney
Sonja Henie

1940

Mickey Rooney
Spencer Tracy
Clark Gable
Gene Autry
Tyrone Power
James Cagney
Bing Crosby
Wallace Beery
Bette Davis
Judy Garland

1941

Mickey Rooney
Clark Gable
Abbott and Costello
Bob Hope
Spencer Tracy
Gene Autry
Gary Cooper
Bette Davis
James Cagney
Judy Garland

1942

Abbott and Costello
Clark Gable
Gary Cooper
Mickey Rooney
Bob Hope
James Cagney
Gene Autry
Betty Grable
Greer Garson
Spencer Tracy

1943

Betty Grable
Bob Hope
Abbott and Costello
Bing Crosby
Gary Cooper
Greer Garson
Humphrey Bogart
James Cagney
Mickey Rooney
Clark Gable

1944

Bing Crosby
Gary Cooper
Bob Hope
Betty Grable
Spencer Tracy
Greer Garson
Humphrey Bogart
Abbott and Costello
Cary Grant
Bette Davis

1945

Bing Crosby
Van Johnson
Greer Garson
Betty Grable
Spencer Tracy
Humphrey Bogart/Gary Cooper
Bob Hope
Judy Garland
Margaret O'Brien
Roy Rogers

1946

Bing Crosby
Ingrid Bergman
Van Johnson
Gary Cooper
Bob Hope
Humphrey Bogart
Greer Garson
Margaret O'Brien
Betty Grable
Roy Rogers

1947

Bing Crosby
Betty Grable
Ingrid Bergman
Gary Cooper
Humphrey Bogart
Bob Hope
Clark Gable
Gregory Peck
Claudette Colbert
Alan Ladd

1948

Bing Crosby
Betty Grable
Abbott and Costello
Gary Cooper
Bob Hope
Humphrey Bogart
Clark Gable
Cary Grant
Spencer Tracy
Ingrid Bergman

1949

Bob Hope
Bing Crosby
Abbott and Costello
John Wayne
Gary Cooper
Cary Grant
Betty Grable
Esther Williams
Humphrey Bogart
Clark Gable

1950

John Wayne
Bob Hope
Bing Crosby
Betty Grable
James Stewart
Abbott and Costello
Clifton Webb
Esther Williams
Spencer Tracy
Randolph Scott

1951

John Wayne
Martin and Lewis
Betty Grable
Abbott and Costello
Bing Crosby
Bob Hope
Randolph Scott
Gary Cooper
Doris Day
Spencer Tracy

1952

Martin and Lewis
Gary Cooper
John Wayne
Bing Crosby
Bob Hope
James Stewart
Doris Day
Gregory Peck
Susan Hayward
Randolph Scott

1953

Gary Cooper
Martin and Lewis
John Wayne
Alan Ladd
Bing Crosby
Marilyn Monroe
James Stewart
Bob Hope
Susan Hayward
Randolph Scott

1954

John Wayne
Martin and Lewis
Gary Cooper
James Stewart
Marilyn Monroe
Alan Ladd
William Holden
Bing Crosby
Jane Wyman
Marlon Brando

1955

James Stewart
Grace Kelly
John Wayne
William Holden
Gary Cooper
Marlon Brando
Martin and Lewis
Humphrey Bogart
June Allyson
Clark Gable

1956

William Holden
John Wayne
James Stewart
Burt Lancaster
Glenn Ford
Martin and Lewis
Gary Cooper
Marilyn Monroe

Kim Novak
Frank Sinatra

1957

Rock Hudson
John Wayne
Pat Boone
Elvis Presley
Frank Sinatra
Gary Cooper
William Holden
James Stewart
Jerry Lewis
Yul Brynner

1958

Glenn Ford
Elizabeth Taylor
Jerry Lewis
Marlon Brando
Rock Hudson
William Holden
Brigitte Bardot
Yul Brynner
James Stewart
Frank Sinatra

1959

Rock Hudson
Cary Grant
James Stewart
Doris Day
Debbie Reynolds
Glenn Ford
Frank Sinatra
John Wayne
Jerry Lewis
Susan Hayward

1960

Doris Day
Rock Hudson
Cary Grant
Elizabeth Taylor
Debbie Reynolds

Tony Curtis
Sandra Dee
Frank Sinatra
Jack Lemmon
John Wayne

1961
Elizabeth Taylor
Rock Hudson
Doris Day
John Wayne
Cary Grant
Sandra Dee
Jerry Lewis
William Holden
Tony Curtis
Elvis Presley

1962
Doris Day
Rock Hudson
Cary Grant
John Wayne
Elvis Presley
Elizabeth Taylor
Jerry Lewis
Frank Sinatra
Sandra Dee
Burt Lancaster

1963
Doris Day
John Wayne
Rock Hudson
Jack Lemmon
Cary Grant
Elizabeth Taylor
Elvis Presley
Sandra Dee
Paul Newman
Jerry Lewis

1964
Doris Day
Jack Lemmon

Rock Hudson
John Wayne
Cary Grant
Elvis Presley
Shirley MacLaine
Ann-Margaret
Paul Newman
Richard Burton

1965
Sean Connery
John Wayne
Doris Day
Julie Andrews
Jack Lemmon
Elvis Presley
Cary Grant
James Stewart
Elizabeth Taylor
Richard Burton

1966
Julie Andrews
Sean Connery
Elizabeth Taylor
Jack Lemmon
Richard Burton
Cary Grant
John Wayne
Doris Day
Paul Newman
Elvis Presley

1967
Julie Andrews
Lee Marvin
Paul Newman
Dean Martin
Sean Connery
Elizabeth Taylor
Sidney Poitier
John Wayne
Richard Burton
Steve McQueen

1968

Sidney Poitier
Paul Newman
Julie Andrews
John Wayne
Clint Eastwood
Dean Martin
Steve McQueen
Jack Lemmon
Lee Marvin
Elizabeth Taylor

1969

Paul Newman
John Wayne
Steve McQueen
Dustin Hoffman
Clint Eastwood
Sidney Poitier
Lee Marvin
Jack Lemmon
Katharine Hepburn
Barbra Streisand

1970

Paul Newman
Clint Eastwood
Steve McQueen
John Wayne
Elliott Gould
Dustin Hoffman
Lee Marvin
Jack Lemmon
Barbra Streisand
Walter Matthau

1971

John Wayne
Clint Eastwood
Paul Newman
Steve McQueen
George C. Scott
Dustin Hoffman
Walter Matthau
Ali MacGraw
Sean Connery
Lee Marvin

1972

Clint Eastwood
George C. Scott
Gene Hackman
John Wayne
Barbra Streisand
Marlon Brando
Paul Newman
Steve McQueen
Dustin Hoffman
Goldie Hawn

1973

Clint Eastwood
Ryan O'Neal
Steve McQueen
Burt Reynolds
Robert Redford
Barbra Streisand
Paul Newman
Charles Bronson
John Wayne
Marlon Brando

1974

Robert Redford
Clint Eastwood
Paul Newman
Barbra Streisand
Steve McQueen
Burt Reynolds
Charles Bronson
Jack Nicholson
Al Pacino
John Wayne

1975

Robert Redford
Barbra Streisand
Al Pacino
Charles Bronson
Paul Newman
Clint Eastwood
Burt Reynolds
Woody Allen
Steve McQueen
Gene Hackman

1976
Robert Redford
Jack Nicholson
Dustin Hoffman
Clint Eastwood
Mel Brooks
Burt Reynolds
Al Pacino
Tatum O'Neal
Woody Allen
Charles Bronson

1977
Sylvester Stallone
Barbra Streisand
Clint Eastwood
Burt Reynolds
Robert Redford
Woody Allen
Mel Brooks
Al Pacino
Diane Keaton
Robert DeNiro

1978
Burt Reynolds
John Travolta
Richard Dreyfuss
Warren Beatty

Clint Eastwood
Woody Allen
Diane Keaton
Jane Fonda
Peter Sellers
Barbra Streisand

1979
Burt Reynolds
Clint Eastwood
Jane Fonda
Woody Allen
Barbra Streisand
Sylvester Stallone
John Travolta
Jill Clayburgh
Roger Moore
Mel Brooks

1980
Burt Reynolds
Robert Redford
Clint Eastwood
Jane Fonda
Dustin Hoffman
John Travolta
Sally Field
Sissy Spacek
Barbra Streisand
Steve Martin

DON'T I KNOW YOU? (1)

Listed below on the left are actors whose supporting or "character" performances in the films listed on the right were outstanding. Match the actors with the films.

1. George C. Scott	A.	*Chinatown*
2. Randy Quaid	B.	*One Flew Over the Cuckoo's Nest*
3. Burgess Meredith	C.	*The Sting*
4. Lee Tracy	D.	*My Fair Lady*
5. Jason Robards	E.	*Lovers and Other Strangers*
6. John Huston	F.	*The French Connection*
7. Marty Feldman	G.	*Anatomy of a Murder*
8. Brad Dourif	H.	*Captain Newman, M.D.*
9. Edmond O'Brien	I.	*Georgy Girl*
10. Robert Shaw	J.	*The Best Man*
11. Roy Scheider	K.	*Smokey and the Bandit*
12. Stanley Holloway	L.	*Tom Jones*
13. Bobby Darrin	M.	*All the President's Men*
14. Richard Castellano	N.	*Who's Afraid of Virginia Woolf?*
15. Hugh Griffith	O.	*Ship of Fools*
16. George Segal	P.	*The Last Detail*
17. James Mason	Q.	*Gone with the Wind*
18. Michael Dunn	R.	*Seven Days in May*
19. Jackie Gleason	S.	*Young Frankenstein*
20. Thomas Mitchell	T.	*Rocky*

Photo 36

Photo 37   86

DON'T I KNOW YOU? (2)

Listed below on the left are actresses whose supporting or "character" performances in the films on the right were outstanding. Match the stars with the films.

1. Maggie Smith	A.	*Farewell, My Lovely*
2. Jane Alexander	B.	M*A*S*H
3. Valentina Cortese	C.	*Gone with the Wind*
4. Talia Shire	D.	*A Man for All Seasons*
5. Ronee Blakley	E.	*To Kill a Mockingbird*
6. Sylvia Miles	F.	*Judgment at Nuremberg*
7. Linda Blair	G.	*They Shoot Horses, Don't They?*
8. Peggy Wood	H.	*The Manchurian Candidate*
9. Madeline Kahn	I.	*Hush Hush, Sweet Charlotte*
10. Sally Kellerman	J.	*Othello*
11. Susannah York	K.	*Tom Jones*
12. Wendy Hiller	L.	*Nashville*
13. Ona Munson	M.	*Day for Night*
14. Agnes Moorehead	N.	*Sweet Bird of Youth*
15. Edith Evans	O.	*Birdman of Alcatraz*
16. Mary Badham	P.	*The Sound of Music*
17. Shirley Knight	Q.	*The Exorcist*
18. Angela Lansbury	R.	*The Godfather, Part II*
19. Thelma Ritter	S.	*Paper Moon*
20. Judy Garland	T.	*All the President's Men*

THE ANIMAL KINGDOM

The performers listed below starred together if films whose titles contain the name of an animal. Identify the films.

1. Liza Minnelli, Wendell Burton.
2. Jack Lemmon, Jack Gilford.
3. Burt Reynolds, Sarah Miles.
4. George C. Scott, Trish Van Devere, Paul Sorvino.
5. Ronald Colman, Joan Bennett, Lilyan Tashman, Montagu Love.
6. Charlton Heston, Roddy McDowall, Kim Hunter.
7. Lee Marvin, Jane Fonda, Michael Callan, Dwayne Hickman.
8. Al Pacino, John Cazale, James Broderick, Charles Durning, Chris Sarandon.
9. Edward Fox, Terence Alexander, Alan Badel, Delphine Seyrig.
10. John Wayne, Katharine Hepburn.
11. Dustin Hoffman, Susan Oliver, David Warner.
12. Peter O'Toole, Katharine Hepburn, Anthony Hopkins, Nigel Terry.
13. Jack Nicholson, Louise Fletcher, William Redfield.
14. Peter Sellers, David Niven, Robert Wagner, Claudia Cardinale, Capucine.
15. George Segal, Barbra Streisand, Robert Klein, Allen Garfield, Roz Kelly.
16. Sandy Dennis, Keir Dullea, Anne Heywood, Glyn Morris.
17. Richard Harris, Judith Anderson, Jean Gucson, Manu Tupou, Corinne Tsopei.
18. Mel Ferrer, Miroslava, Anthony Quinn.
19. Humphrey Bogart, Peter Lorre, Mary Astor.
20. Peter Sellers, Peter O'Toole, Romy Schneider. Capucine, Paula Prentiss.

Photo 38

THE PLAY'S THE THING

Listed below are the names of characters featured in films based on the work of Tennessee Williams. Name the star who played each role.

1. Amanda Wingate in *The Glass Menagerie*
2. Chance Wayne in *Sweet Bird of Youth*
3. Alma Winemiller in *Summer and Smoke*
4. Dr. Cukrowicz in *Suddenly Last Summer*
5. Mrs. Venable in *Suddenly Last Summer*
6. Rev. T. Lawrence Shannon in *Night of the Iguana*
7. Alexandra Del Lago in *Sweet Bird of Youth*
8. Brick Pollitt in *Cat on a Hot Tin Roof*
9. Stella Kowalski in *A Streetcar Named Desire*
10. Paolo in *The Roman Spring of Mrs. Stone*
11. Maggie Pollitt in *Cat on a Hot Tin Roof*
12. Val Xavier in *The Fugitive Kind*
13. Serafina Della Rose in *The Rose Tattoo*
14. Tom Wingate in *The Glass Menagerie*
15. Catherine Holly in *Suddenly Last Summer*
16. Big Daddy Pollitt in *Cat on a Hot Tin Roof*
17. Maxine Faulk in *Night of the Iguana*
18. John Buchanan in *Summer and Smoke*
19. Mrs. Flora Goforth in *Boom!*
20. Stanley Kowalski in *A Streetcar Named Desire*

Photo 39

TALL IN THE SADDLE

Identify the stars who played the following title roles.

1. *Davy Crockett—King of the Wild Frontier*
2. *Hombre*
3. *Navajo Joe*
4. *The Ballad of Cable Hogue*
5. *Chisum*
6. *Billy Two Hats*
7. *Dirty Dingus Magee*
8. *The Man Who Loved Cat Dancing*
9. *Cahill, United States Marshal*
10. *Davy Crockett—Indian Scout*
11. *The Sheepman*
12. *Alias Jesse James*
13. *The Cimarron Kid*
14. *Nevada Smith*
15. *Trooper Hook*
16. *Sergeant Rutledge*
17. *Alvarez Kelly*
18. *Shane*
19. *Pat Garrett and Billy the Kid*
20. *Pat Garrett and Billy the Kid*

LITTLE BROTHERS

The stars listed on the left have played the younger brothers of the stars listed on the right. Match the stars and identify the films involved.

1.	Arthur Kennedy	A.	Phyllis Thaxter
2.	Audie Murphy	B.	Lana Turner
3.	Mickey Rooney	C.	Jason Robards
4.	Butch Jenkins	D.	Shirley Temple
5.	Richard Jaekel	E.	James Cagney
6.	Robert Walker	F.	Johnny Ray
7.	Lew Ayres	G.	Luther Adler
8.	James Cagney	H.	James Stewart
9.	Rand Brooks	I.	Jean Harlow
10.	Robert Wagner	J.	Kevin McCarthy
11.	Alan Curtis	K.	Peter Lawford
12.	Dean Stockwell	L.	Katharine Hepburn
13.	Cameron Mitchell	M.	Paul Newman
14.	Dean Martin	N.	Gary Cooper
15.	Donald O'Connor	O.	Henry Fonda
16.	Jackie Cooper	P.	Don Ameche
17.	Tyrone Power	Q.	Richard Widmark
18.	Richard Conte	R.	Olivia de Havilland
19.	Ray Milland	S.	Pat O'Brien
20.	Johnny Russell	T.	Wendy Hiller

Photo 40

KID SISTERS

The stars listed on the left have played the younger sisters of the stars listed on the right. Match the stars and identify the films involved.

1. Margaret O'Brien	A. Alexis Smith
2. Virginia Weidler	B. Rosalind Russell
3. Joan Leslie	C. Lola Lane
4. Jeanne Cagney	D. Dick Haymes
5. Diana Lynn	E. Arthur Kennedy
6. Evelyn Keyes	F. Barbara Stanwyck
7. Jeanne Crain	G. Judy Garland
8. Carole Landis	H. Robert Young
9. Joan Fontaine	I. Joan Caulfield
10. Janet Gaynor	J. Ida Lupino
11. Anne Shirley	K. Betty Garrett
12. Laraine Day	L. Robert Sterling
13. Nancy Coleman	M. Katharine Hepburn
14. Katharine Hepburn	N. James Cagney
15. June Allyson	O. Rita Johnson
16. Janet Blair	P. Carole Lombard
17. Janet Leigh	Q. Douglas Fairbanks, Jr.
18. Mona Freeman	R. Doris Nolan
19. Jane Wyman	S. Betty Grable
20. Priscilla Lane	T. Vivien Leigh

Photo 41

LIGHTS, ACTION . . . FORD

Listed below are the stars of films directed by John Ford. Identify the films.

1. John Wayne, Maureen O'Hara, Victor McLaglen, Barry Fitzgerald, Mildred Natwick.
2. Roddy McDowall, Walter Pidgeon, Maureen O'Hara, Donald Crisp, Sara Allgood.
3. Henry Fonda, Jane Darwell, John Carradine, Dorris Bowden, Charley Grapewin.
4. Henry Fonda, Linda Darnell, Victor Mature, Walter Brennan, Tim Holt.
5. James Stewart, John Wayne, Vera Miles, Lee Marvin, Edmond O'Brien.
6. Clark Gable, Ava Gardner, Grace Kelly, Donald Sinden.
7. Tyrone Power, Maureen O'Hara, Ward Bond, Robert Francis, Donald Crisp.
8. Victor McLaglen, Preston Foster, Wallace Ford, Margot Grahame, Una O'Connor.
9. Victor McLaglen, Wallace Ford, Boris Karloff, Reginald Denny.
10. Katharine Hepburn, Fredric March, Florence Eldredge, Donald Crisp.
11. Barbara Stanwyck, Preston Foster, Barry Fitzgerald, Una O'Connor, J. M. Kerrigan.
12. Dorothy Lamour, Jon Hall, Raymond Massey, Mary Astor, Thomas Mitchell.
13. Shirley Temple, Victor McLaglen, Cesar Romero, June Lang, Michael Whalen.
14. Claudette Colbert, Henry Fonda, Edna May Oliver, Ward Bond, John Carradine.
15. John Wayne, Claire Trevor, Thomas Mitchell, Tim Holt, Louise Platt, Andy Devine.
16. John Wayne, Henry Fonda, Shirley Temple, John Agar, Anna Lee, Ward Bond.
17. John Wayne, Maureen O'Hara, Claude Jarmin, Jr., Victor McLaglen, Ben Johnson.
18. Henry Fonda, James Cagney, William Powell, Jack Lemmon, Betsy Palmer.
19. Charley Grapewin, Marjorie Rambeau, Gene Tierney, Ward Bond, William Tracy.
20. Henry Fonda, Alice Brady, Marjorie Weaver, Donald Meek, Richard Cromwell.

LIGHTS, ACTION . . . HITCHCOCK

Listed below are the stars of films directed by Alfred Hitchock. Identify the films.

1. Tippi Hendren, Rod Taylor, Suzanne Pleshette, Jessica Tandy, Charles McGraw.
2. Tony Perkins, Janet Leigh, Vera Miles, John Gavin, Martin Balsam.
3. Cary Grant, Eva Marie Saint, James Mason, Jessie Royce Landis, Leo G. Carroll.
4. James Stewart, Kim Novak, Barbara Bel Geddes, Tom Helmore, Henry Jones.
5. Henry Fonda, Vera Miles, Anthony Quayle, Harold J. Stone.
6. James Stewart, Doris Day, Brenda de Banzie, Bernard Miles, Ralph Truman.
7. Barbara Harris, Bruce Dern, Karen Black, William Devane.
8. Jon Finch, Barry Foster, Alex McGowen, Vivien Merchant.
9. Paul Newman, Julie Andrews, Lila Kedrova.
10. Edmund Gwenn, John Forsythe, Shirley MacLaine, Mildred Natwick.
11. Cary Grant, Grace Kelly, Jessie Royce Landis, John Williams.
12. James Stewart, Grace Kelly, Wendell Corey, Thelma Ritter, Raymond Burr.
13. Ray Milland, Grace Kelly, Robert Cummings, John Williams.
14. Robert Walker, Farley Granger, Ruth Roman, Leo G. Carroll, Patricia Hitchcock.
15. Marlene Dietrich, Jane Wyman, Richard Todd, Michael Wilding, Alastair Sim.
16. Cary Grant, Ingrid Bergman, Claude Rains, Louis Calhern, Madame Konstantin.
17. Ingrid Bergman, Gregory Peck, Michael Chekhov, Jean Acker, Rhonda Fleming.
18. Tallulah Bankhead, John Hodiak, William Bendix, Walter Slezak, Mary Anderson.
19. Cary Grant, Joan Fontaine, Cedric Hardwicke, Nigel Bruce, Dame May Whitty.
20. Laurence Olivier, Joan Fontaine, Judith Anderson, George Sanders.

LIGHTS, ACTION . . . HUSTON

Listed below are the stars of films directed by John Huston. Identify the films.

1. Humphrey Bogart, Mary Astor, Sydney Greenstreet, Peter Lorre, Lee Patrick.
2. Elizabeth Taylor, Marlon Brando, Julie Harris, Robert Forster, Brian Keith.
3. Humphrey Bogart, Walter Huston, Tim Holt, Bruce Bennett, Barton MacLane.
4. Richard Burton, Ava Gardner, Deborah Kerr, Sue Lyon, Grayson Hall.
5. Montgomery Clift, Susannah York, Larry Parks, David McCallum, Susan Kohner.
6. Humphrey Bogart, Jennifer Jones, Gina Lollobrigida, Robert Morley, Peter Lorre.
7. George C. Scott, Clive Brook, Dana Wynter, Herbert Marshall, Tony Curtis, Kirk Douglas, Burt Lancaster, Robert Mitchum, Frank Sinatra.
8. Humphrey Bogart, Katharine Hepburn, Robert Morley.
9. Bette Davis, Olivia de Havilland, George Brent, Dennis Morgan, Charles Coburn.
10. Audrey Hepburn, Burt Lancaster, Lillian Gish, Audie Murphy, John Saxon.
11. Humphrey Bogart, Lauren Bacall, Edward G. Robinson, Claire Trevor, Lionel Barrymore.
12. Trevor Howard, Errol Flynn, Juliette Greco, Eddie Albert, Orson Welles.
13. Deborah Kerr, Robert Mitchum.
14. Gregory Peck, Richard Basehart, Orson Welles, Leo Genn.
15. Jose Ferrer, Zsa Zsa Gabor, Suzanne Flon, Colette Marchand, Christopher Lee.
16. Sterling Hayden, Louis Calhern, Jean Hagen, Marilyn Monroe, Sam Jaffe.
17. Audie Murphy, Bill Mauldin, John Dierkes, Royal Dano, Andy Devine.
18. Clark Gable, Marilyn Monroe, Montgomery Clift, Thelma Ritter, Eli Wallach.
19. Michael Parks, Ulla Bergryd, Richard Harris, John Huston, Ava Gardner.
20. Jennifer Jones, John Garfield, Pedro Armendariz, Gilbert Roland, Ramon Novarro.

LIGHTS, ACTION . . . CUKOR

Listed below are the stars of films directed by George Cukor. Identify the films.

1. Audrey Hepburn, Rex Harrison, Stanley Holloway, Wilfred Hyde-White.
2. Judy Garland, James Mason, Charles Bickford, Jack Carson, Tommy Noonan.
3. Ronald Colman, Signe Hasso, Edmond O'Brien, Shelley Winters.
4. Norma Shearer, Joan Crawford, Rosalind Russell, Paulette Goddard, Joan Fontaine.
5. Gene Kelly, Mitzi Gaynor, Kay Kendall, Taina Elg.
6. Anna Magnani, Anthony Quinn, Tony Franciosa, Dolores Hart.
7. Katharine Hepburn, Spencer Tracy, Judy Holliday, Jean Hagen, Tom Ewell.
8. Greta Garbo, Melvyn Douglas, Constance Bennett, Robert Sterling.
9. Katharine Hepburn, Douglass Montgomery, Paul Lukas, Joan Bennett, Jean Parker.
10. Joan Crawford, Melvyn Douglas, Conrad Veidt, Osa Massen.
11. Greta Garbo, Robert Taylor, Laura Hope Crews, Lionel Barrymore, Henry Daniell.
12. John and Lionel Barrymore, Marie Dressler, Jean Harlow, Wallace Beery, Billie Burke.
13. Freddie Bartholomew, W. C. Fields, Frank Lawton, Elizabeth Allan, Basil Rathbone.
14. Norma Shearer, Leslie Howard, John Barrymore, Edna May Oliver, Ralph Forbes.
15. Joan Crawford, Fredric March, Ruth Hussey, Rita Quigley, Rita Hayworth.
16. Katharine Hepburn, Cary Grant, James Stewart, Ruth Hussey, John Howard.
17. Ingrid Bergman, Charles Boyer, Joseph Cotten, Angela Lansbury.
18. Judy Holliday, Broderick Crawford, William Holden, Howard St. John.
19. Katharine Hepburn, Spencer Tracy, Aldo Ray, William Ching, Jim Backus.
20. Katharine Hepburn, Cary Grant, Lew Ayres, Doris Nolan, Binnie Barnes.

GUMSHOES (1)

Listed below are screen detectives and films in which they appeared. Identify the stars who played these detectives.

1. Nick Charles in *The Thin Man*.
2. Philip Marlowe in *Murder, My Sweet*.
3. Philip Marlowe in *Farewell, My Lovely*.
4. Philip Marlowe in *The Long Goodbye*.
5. Philip Marlowe in *The Big Sleep*.
6. Philip Marlowe in *Lady in the Lake*.
7. Philip Marlowe in *The Brasher Doubloon*.
8. Philip Marlowe in *Marlowe*.
9. Mrs. North in *Mr. and Mrs. North*.
10. Tony Rome in *Lady in Cement*.
11. Sam Spade in *The Maltese Falcon*.
12. Sam Spade, Jr. in *The Black Bird*.
13. Flint in *Our Man Flint*.
14. Matt Helm in *Murderers Row*.
15. James Bond in *You Only Live Twice*.
16. James Bond in *The Spy Who Loved Me*.
17. James Bond in *Casino Royale*.
18. Inspector Clouseau in *The Pink Panther*.
19. Hercule Poirot in *Murder on the Orient Express*.
20. Hercule Poirot in *The Alphabet Murders*.

GUMSHOES (2)

Listed below are screen detectives and films in which they appeared. Identify the stars who played these detectives.

1. Sherlock Holmes in *The Seven-Per-Cent Solution*.
2. Sherlock Holmes in *The Hound of the Baskervilles* (1939).
3. Sherlock Holmes in *The Hound of the Baskervilles* (1959).
4. Harper in *The Drowning Pool*.
5. Nancy Drew in *Nancy Drew, Detective*.
6. Charlie Chan in *Charlie Chan at the Opera*.
7. Charlie Chan in *Charlie Chan in Panama*.
8. Charlie Chan in *Chinese Ring*.
9. Mr. Moto in *Think Fast, Mr. Moto*.
10. Bulldog Drummond in *Bulldog Drummond Strikes Back*.
11. Bulldog Drummond in *Bulldog Drummond Escapes*.
12. Bulldog Drummond in *Bulldog Drummond Comes Back*.
13. Perry Mason in *The Case of the Velvet Claws*.
14. Perry Mason in *The Case of The Black Cat*.
15. Perry Mason in *The Case of the Stuttering Bishop*.
16. Philo Vance in *The Canary Murder Case*.
17. Philo Vance in *The Garden Murder Case*.
18. Philo Vance in *The Dragon Murder Case*.
19. Ellery Queen in *Ellery Queen's Penthouse Mystery*.
20. Ellery Queen in *A Desperate Chance for Ellery Queen*.

99   Photo 42

CHORUS LINES (1)

Listed below are the casts of Hollywood musical films. Identify the films.

1. Fred Astaire, Cyd Charisse, Nanette Fabray, Oscar Levant, Jack Buchanan.
2. Bing Crosby, Fred Astaire, Marjorie Reynolds, Virginia Dale.
3. Alice Faye, Tyrone Power, Ethel Merman, Don Ameche.
4. Ethel Merman, Marilyn Monroe, Dan Dailey, Donald O'Connor, Mitzi Gaynor.
5. Judy Garland, Bert Lahr, Ray Bolger, Jack Haley, Frank Morgan.
6. Fred Astaire, Ginger Rogers, Irene Dunne, Randolph Scott.
7. James Cagney, Joan Blondell, Dick Powell, Ruby Keeler, Claire Dodd.
8. Judy Garland, Fred Astaire, Ann Miller, Peter Lawford.
9. Howard Keel, Kathryn Grayson, Ann Miller, Tommy Rall, Keenan Wynn.
10. Howard Keel, Kathryn Grayson, Ava Gardner, Joe E. Brown, the Champions.
11. Betty Grable, June Haver, John Payne, S. Z. Sakall.
12. Alice Faye, Betty Grable, John Payne, Jack Oakie.
13. Warner Baxter, Bebe Daniels, Ruby Keeler, Dick Powell, Ginger Rogers, Una Merkel.
14. Gene Kelly, Debbie Reynolds, Donald O'Connor, Jean Hagen, Cyd Charisse.
15. Bing Crosby, Danny Kaye, Vera-Ellen, Rosemary Clooney.
16. Bing Crosby, Bob Hope, Dorothy Lamour, Anthony Quinn, Dona Drake.
17. Judy Garland, Margaret O'Brien, Tom Drake, Mary Astor, Lucille Bremer.
18. Gene Kelly, Rita Hayworth, Lee Bowman, Eve Arden, Phil Silvers.
19. Howard Keel, Jane Powell, Russ Tamblyn, Jeff Richards, Marc Platt, Jacques D'Ambois.
20. Leslie Caron, Louis Jordan, Maurice Chevalier, Hermione Gingold.

101   Photo 43

CHORUS LINES (2)

Listed below are the casts of Hollywood musical films. Identify the films.

1. Julie Andrews, Dick Van Dyke, Ed Wynn, Glynis Johns, Hermione Baddeley.
2. Audrey Hepburn, Rex Harrison, Stanley Holloway, Wilfred Hyde-White.
3. Natalie Wood, Richard Beymer, Rita Moreno, George Chakiris, Russ Tamblyn.
4. Frank Sinatra, Marlon Brando, Jean Simmons, Vivian Blaine.
5. Gene Kelly, Leslie Caron, Oscar Levant, Georges Guetary, Nina Foch.
6. Doris Day, John Raitt, Carol Haney, Eddie Foy, Jr., Reta Shaw.
7. Judy Garland, Lana Turner, Hedy Lamarr, James Stewart, Tony Martin.
8. James Cagney, Joan Leslie, Walter Huston, Rosemary DeCamp, Jeanne Cagney.
9. Dorothy Dandridge, Harry Belafonte, Pearl Bailey, Diahann Carroll.
10. Doris Day, James Cagney, Cameron Mitchell.
11. Frank Sinatra, Shirley MacLaine, Maurice Chevalier, Louis Jourdan, Juliet Prowse.
12. Gordon MacRae, Shirley Jones, Gloria Grahame, Gene Nelson, Charlotte Greenwood.
13. Gordon MacRae, Shirley Jones, Robert Rounseville, Cameron Mitchell, Barbara Ruick.
14. Jane Powell, Elizabeth Taylor, Wallace Beery, Carmen Miranda, Robert Stack.
15. The Marx Brothers, Kitty Carlisle, Allan Jones, Margaret Dumont.
16. Jeanne Crain, Dana Andrews, Dick Haymes, Vivian Blaine, Fay Bainter.
17. Mitzi Gaynor, Rossano Brazzi, John Kerr, Ray Walston, Juanita Hall, France Nuyen.
18. Fred Astaire, Jane Powell, Peter Lawford, Sarah Churchill, Keenan Wynn.
19. Cary Grant, Alexis Smith, Ginny Simms, Jane Wyman, Mary Martin, Monty Woolley.
20. Betty Grable, Dan Dailey, Mona Freeman, Connie Marshall, Vanessa Brown.

Photo 44

THEY'RE PLAYING THEIR SONGS (1)

Listed below on the left are songs which were performed in various films by the stars on the right. Match the singers with the songs and identify the films in which the songs were sung. (Yes, some of them were dubbed.)

1. "White Christmas"
2. "Put the Blame on Mame"
3. "High Hopes"
4. "Get Happy"
5. "On the Good Ship Lollipop"
6. "Que Sera, Sera"
7. "That's Amore"
8. "Supercalifragilisticexpialido-cious"
9. "Oh, What a Beautiful Morning"
10. "Once in Love with Amy"
11. "I'm in Love with a Wonderful Guy"
12. "The Donkey Serenade"
13. "Whatever Lola Wants"
14. "Again"
15. "(All of a Sudden) My Heart Sings"
16. "Too Darn Hot"
17. "Loverly"
18. "Easy to Love"
19. "I Only Have Eyes for You"
20. "Would You?"

A. Doris Day
B. Julie Andrews
C. Ray Bolger
D. Gwen Verdon
E. Kathryn Grayson
F. Allan Jones
G. Mitzi Gaynor
H. Bing Crosby
I. Ann Miller
J. Judy Garland
K. Audrey Hepburn
L. Jeanette MacDonald
M. James Stewart
N. Rita Hayworth
O. Dick Powell
P. Dean Martin
Q. Ida Lupino
R. Gordon MacRae
S. Frank Sinatra
T. Shirley Temple

Photo 45

Photo 46

THEY'RE PLAYING THEIR SONGS (2)

Listed below on the left are songs which were performed in various films by the stars on the right. Match the singers with the songs and identify the films in which the songs were sung. (Yes, some of them were dubbed.)

1. "I Wish I Didn't Love You So"
2. "My Favorite Things"
3. "Talk to the Animals"
4. "Moon River"
5. "I've Got You Under My Skin"
6. "The Boy Next Door"
7. "Zip"
8. "Somethin's Gotta Give"
9. "Take It from There"
10. "Now It Can Be Told"
11. "You Keep Coming Back Like a Song"
12. "Buttons and Bows"
13. "The Last Time I Saw Paris"
14. "Maybe This Time"
15. "Did I Remember?"
16. "As Time Goes By"
17. "Ole Buttermilk Sky"
18. "Love Letters in the Sand"
19. "A Person Could Develop a Cold"
20. "Thank Heaven for Little Girls"

A. Judy Garland
B. Audrey Hepburn
C. Fred Astaire
D. Alice Faye
E. Rita Hayworth
F. Bob Hope
G. Liza Minnelli
H. Hoagy Carmichael
I. Ann Sothern
J. Jean Harlow
K. Virginia Bruce

L. Julie Andrews
M. Vivian Blaine
N. Dooley Wilson
O. Pat Boone
P. Maurice Chevalier
Q. Bing Crosby
R. Betty Hutton
S. Betty Grable
T. Rex Harrison

SPEAK EASY

Listed below are the stars of films about the "Roaring Twenties." Identify the films.

1. James Cagney, Priscilla Lane, Jeffrey Lynn, Gladys George, Humphrey Bogart.
2. James Stewart, Patricia Smith, Murray Hamilton, Marc Connelly.
3. James Cagney, Jean Harlow, Joan Blondell, Mae Clarke, Eddie Woods.
4. Margaret Sullivan, Douglass Montgomery, Alan Hale, Catherine Doucet.
5. Edward G. Robinson, Douglas Fairbanks, Jr., Glenda Farrell.
6. Margaret Sullavan, Robert Taylor, Franchot Tone, Robert Young, Lionel Atwill.
7. Robert Redford, Paul Newman, Robert Shaw, Eileen Brennan.
8. Alice Faye, John Payne, Jack Oakie, Mary Beth Hughes, Cesar Romero.
9. Robert Redford, Mia Farrow, Sam Waterston, Karen Black.
10. Julie Andrews, John Gavin, Mary Tyler Moore, James Fox, Carol Channing.
11. Gene Kelly, Debbie Reynolds, Donald O'Connor, Jean Hagen.
12. Paul Muni, Ann Dvorak, Karen Morley, George Raft.
13. Marilyn Monroe, Tony Curtis, Jack Lemmon, Joe E. Brown.
14. Jack Webb, Janet Leigh, Peggy Lee, Edmond O'Brien, Lee Marvin, Andy Devine.
15. Anne Baxter, Dan Dailey, Anne Revere, Buster Keaton.
16. Alice Faye, Don Ameche, Mack Sennett, Stuart Erwin, Buster Keaton.
17. Bob Hope, Vera Miles, Alexis Smith, Paul Douglas.
18. Jeanne Crain, Glenn Langan, Lynn Bari, Esther Dale.
19. Ginger Rogers, George Montgomery, Adolphe Menjou, Lynne Overman.
20. James Cagney, Doris Day, Cameron Mitchell, Robert Keith, Tom Tully.

Photo 47

107

BROTHER, CAN YOU SPARE A DIME?

Listed below are the stars of films set during the 1930s. Identify the films.

1. Henry Fonda, Jane Darwell, John Carradine, Charley Grapewin, Dorris Bowdon.
2. Margaret Sullavan, James Stewart, Robert Young, Robert Stack, Frank Morgan.
3. Ryan O'Neal, Tatum O'Neal, Madeline Kahn.
4. Henry Fonda, Madeleine Carroll, Leo Carrillo, John Halliday.
5. Warner Baxter, Madge Evans, Shirley Temple, James Dunn, John Boles.
6. Gary Cooper, Ingrid Bergman, Katina Paxinou, Akim Tamiroff.
7. Carole Lombard, William Powell, Gail Patrick, Alice Brady, Mischa Auer.
8. Spencer Tracy, Loretta Young, Marjorie Rambeau, Arthur Hoyl.
9. Warren Beatty, Faye Dunaway, Estelle Parsons, Michael J. Pollard.
10. Broderick Crawford, John Ireland, Mercedes McCambridge, Joanne Dru.
11. Karen Morley, Tom Steele, John Qualen, Barbara Pepper.
12. James Cagney, Ann Dvorak, Margaret Lindsay, Robert Armstrong.
13. Charley Grapewin, Marjorie Rambeau, Gene Tierney, Ward Bond, William Tracy.
14. Lew Ayres, Dorothy Lamour, Anthony Quinn, Gilbert Roland, Karen Morley.
15. Mickey Rooney, Judy Garland, Lana Turner, Ann Rutherford, Lewis Stone.
16. Spencer Tracy, Sylvia Sidney, Frank Albertson, Walter Abel, Bruce Cabot.
17. Humphrey Bogart, Erin O'Brien-Moore, Dick Foran, Ann Sheridan.
18. Jane Fonda, Michael Sarrazin, Susannah York, Gig Young, Bruce Dern.
19. Claudette Colbert, Warren William, Louise Beavers, Rochelle Hudson.

20. Claude Rains, Gloria Dickson, Edward Norris, Lana Turner, Otto Kruger.

WAR AND PEACE

Listed below are the stars of films set during the 1940s. Identify the films.

1. Fredric March, Myrna Loy, Dana Andrews, Teresa Wright, Harold Russell.
2. Marlon Brando, Teresa Wright, Jack Webb, Everett Sloane.
3. James Edwards, Douglas Dick, Steve Brodie, Lloyd Bridges.
4. Arthur Kennedy, Peggy Dow, Julie Adams, James Edwards.
5. Clark Gable, Deborah Kerr, Ava Gardner, Sydney Greenstreet, Adolphe Menjou.
6. Gregory Peck, Jennifer Jones, Fredric March, Marisa Pavan, Ann Harding.
7. Preston Foster, Lloyd Nolan, William Bendix, Richard Conte, Anthony Quinn.
8. Gregory Peck, Dorothy McGuire, John Garfield, Celeste Holm, Anne Revere.
9. Dana Andrews, Richard Conte, Sterling Holloway, John Ireland.
10. Dana Andrews, Farley Granger, Sam Levene, Richard Conte, Marshall Thompson.
11. John Garfield, Eleanor Parker, Dane Clark, Rosemary DeCamp.
12. Audie Murphy, Marshall Thompson, Susan Kohner, Charles Drake, Jack Kelly.

Photo 48

13. Steve McQueen, Shirley Anne Field, Robert Wagner.
14. Franchot Tone, Anne Baxter, Erich von Stroheim, Akim Tamiroff.
15. Spencer Tracy, Van Johnson, Robert Walker, Phyllis Thaxter, Robert Mitchum.
16. James Mason, Cedric Hardwicke, Jessica Tandy, Luther Adler.
17. Gene Kelly, Frank Sinatra, Kathryn Grayson, Dean Stockwell, Jose Iturbi.
18. Edward G. Robinson, Burt Lancaster, Howard Duff, Mady Christians, Louisa Horton.
19. Greer Garson, Walter Pidgeon, Teresa Wright, Richard Ney, May Whitty.
20. Tallulah Bankhead, John Hodiak, William Bendix, Walter Slezak, Mary Anderson.

MARLON, ALSO STARRING . . .

The performers listed on the left have played in the Marlon Brando films listed on the right. Match the stars and the films.

1. Jack Webb	A. *Viva Zapata*
2. Greer Garson	B. *The Wild One*
3. Merle Oberon	C. *The Teahouse of the August Moon*
4. Hope Lange	D. *A Countess from Hong Kong*
5. Richard Harris	E. *The Godfather*
6. Robert Redford	F. *On the Waterfront*
7. Kim Hunter	G. *The Missouri Breaks*
8. David Niven	H. *Sayonara*
9. Mary Murphy	I. *Last Tango in Paris*
10. James Caan	J. *The Night of the Following Day*
11. Margo	K. *Reflections in a Golden Eye*
12. Maria Schneider	L. *Julius Caesar*
13. Vivian Blaine	M. *The Chase*
14. Jack Nicholson	N. *Bedtime Story*
15. Rita Moreno	O. *The Men*
16. Glenn Ford	P. *Mutiny on the Bounty*
17. Julie Harris	Q. *Desiree*
18. Sydney Chaplin	R. *The Young Lions*
19. Red Buttons	S. *Guys and Dolls*
20. Eva Marie Saint	T. *A Streetcar Named Desire*

Photo 49

111

ELIZABETH, ALSO STARRING . . .

The performers listed on the left have played in the Elizabeth Taylor films listed on the right. Match the stars and films.

1. Noel Coward	A. *X, Y and Zee*
2. Mia Farrow	B. *The Only Game in Town*
3. George Raft	C. *The Comedians*
4. Henry Fonda	D. *The V.I.P.s*
5. Julie Harris	E. *Night Watch*
6. Peter O'Toole	F. *Suddenly Last Summer*
7. Sandy Dennis	G. *Cat on a Hot Tin Roof*
8. Michael Caine	H. *The Last Time I Saw Paris*
9. Maggie Smith	I. *Boom!*
10. Eddie Fisher	J. *Ivanhoe*
11. Judith Anderson	K. *The Girl Who Had Everything*
12. Joan Fontaine	L. *Rhapsody*
13. Alec Guinness	M. *Giant*
14. William Powell	N. *Ash Wednesday*
15. Donna Reed	O. *Butterfield 8*
16. Warren Beatty	P. *Who's Afraid of Virginia Woolf?*
17. Katharine Hepburn	Q. *Hammersmith Is Out*
18. Vittorio Gassman	R. *Secret Ceremony*
19. Jane Withers	S. *Reflections in a Golden Eye*
20. Laurence Harvey	T. *Under Milk Wood*

Photo 50

CARY, ALSO STARRING . . .

The performers listed on the left have played in the Cary Grant films listed on the right. Match the stars and the films.

1.	Samantha Eggar	A.	Houseboat
2.	Robert Mitchum	B.	North by Northwest
3.	Leslie Caron	C.	People Will Talk
4.	James Coburn	D.	Night and Day
5.	Grace Kelly	E.	That Touch of Mink
6.	Shirley Temple	F.	None But the Lonely Heart
7.	Jeanne Crain	G.	The Pride and the Passion
8.	Jayne Mansfield	H.	Monkey Business
9.	Mary Martin	I.	Destination Tokyo
10.	Martha Hyer	J.	Crisis
11.	Ethel Barrymore	K.	Dream Wife
12.	John Garfield	L.	I Was a Male War Bride
13.	Tony Curtis	M.	Walk, Don't Run
14.	Jose Ferrer	N.	The Bachelor and the Bobby-Soxer
15.	Betta St. John	O.	Kiss Them for Me
16.	Eva Marie Saint	P.	The Grass Is Greener
17.	Marilyn Monroe	Q.	Father Goose
18.	Ann Sheridan	R.	Charade
19.	Gig Young	S.	Operation Petticoat
20.	Frank Sinatra	T.	To Catch a Thief

Photo 51

113

INGRID, ALSO STARRING . . .

The performers listed on the left have played in the Ingrid Bergman films listed on the right. Match the stars and the films.

1. Fritz Weaver	A. *Under Capricorn*
2. Anthony Perkins	B. *Indiscreet*
3. Valentina Cortese	C. *The Inn of the Sixth Happiness*
4. Helen Hayes	D. *Saratoga Trunk*
5. Jose Ferrer	E. *Notorious*
6. Bing Crosby	F. *Cactus Flower*
7. Michael Wilding	G. *Arch of Triumph*
8. Geraldine Brooks	H. *For Whom the Bell Tolls*
9. Lana Turner	I. *Casablanca*
10. Sydney Greenstreet	J. *Gaslight*
11. Omar Sharif	K. *Spellbound*
12. Katina Paxinou	L. *Dr. Jekyll and Mr. Hyde*
13. Madame Konstantin	M. *The Bells of St. Mary's*
14. Angela Lansbury	N. *A Walk in the Spring Rain*
15. Charles Laughton	O. *The Visit*
16. Flora Robson	P. *Stromboli*
17. Gregory Peck	Q. *Joan of Arc*
18. Phyllis Calvert	R. *Anastasia*
19. Robert Donat	S. *The Yellow Rolls Royce*
20. Goldie Hawn	T. *Goodbye Again*

Photo 52

GARLAND, ALSO STARRING . . .

The performers listed on the left have played in the Judy Garland films listed on the right. Match the stars with the films.

1. Charles Bickford		A.	Meet Me in St. Louis
2. Gloria de Haven		B.	Pigskin Parade
3. S. Z. Sakall		C.	Girl Crazy
4. Ann Miller		D.	Broadway Melody of 1938
5. Richard Carlson		E.	The Wizard of Oz
6. Angela Lansbury		F.	Judgment at Nuremberg
7. Allan Jones		G.	The Clock
8. Margaret O'Brien		H.	Ziegfeld Girl
9. Robert Taylor		I.	Babes in Arms
10. June Allyson		J.	I Could Go on Singing
11. Robert Walker		K.	A Child Is Waiting
12. Ann Rutherford		L.	In the Good Old Summertime
13. Tony Martin		M.	The Pirate
14. Betty Grable		N.	A Star Is Born
15. Dirk Bogarde		O.	Everybody Sing
16. Margaret Hamilton		P.	Love Finds Andy Hardy
17. Gena Rowlands		Q.	Presenting Lily Mars
18. June Preisser		R.	Summer Stock
19. Montgomery Clift		S.	The Harvey Girls
20. Gladys Cooper		T.	Easter Parade

Photo 53

CAGNEY, ALSO STARRING . . .

The performers listed on the left have played in the James Cagney films listed on the right. Match the stars with the films.

1. Horst Buchholz	A. *Man of a Thousand Faces*
2. Dana Wynter	B. *Run for Cover*
3. Dennis Weaver	C. *Come Fill the Cup*
4. Shirley Jones	D. *White Heat*
5. Jack Lemmon	E. *Tribute to a Bad Man*
6. Dorothy Malone	F. *13 Rue Madeleine*
7. Gig Young	G. *Blood on the Sun*
8. Viveca Lindfors	H. *City for Conquest*
9. Gordon MacRae	I. *Shake Hands with the Devil*
10. Corinne Calvet	J. *The Public Enemy*
11. George Brent	K. *Jimmy the Gent*
12. Irene Papas	L. *One Two Three*
13. Arthur Kennedy	M. *The Strawberry Blonde*
14. Margaret Wycherly	N. *These Wilder Years*
15. Jean Harlow	O. *The Fighting 69th*
16. Annabella	P. *Mr. Roberts*
17. Bette Davis	Q. *The West Point Story*
18. Sylvia Sidney	R. *The Gallant Hours*
19. Barbara Stanwyck	S. *What Price Glory*
20. Rita Hayworth	T. *Never Steal Anything Small*

Photo 54

117

DIETRICH, ALSO STARRING . . .

The performers listed on the left have played in the Marlene Dietrich films listed on the right. Match the stars and the films.

1.	Adolphe Menjou	A.	*Dishonored*
2.	Elsa Lanchester	B.	*Golden Earrings*
3.	Vittorio De Sica	C.	*Kismet*
4.	Judy Garland	D.	*Stage Fright*
5.	Mel Ferrer	E.	*Blonde Venus*
6.	Jane Wyman	F.	*Seven Sinners*
7.	Victor McLaglen	G.	*Song of Songs*
8.	Jean Arthur	H.	*Pittsburgh*
9.	Ray Milland	I.	*Destry Rides Again*
10.	Anna May Wong	J.	*Manpower*
11.	Aline MacMahon	K.	*Judgment at Nuremberg*
12.	James Craig	L.	*Knight Without Armor*
13.	Cary Grant	M.	*Morocco*
14.	Eve Arden	N.	*The Flame of New Orleans*
15.	Randolph Scott	O.	*Witness for the Prosecution*
16.	Una Merkel	P.	*The Lady Is Willing*
17.	Brian Aherne	Q.	*Shanghai Express*
18.	Robert Donat	R.	*Rancho Notorious*
19.	Bruce Cabot	S.	*A Foreign Affair*
20.	Mischa Auer	T.	*The Monte Carlo Story*

Photo 55

COOPER, ALSO STARRING . . .

The performers listed on the left have played in the Gary Cooper films listed on the right. Match the stars and the films.

1. Deborah Kerr
2. Charlton Heston
3. Elizabeth Montgomery
4. Anthony Perkins
5. Julie London
6. Tab Hunter
7. Lauren Bacall
8. Lloyd Bridges
9. Jane Wyatt
10. Maurice Chevalier
11. Suzy Parker
12. Burt Lancaster
13. Jean Arthur
14. Robert Alda
15. Paulette Goddard
16. Dana Andrews
17. David Niven
18. Merle Oberon
19. Ray Milland
20. Fay Wray

A. *Bright Leaf*
B. *Love in the Afternoon*
C. *Vera Cruz*
D. *Mr. Deeds Goes to Town*
E. *Cloak and Dagger*
F. *Beau Geste*
G. *Ten North Frederick*
H. *One Sunday Afternoon*
I. *Unconquered*
J. *The Cowboy and the Lady*
K. *Ball of Fire*
L. *The Wreck of the Mary Deare*
M. *The Real Glory*
N. *Man of the West*
O. *The Naked Edge*
P. *You're in the Navy Now*
Q. *High Noon*
R. *Friendly Persuasion*
S. *They Came to Cordura*
T. *The Court Martial of Billy Mitchell*

Photo 56

MUSIC TO OUR EARS

The advent of sound, or the "talkies," in 1927 brought on a rash of musicals in 1928 and 1929. Listed below are the casts of some of these early sound musicals. Identify the films.

1. Betty Compson, Joe E. Brown, Louise Fazenda, Sally O'Neil, Ethel Waters.
2. Al Jolson, May McAvoy, Warner Oland, Eugenie Besserer.
3. Bessie Love, Anita Page, Charles King, Jed Prouty.
4. Texas Guinan, John Davidson, Lila Lee, Eddie Foy, Jr., George Raft.
5. Laura LaPlante, Joseph Schildkraut, Otis Harlan, Alma Rubens.
6. John Boles, Carlotta King, Louise Fazenda, Johnny Arthur.
7. Charles "Buddy" Rogers, Nancy Carroll, Jack Oakie, Skeets Gallagher.
8. Fannie Brice, Guinn Williams, Edna Murphy, Richard Tucker.
9. Alice White, Donald Reed, Lee Moran, Charles Delaney.
10. Winnie Lightner, Ann Pennington, Nick Lucas, Conway Taerle.
11. Alice White, Charles Delaney, Fred Kohler, Sally Eilers.
12. Marion Davies, Lawrence Gray, George Baxter, Cliff Edwards.
13. Bebe Daniels, John Boles, Wheeler and Woolsey, Don Alvarado, Dorothy Lee.
14. J. Harold Murray, Norma Terris, Walter Catlett.
15. Nancy Carroll, Stanley Smith, Helen Kane, Jack Oakie.
16. Jeanette MacDonald, Maurice Chevalier, Lupino Lane, Lillian Roth.
17. Janet Gaynor, Charles Farrell, Sharon Lynn, El Brendell, Marjorie White.
18. Marilyn Miller, Lawrence Gray, Joe E. Brown.
19. Al Jolson, Betty Bronson, Josephine Dunn, Davey Lee.
20. George Jessel, Rosa Rosanova, Margaret Quimby.

Photo 57

A NOVEL IDEA (1)

Listed below are the stars of films of the '20s which were based on well-known books. Identify the films.

1. Douglas Fairbanks, Marguerite de la Motte, Barbara LaMarr, Adolphe Menjou.
2. Jackie Coogan, Lon Chaney, Gladys Brockwell, Lionel Belmore, Esther Ralston.
3. Lillian Gish, Lars Hansen, Henry B. Walthall.
4. Greta Garbo, John Gilbert, George Fawcett, Philippe de Lacy.
5. Lillian Gish, Richard Barthelmess, Lowell Sherman, Burr McIntosh.
6. John Barrymore, Dolores Costello.
7. Betty Bronson, Mary Brian, Philippe de Lacy.
8. Ronald Colman, Neil Hamilton, Ralph Forbes, Mary Brian, Alice Joyce.
9. Norma Talmadge, Gilbert Roland, Maurice Costello, Lilyan Tashman.
10. Ramon Novarro, Francis X. Bushman, May McAvoy, Carmel Myers.
11. Lon Chaney, Patsy Ruth Miller, Norman Kerry, Kate Lester.
12. Wallace Beery, Barbara Bedford, Lillian Hall, Harry Lorraine, Boris Karloff.
13. Lon Chaney, Mary Philbin, Norman Kerry, Gibson Gowland.
14. Douglas Fairbanks, Marguerite de la Motte, Belle Bennett, Dorothy Revier.
15. May McAvoy, Richard Barthelmess, Ida Waterman, Holmes Herbert.
16. Laura La Plante, Joseph Schildkraut, Otis Harlan, Alma Rubens.
17. Colleen Moore, Wallace Beery, Ben Lyon, John Bowers.
18. Ramon Novarro, Alice Terry, Lewis Stone, Julia Swayne Gordon.
19. Dolores Del Rio, Warner Baxter, Roland Drew, Vera Lewis.
20. Gary Cooper, Mary Brian, Walter Huston, Richard Arlen.

A NOVEL IDEA (2)

Listed below are the stars of films of the '30s which were based on well-known books. Identify the films.

1. Fredric March, Olivia de Havilland, Claude Rains, Gale Sondergaard.
2. Clark Gable, Vivien Leigh, Leslie Howard, Olivia de Havilland.
3. Paul Muni, Luise Rainer, Walter Connolly, Tilly Losch.
4. Barbara Stanwyck, John Boles, Anne Shirley, Alan Hale, Barbara O'Neil.

Photo 58

5. Irene Dunne, Robert Taylor, Betty Furness.
6. Ronald Colman, Elizabeth Allen, Donald Woods, Edna May Oliver.
7. Robert Donat, Greer Garson, Paul Henreid, Terry Kilburn.
8. Ronald Colman, Jane Wyatt, Sam Jaffe, H. B. Warner, Margo.
9. Gary Cooper, Ray Milland, Robert Preston, Susan Hayward, Brian Donlevy.
10. Clark Gable, Charles Laughton, Franchot Tone, Movita.
11. Ronald Colman, Madeleine Carroll, Douglas Fairbanks, Jr., Raymond Massey.
12. Greta Garbo, Robert Taylor, Henry Daniell, Lionel Barrymore.
13. Tyrone Power, Myrna Loy, George Brent, Brenda Joyce, Maria Ouspenskaya.
14. Greta Garbo, Fredric March, Basil Rathbone, Freddie Bartholomew.
15. Spencer Tracy, Freddie Bartholomew, Lionel Barrymore, Mickey Rooney.
16. Merle Oberon, Laurence Olivier, David Niven, Geraldine Fitzgerald.
17. Fay Bainter, Claude Rains, Jackie Cooper, Bonita Granville.
18. Bette Davis, Leslie Howard, Frances Dee, Reginald Denny.
19. Irene Dunne, Allan Jones, Helen Morgan, Donald Woods, Paul Robeson.
20. Greta Garbo, John and Lionel Barrymore, Joan Crawford, Wallace Beery.

A NOVEL IDEA (3)

Listed below are the stars of films of the '30s which were based on well-known books. Identify the films.

1. Lew Ayres, Louis Wolheim, William Bakewell, Slim Summerville.
2. Errol Flynn, Olivia de Havilland, Lionel Atwill, Basil Rathbone.
3. Bette Davis, Miriam Hopkins, George Brent, Jane Bryan, Louise Fazenda.
4. Errol Flynn, the Mauch twins, Claude Rains, Alan Hale.
5. Margaret Sullavan, Robert Taylor, Robert Young, Franchot Tone.
6. Fredric March, Miriam Hopkins, Rose Hobart, Halliwell Hobbes.
7. Warner Baxter, Freddie Bartholomew, Arlene Whelan.
8. Claudette Colbert, Warren William, Rochelle Hudson, Louise Beavers.
9. Gary Cooper, Helen Hayes, Adolphe Menjou.
10. Claudette Colbert, Charles Boyer, Joan Bennett, Joel McCrea.
11. Fredric March, Charles Laughton, Rochelle Hudson.
12. Katharine Hepburn, Douglass Montgomery, Joan Bennett, Frances Dee.
13. Josephine Hutchinson, Pat O'Brien, Ross Alexander.
14. Guy Kibbee, Aline MacMahon, Claire Dodd, Nan Grey.
15. Walter Huston, Ruth Chatterton, Mary Astor, David Niven.
16. Leslie Howard, Merle Oberon, Joan Gardner, Anthony Bushell.
17. Bette Davis, Warren William, Alison Skipworth, Arthur Treacher.
18. Miriam Hopkins, Frances Dee, Alan Mowbray, Cedric Hardwicke.
19. William Powell, Myrna Loy, Maureen O'Sullivan, Nat Pendleton, Cesar Romero.
20. Claudette Colbert, Henry Fonda, Edna May Oliver, Ward Bond, Brian Donlevy.

Photo 59

Photo 60

A NOVEL IDEA (4)

Listed below are the casts of films of the '40s which were based on well-known books. Identify the films.

1. Spencer Tracy, Katharine Hepburn, Melvyn Douglas, Robert Walker.
2. Lynn Bari, Nazimova, Akim Tamiroff, Francis Lederer, Louis Calhern.
3. Ginger Rogers, Dennis Morgan, James Craig, Ernest Cossart.
4. Gary Cooper, Ingrid Bergman, Katina Paxinou, Akim Tamiroff.
5. Gregory Peck, Dorothy McGuire, John Garfield, Celeste Holm.
6. Gary Cooper, Patricia Neal, Raymond Massey.
7. Ray Milland, Jane Wyman, Philip Terry, Howard da Silva.
8. Joan Crawford, Ann Blyth, Zachary Scott, Jack Carson, Eve Arden.
9. Gary Cooper, Ingrid Bergman, Flora Robson, Jerry Austin, Florence Bates.
10. Walter Pidgeon, Roddy McDowall, Maureen O'Hara, Donald Crisp.
11. Henry Fonda, Jane Darwell, John Carradine, Charley Grapewin.
12. Charley Grapewin, Gene Tierney, Ward Bond, Elizabeth Patterson.
13. Greer Garson, Laurence Olivier, Maureen O'Sullivan, Mary Boland.
14. Joan Fontaine, Orson Welles, Margaret O'Brien, Peggy Ann Garner.
15. Peggy Ann Garner, Dorothy McGuire, James Dunn, Joan Blondell, Lloyd Nolan.
16. Spencer Tracy, Lana Turner, Zachary Scott, Tom Drake, Mary Astor.
17. Lana Turner, Van Heflin, Donna Reed, Richard Hart.
18. Linda Darnell, Cornel Wilde, George Sanders, Richard Greene.
19. Charles Laughton, Maureen O'Hara, Edmond O'Brien.
20. Laurence Olivier, Joan Fontaine, Judith Anderson, George Sanders.

A NOVEL IDEA (5)

Listed below are the casts of films of the '40s which were based on well-known books. Identify the films.

1. Clark Gable, Deborah Kerr, Adolphe Menjou, Ava Gardner.
2. Fred MacMurray, Frank Sinatra, Alida Valli, Lee J. Cobb.
3. Gregory Peck, Jane Wyman, Claude Jarmin, Jr.
4. Ann Sheridan, Ronald Reagan, Robert Cummings, Betty Field, Claude Rains.
5. Katharine Hepburn, Walter Huston, Turhan Bey, Aline MacMahon.
6. Mickey Rooney, Butch Jenkins, Frank Morgan, James Craig, Donna Reed.
7. Olivia de Havilland, Montgomery Clift, Ralph Richardson, Miriam Hopkins.
8. Randolph Scott, Ellen Drew, Ruth Warrick, Anthony Quinn.
9. Olivia de Havilland, Mark Stevens, Leo Genn, Celeste Holm.
10. Barbara Stanwyck, Michael O'Shea, Iris Adrian, Gloria Dickson.
11. Hedy Lamarr, Robert Young, Ruth Hussey, Van Heflin.
12. Barbara Stanwyck, Van Heflin, Richard Hart, Cyd Charisse.
13. Ingrid Bergman, Charles Boyer, Charles Laughton, Louis Calhern.
14. Greer Garson, Gregory Peck, Preston Foster, Donald Crisp.
15. Preston Foster, William Bendix, Lloyd Nolan, Anthony Quinn, Richard Conte.
16. Joan Crawford, Henry Fonda, Dana Andrews, Ruth Warrick.
17. Barbara Stanwyck, Fred MacMurray, Edward G. Robinson.
18. June Allyson, Peter Lawford, Elizabeth Taylor, Margaret O'Brien.
19. Ronald Colman, Greer Garson, Susan Peters.
20. Errol Flynn, Ann Sheridan, Walter Huston, Judith Anderson, Helmut Dantine.

Photo 61

126

WHERE IN THE WORLD?

Listed below are the stars of films whose titles contain the name of a place. Identify the films.

1. Tyrone Power, Don Ameche, Alice Faye.
2. Raymond Massey, Ruth Gordon, Gene Lockhart.
3. Jack Nicholson, Faye Dunaway, John Huston.
4. Marlon Brando, Maria Schneider, Jean-Pierre Leaud.
5. Henry Gibson, Ronee Blakley, Lily Tomlin, Keith Carradine.
6. Lenny Baker, Ellen Greene, Shelley Winters.
7. George Segal, Elliott Gould, Ann Prentiss, Gwen Welles.
8. Charles Boyer, Hedy Lamarr, Gene Lockhart.
9. Gordon MacRae, Shirley Jones, Gloria Grahame.
10. Peter O'Toole, Alec Guinness, Anthony Quinn, Jack Hawkins.
11. Ronald Reagan, Eddie Albert, Milburn Stone.
12. George Sanders, Marguerite Chapman, Gale Sondergaard.
13. Clark Gable, Spencer Tracy, Jeanette MacDonald.
14. Liza Minnelli, Robert DeNiro.
15. Gregory Peck, Audrey Hepburn, Eddie Albert.
16. Sylvester Stallone, Perry King, Henry Winkler, Paul Mace.
17. Barbara Stanwyck, Robert Ryan, Reginald Denny.
18. Bing Crosby, Bob Hope, Dorothy Lamour, Anthony Quinn, Jerry Colonna.
19. Max von Sydow, Julie Andrews, Richard Harris, Chuck Connors.
20. Charlton Heston, Yvette Mimieux, George Chakiris, France Nuyen.

Photo 62

MISSING LINKS

The missing words complete the movie titles. Fill in the blanks and forty film titles will be identified.

1. My Foolish _____ is a Lonely Hunter
2. The Last Time I Saw _____ Blues
3. Long Day's Journey into _____ at the Opera
4. The African _____ Christina
5. Some Like it _____ Rock
6. Mr. Deeds Goes to _____ Without Pity
7. How Green Was My _____ of the Dolls
8. The Thin _____ with the Golden Gun
9. Anne of the Thousand _____ of Wine and Roses
10. The Scarlet _____ to Three Wives
11. A Doll's _____ of Seven Gables
12. Diamonds are _____ Amber
13. Five Miles to _____ Cowboy
14. All That _____ Singer
15. Soldier _____ Hawaii
16. Sunday Bloody _____ in New York
17. My Fair _____ from Shanghai
18. Life With _____ of the Bride
19. Endless _____ and Death
20. Imitation of _____ at the Top

Photo 63

MUSICAL MOMENTS

The stars listed on the left sang the songs listed on the right in musical movies. Match the stars with the songs and identify the films.

1. Liza Minnelli and Joel Grey
2. Rosalind Russell

3. Nat King Cole and Stubby Kaye
4. Shirley MacLaine
5. Franco Nero
6. Shani Wallis
7. Julie Andrews
8. Willie Nelson
9. Barbra Streisand
10. Diana Ross

11. Lucille Ball and Beatrice Arthur
12. Peter O'Toole
13. Liza Minnelli
14. Carol Channing
15. Marilyn Monroe
16. Bette Midler

17. Keith Carradine
18. Rex Harrison
19. Elizabeth Taylor
20. Judy Garland

A. "Burlington Bertie from Bow"
B. "Do You Know Where You're Going To?"
C. "Evergreen"
D. "The Impossible Dream"
E. "I'm a Jazz Baby"
F. "Hello Bluebird"
G. "Maybe This Time"
H. "Send in the Clowns"
I. "I'm Easy"
J. "Money Makes the World Go Around"
K. "I've Grown Accustomed to Her Face"
L. "As Long as He Needs Me"
M. "I'm Through with Love"
N. "Ballad of Cat Ballou"
O. "If Ever I Would Leave You"
P. "Everything's Coming Up Roses"
Q. "When a Man Loves a Woman"
R. "Bosom Buddies"
S. "On the Road Again"
T. "If My Friends Could See Me Now"

EVERYTHING IS RELATIVE

In the fifty years of Oscar awards there have been many "firsts," other than the obvious mention of Janet Gaynor and Emil Jannings as the first Oscar winners in the acting category. And often these firsts have been topped, as in the case of Walter Brennan being the first in the acting field to win three Oscars, his last being in 1940 for *The Westerner*. He remained unique in this field until Katharine Hepburn captured her third Oscar in 1968 for *The Lion in Winter*. Then Ingrid Bergman copped her third Oscar in 1974 for *Murder on the Orient Express*. But at least Mr. Brennan, who passed away in 1974, still remains the only *actor* to win three statues.

When Ethel Barrymore won her Oscar in 1944 for *None But the Lonely Heart*, she and brother Lionel became the only brother and sister to win acting Oscars, Lionel having won several years earlier in 1930/31 for *A Free Soul*. Active today are brother and sister Warren Beatty and Shirley MacLaine who could conceivably match this record. MacLaine has been nominated three times already for *Some Came Running* (1958), for *The Apartment* (1960), and for *Irma La Douce* (1963), while Beatty has been nominated for *Bonnie and Clyde* (1967) and *Heaven Can Wait* (1978), which he starred in, co-produced, co-directed, and co-wrote. Actress Norma Shearer won the best actress award in 1929/30 for *The Divorcee* and her brother Douglas, sound recorder and technician, has won five Oscars for

Photo 64

Photo 65

sound recording and two for special effects. His earliest Oscar was in 1929/30 also, for *The Big House*, making the Shearers the first in the brother-sister category to win Academy Awards in the same year.

To date, Vivien Leigh and Laurence Olivier are the only couple to both win Oscars while they were married to one another: Vivien for *A Streetcar Named Desire* (1951) and Olivier for *Hamlet* (1948). They were not yet married when she received her first one for *Gone With the Wind* in March of 1940 (they were married that August). Ocsar winner Joanne Woodward (*Three Faces of Eve*, 1957) and husband Paul Newman, long overdue for an Oscar, could match this record. In 1931/32, the famous married acting pair, Lynn Fontanne and Alfred Lunt were nominated for *The Guardsman* but did not win. That year Helen Hayes won for best actress and the Oscar for best actor went to two performers, Fredric March and Wallace Beery. That was the only tie in the Academy's history until 1968 when Barbra Streisand and Katharine Hepburn both won best actress honors.

In 1970 Helen Hayes won the best supporting actress award for *Airport*, making her the first actress to win in both supporting and best actress categories. Ingrid Bergman took best actress honors in 1956 for her performance in *Anastasia* and in 1974 she won the best supporting actress award

131

Photo 66

132

for *Murder on the Orient Express*. Jack Lemmon, by his 1973 win for best actor in *Save the Tiger*, became the first actor to win in both categories, since he had previously won the supporting actor prize for *Mister Roberts* in 1955. Robert DeNiro won the 1974 best supporting actor award for *The Godfather, Part II* and the best actor Oscar for *Raging Bull* (1980).

Walter and John Huston were the only father-son Oscar winners; Walter winning the supporting actor award and John winning Oscars for his directing and writing duties in the same film, *Treasure of Sierra Madre* (1948), until the Coppolas, Francis and his father Carmine, won in 1974 for *The Godfather, Part II*—Francis for directing and writing and Carmine for music scoring. Carmine's daughter, Francis' sister, Talia Shire has been nominated for two Oscars; in 1974 for best supporting actress in the film for which her father and brother won their awards. She was nominated for the best actress Oscar in 1976 for her performance in *Rocky*.

A father-daughter Oscar winning pair is made up of father, John Mills, best supporting actor for *Ryan's Daughter* in 1970, and daughter Hayley, recepient of an honorary Oscar for *Pollyanna* (1960). Tatum O'Neal, who won the best supporting actress award in 1973 for *Paper Moon*, and her father, Ryan O'Neal, could possibly become an Oscar winning family pair. Ryan O'Neal already has one nomination to his credit, *Love Story* (1970)—best actor.

Michael Douglas, son of actor Kirk, won an Oscar as producer of 1975's *One Flew Over the Cuckoo's Nest*, but Kirk, nominated three times for best actor, has yet to win, although the possibility remains for them to make up a winning father-son combination. Kirk was nominated for his performances in *Champion* (1949), *The Bad and the Beautiful* (1952), and *Lust for Life* (1956).

In a category by themselves is the mother-father-daughter combination of Judy Garland, Vincente Minnelli, and Liza Minnelli. Although Judy lost in her bid for best actress in *A Star Is Born* in 1954 and for best supporting actress in *Judgment at Nuremberg* in 1961, she did receive a juvenile Oscar in 1939 for *The Wizard of Oz*. Vincente won the director's Oscar in 1958 for *Gigi*, and, of course, Liza won the best actress award in 1973 for *Cabaret*, having previously lost in 1969 for *The Sterile Cuckoo*.

Joan Fontaine and Olivia de Havilland remain the only sisters to tote home Oscars, Joan for 1941's *Suspicion* and Olivia for 1946's *To Each His Own* and 1949's *The Heiress*. But the Redgrave sisters could equal the record. Lynn has been nominated once in 1966 for *Georgy Girl* and Vanessa has three nominations; in 1966 for *Morgan*, in 1968 for *Isadora*, and in 1971 for *Mary, Queen of Scots*. Vanessa won an Oscar in the best supporting actress category for *Julia* (1977). Both sister pairings were in competition against one another; the de Havilland-Fontaine duo in 1941 and the Red-graves in 1966. The Redgrave's pere, Michael, was also nominated for best actor back in 1947 for *Mourning Becomes Electra*.

In fields other than acting, the husband-wife team of art director Wiard Ihnen and costume designer Edith Head are both Oscar winners. Writer Charles MacArthur, late husband of two-time winner, actress Helen Hayes, won an Oscar in 1935 for best original story, *The Scoundrel*, along with his oft-time partner, Ben Hecht. The husband and wife team of lyricists Alan and Marilyn Bergman won an Oscar, along with composer Michel Le-Grand, for 1968's "The Windmills of Your Mind" from *The Thomas Crown Affair*, and a second one, with composer Marvin Hamlisch, for 1973's best song, "The Way We Were." Also, the song-writing brother team of Richard M. and Robert B. Sherman won 1964's best song Oscar, for "Chim Chim Cher-ee," from *Mary Poppins*. The husband-wife team of Garson Kanin and Ruth Gordon have won three nominations for best writing: in 1947 for *A Double Life*, in 1950 for *Adam's Rib*, and in 1952 for *Pat and Mike*. Miss Gordon herself won an Oscar for best supporting actress in 1968's *Rosemary's Baby*.

John Carradine's sons, Keith and David, are very much active in the film industry and, although John has never won an Oscar, Keith already has one for his song, "I'm Easy" from 1975's *Nashville*, and John still acts occasionally. Henry Fonda, never an Oscar winner, may still win and join daughter Jane who has Oscars for 1971's best actress award in *Klute*, and the best actress award in 1978 for *Coming Home*, or his son Peter may win for either acting or directing. And the Bridges family, father Lloyd and sons Jeff and Beau, are all still very much active and could upset records, since Jeff has already received two nominations as best supporting actor—in 1971 for *The Last Picture Show* and in 1974 for *Thunderbolt and Lightfoot*.

TO THEIR CREDIT

Of the forty-nine films that have won Oscars for best picture of the year, only Clark Gable, nicknamed "The King," has starred in three: *It Happened One Night* (1934), *Mutiny on the Bounty* (1935), and *Gone With the Wind* (1939).

Of the hundreds of films that have been nominated for best film, Gary Cooper has starred in more than any other star, with a total of nine to his credit. He is followed by Spencer Tracy, Gregory Peck, and William Holden with eight apiece. On the distaff side, Bette Davis leads with seven starring films, along with Elizabeth Taylor followed by Katharine Hepburn with six. The breakdown reads as follows:

Gary Cooper (9)
Wings (1927/28)
A Farewell to Arms (1932/33)
Lives of a Bengal Lancer (1935)
Mr. Deeds Goes to Town (1936)
Sergeant York (1941)
The Pride of the Yankees (1942)
For Whom the Bell Tolls (1943)
High Noon (1952)
Friendly Persuasion (1956)

Gregory Peck (8)
Spellbound (1945)
The Yearling (1946)
Gentleman's Agreement (1947)
Twelve O'Clock High (1949)
Roman Holiday (1953)
The Guns of Navarone (1961)
To Kill a Mockingbird (1962)
How the West Was Won (1963)

Spencer Tracy (8)
Libeled Lady (1936)
San Francisco (1936)
Captains Courageous (1937)
Boys Town (1938)
Test Pilot (1938)
Father of the Bride (1950)
Judgment at Nuremberg (1961)
Guess Who's Coming to Dinner (1967)

William Holden (8)
Our Town (1940)
Born Yesterday (1950)
Sunset Boulevard (1950)
The Country Girl (1954)
Love Is a Many Splendored Thing (1955)
Picnic (1955)
The Bridge on the River Kwai (1957)
Network (1976)

Bette Davis (7)
Jezebel (1938)
Dark Victory (1939)
All This and Heaven, Too (1940)
The Letter (1940)
The Little Foxes (1941)
Watch on the Rhine (1943)
All About Eve (1950)

Elizabeth Taylor (7)
Father of the Bride (1950)
A Place in the Sun (1951)
Ivanhoe (1952)
Giant (1956)
Cat On a Hot Tin Roof (1958)
Cleopatra (1963)
Who's Afraid of Virginia Wolf? (1966)

Katharine Hepburn (6)
Little Women (1932/33)
Alice Adams (1935)
Stage Door (1937)
The Philadelphia Story (1940)
Guess Who's Coming to Dinner (1967)
The Lion in Winter (1968)

OSCAR JINX?

Is the Oscar a jinx? Movie columnists and fan magazine writers have cited the decline of Oscar winners of the past, such as: Emil Jannings (first male recipient), Luise Rainer, Paul Muni, Gale Sondergaard, Anne Revere, Katina Paxinou, Kim Hunter—even James Dunn and Celeste Holm. One writer who shall remain nameless even went as far as including the name of Harold Russell, armless paraplegic veteran, who played himself and won an Oscar for best supporting actor of 1946 in *The Best Years of Our Lives*. Mr. Russell never aspired to be an actor, and the award was a testament to the man himself for his courage and dignity and inspiration to handicapped veterans. An examination of the facts makes such headlines and lists ridiculous and points them out for what they are—mere publicity hawking.

It is a fact that even an Academy Award nomination is a tremendous boost to an actor's career and that a "win" is synonymous with good old hard cash in the bank. Mercedes McCambridge, after her 1949 Oscar for best supporting actress in *All The King's Men*, admitted, " . . . it is bound to do a person some good. I am very grateful to the award. Before I won it, my salary was $750 a week. Now it is considerably more." Studios always promote an actor's Oscar to the hilt, especially in their advertising. When Ginger Rogers and James Stewart won the 1940 awards for *Kitty Foyle* and *The Philadelphia Story* respectively, RKO quickly re-released the film they had made together two years previously, *Vivacious Lady*, to gather more coin at the box office on the strength of their Oscars. The ads for *All About Eve* were replete with pictures of eight miniature Oscars beside everyone's name—two for Bette Davis, one each for Anne Baxter, Celeste Holm, and two each for producer Darryl F. Zanuck and director-screenwriter Joseph L. Mankiewicz. After Humphrey Bogart won his Oscar for *The African Queen*, Paramount played up the *three* Oscar-winner aspect in their ads for *Sabrina*, with Bogey and his co-stars, Audrey Hepburn, winner for *Roman Holiday*, and William Holden, winner for *Stalag 17*. The award winning film of each year is immediately re-released to earn additional money. Back in 1953, director Howard Hawks said, ". . . . Other than the acting awards, the Oscars, in my opinion, don't mean a lot at the box office to the individual winners. But the best production award—that means plenty. Remember *Gentleman's Agreement*? When that one was released back in 1947, it was laying an egg. Then in March 1948, it got the Oscar as best production, and you know what happened. It cleaned up. I'd say that the best-production Oscar means at least a million dollars added gross revenue for any film. And a picture that can advertise 'best actor' or 'best actress' is just about as lucky." In today's escalating price market, *Variety* now estimates that an Oscar can mean additional revenues of from $5 million to $10 million. A case in point was United Artists' *One Flew Over the Cuckoo's Nest*, which added over $20 million to its total gross after winning the 1975 Oscar.

In the case of individual actors and actresses, mitigating circumstances, not a "jinxed" Oscar, had control over their destinies. Emil Jannings, winner of the 1927/28 best actor award for *The Way of All Flesh* and *The Last Command*, was a German silent film star who was brought to Hollywood on the strength of his great performances in the German films, *The Sins of Man* and *The Patriot*. He never learned the English language, so when sound films were perfected, he returned to his native Germany and resumed his European career. One of his first talking roles was as the professor in *The Blue Angel*, with Marlene Dietrich as Lola Lola, the role that brought her to Hollywood. Miss Dietrich perfected her English and became one of the top stars of the cinema, even winning a nomination in 1930/31 for *Morocco*. Several foreign films of the silent era found their careers ended when talkies arrived. Vilma Banky and Pola Negri, two of the loveliest stars of the twenties, had accents too heavy and guttural to be understood by the masses. Miss Banky graciously retired; Miss Negri struggled to overcome her accent but never attained her former heights. The fickle public, however, found Greta Garbo's deep and heavy accent intriguing when she first spoke in 1930's *Anna Christie*, for which she won a nomination.

The unfortunate "blacklists" of the late forties and early fifties were responsible for the decline of many film careers, not only in the acting profession, but in other stations as well, including writing and directing. Because they were once affiliated with "red" organizations in their pasts, or were alleged to have been, supporting actress winners Gale Sondergaard, Anne Revere, and Lee Grant all had to fight valiantly to keep their careers going and their heads above water. But they were not alone—actors Larry Parks, Howard Da Silva, and Lionel Stander were also besmirched. Grant, nominated in 1951 for *Detective Story*, finally won in 1975 for *Shampoo*.

Luise Rainer can blame her career's collapse on two things—bad scripts and the public's apathy for her fragile European style, and not on her two Oscars. She was the first actress to ever win in two consecutive years; in 1936 for her portrayal of Anna Held in *The Great Ziegfeld*, and in 1937 for her portrayal of the Chinese peasant, O-lan, in Pearl Buck's prize-winning, *The Good Earth*. Four exceedingly dull and pathetic roles followed. Even pairing her with Oscar winner Spencer Tracy couldn't save the 1937 film, *The Big City*. And the three following "costume" films all hastened the demise of her career: *The Emperor's Candlesticks* (1937), with William Powell; *The Great Waltz* (1938), with Fernand Gravet; and *The Toy Wife* (1938), with Melvyn Douglas and Robert Young. Had MGM followed up her two wins with *Dramatic School*, her late 1938 release and her only subsequent noteworthy role, they might have salvaged her career. But the history of Hollywood is replete with European actresses who failed to capture the American audience's fancy, most notably being Anna Sten, Simone Simon, and Danielle Darrieux, none of whom ever won an Oscar. It is to Miss Darrieux's credit that she returned to her native France after her American debut in *The Rage of Paris* (1938) and continued her lengthy stardom abroad.

The disease of alcoholism was largely responsible for the waning careers of Oscar winners Broderick Crawford (*All the King's Men*), Mercedes McCambridge (*All the King's Men*), and Kim Hunter (*A Streetcar Named Desire*), not an Oscar jinx. Also true in the instance of these three is the fact that they are all strong *character* personalities, and not easily worked into the average script. That all three have successfully risen above their affliction is admirable, since alcoholism has ruined many a Hollywood career. Mary Carlisle, Gail Russell, Diana Barrymore, and Frances Farmer were all victims of the bottle, and none of them was ever nominated for an award. However, Oscar-winner Bing Crosby (Going My Way) was quite a "tippler" in his early career, but wisely put the cork back in the bottle, and certainly no one can say the 1943 Oscar in any way "jinxed" his career. Two other stars who successfully overcame the disease and who were Oscar-nominated were singer-actress Lillian Roth and leading-man Robert Young. They both have been very explicit in detailing the effects of alcohol on their lives and careers in the hope that their experiences might help others. Miss Roth's autobiography, I'll Cry Tomorrow, was tellingly filmed in 1955 and Susan Hayward won a deserved nomination for her portrayal of Lillian's struggle. Robert Young found his greater fame in a latter-day TV career in two successful series, Father Knows Best and Marcus Welby, M.D., winning three Emmy awards.

Actresses Katina Paxinou (best supporting actress for For Whom the Bell Tolls), Anna Magnani (best actress The Rose Tattoo), and Lila Kedrova (best supporting actress for Zorba the Greek) are three other strong and definitive stars for whom Hollywood roles were few and far between. They have each had greater successes in European films. Likewise, Celeste Holm, winner for best supporting actress in Gentleman's Agreement and nominated for Come to the Stable and All About Eve, is not in the mold of a typical Hollywood star. But her lengthy career on stage, in films, and TV, in addition to her many New York charitable works, has certainly never seen a blight since she brought home her Oscar. And, although James Dunn found little Hollywood work after winning his Oscar for best supporting actor in A Tree Grows in Brooklyn, he found later success in the TV series, It's a Great Life.

The myth of the Oscar jinx fits into the same category as the allegation that blondes, because of the misnomer "dumb blonde," seldom get dramatic roles. Refuting that theory are a host of Oscar winners, going as far back as Mary Pickford (Coquette), and continuing with: Bette Davis (Dangerous and Jezebel), Joan Fontaine (Suspicion), Shirley Booth (Come Back, Little Sheba), Dorothy Malone (Written on the Wind), Eva Marie Saint (On the Waterfront), Gloria Grahame (The Bad and the Beautiful), Ingrid Bergman (Gaslight, Anastasia, and Murder on the Orient Express), Claire Trevor (Key Largo), Celeste Holm (Gentleman's Agreement), Judy Holliday (Born Yesterday), and Grace Kelly (The Country Girl). It is true that Ginger Rogers darkened her tresses to win her Oscar for Kitty Foyle, but she afterward returned to her lighter shade. But, as if offsetting that instance, dark-haired Vivien Leigh won her second Oscar as a blonde Blanche DuBois in A Streetcar Named Desire.

HOPE SPRINGS ETERNAL

Contrary to popular belief, Bob Hope has not always been the Master of Ceremonies at the annual Oscar presentation. It only *seems* that way: his last full-time emcee stint was in 1968. Unfortunately for the Academy and viewers, conflicting contractual commitments barred him in recent years from participating except as a token "guest of the Oscar," as recent multiple emcees have been designated.

Hope's style and topical wit were very much akin to that of the 1934 emcee, Will Rogers, although the latter seems cut from a rustic bolt of cloth when compared to Bob's sophisticated pattern. Both humorists poked fun not only at Hollywood's higher-ups, but also at the powers-that-be in Washington. Lionel Barrymore, 1933's emcee, and Irvin S. Cobb, 1935's emcee, both attempted jocularity in the Rogers/Hope style, but suffered by comparison. Frank Capra often hosted the festivities himself during the five years when he was president of the Academy (1935–40).

Bob's first "total-hosting" stint was as far back as 1941 when the occasion was much smaller in scope, still being held in the form of a dinner-banquet broadcast on local radio. In 1944, the festivities moved to an auditorium for the first time, Graumann's Chinese Theater, and the following year it was broadcast nationwide. In 1949, the affair, a small one, was held in the Academy's own theater, then in 1950 it moved to the Pantages Theater, where it was held for the next eleven years. It was here in 1953 that the first Oscarcast was televised, with the inevitable and inimitable Bob Hope as Master of Ceremonies. The affair then moved to the Santa Monica Auditorium in 1961 to accommodate the ever-growing crowds and remained there until 1969, when it moved back to the Hollywood area to the new Dorothy Chandler Pavilion at the Los Angeles Music Center.

Over the years of televising, other comedians have handled the emcee chore: Donald O'Connor (1954); Jerry Lewis (1956, 1957); Frank Sinatra (1963); and Jack Lemmon (1964). Back in radio days, Jack Benny was emcee in 1947. For three years, the TV show was split between Hollywood and New York, employing dual hosts. In 1955 it was Bob Hope and Jack Webb; in 1956 it was Jerry Lewis and Claudette Colbert; and in 1957 it was Jerry Lewis and Celeste Holm. This awkward form of split-televising proved

Photo 67

unsatisfactory and was dropped. In 1958, the first use of multiple hosts, was employed. That year the co-hosts were Bob Hope, Rosalind Russell, James Stewart, David Niven, and Jack Lemmon. In 1959 there were six hosts: Hope, Jerry Lewis, David Niven, Mort Sahl, Laurence Olivier, and Tony Randall. Multiple hosts became a virtual crowd in 1971 when the public was treated to 34—count them, 34—"Friends of the Oscar." In more recent years, the number has dropped to four and once to five (Goldie Hawn and George Segal did a dual-hosting segment in the 1976 show).

Bob Hope's participation in the annual events started with his appearance as a presenter back in 1939, when he gave out the awards for best short subjects of 1938. That was the year when the song which was to become his theme song, *Thanks for the Memory*, won the Oscar as best song of the year. (Bob and Shirley Ross had sung the tune in *The Big Broadcast of 1938*.) Other humor that year was provided by Edgar Bergen and his dummy, Charlie McCarthy, who were there to present special "youth" awards to Deanna Durbin and Mickey Rooney. Rooney was not present, so his miniature Oscar was accepted by Edgar's other dummy, Mortimer Snerd.

The next year, 1940, Hope was also on hand and, as *Gone With the Wind* continued to rack up award after award, Hope quipped that the affair was really a "benefit for David O. Selznick," producer of that epic film, which won ten Oscars. Selznick himself won the Irving Thalberg Memorial Award.

In 1941, Hope was not only the official Master of Ceremonies, opening with the remark, "I'm very happy to be here for my annual insult," but he was also honored for the first of five times by the Academy with a silver plaque for "his unselfish service to the motion picture industry." In 1945 he was given a lifetime membership in the Academy; in 1954 he was given an Honorary Oscar for "his contribution to the laughter of the world, his services to the motion picture industry, and his devotion to the American premise." In 1960 he was awarded the Jean Hersholt Humanitarian Award for "outstanding service to his fellow man," and in 1966 he received the only gold medal bestowed for "unique and distinctive service to the Academy and the industry." In addition to the miniature Oscar a gatecrasher left behind in 1962, Hope also received a one-inch tall Oscar from the Academy as a joke in 1946.

Not to detract from Hope's aplomb and *savoir-faire*, due credit should be given to the host of writers who, over the years, have supplied his one-liners and topical quips. The partial list includes many who have gone on to become directors and producers: Wilkie Mahoney (his first writer), Ted McKay, Mel Shavelson, Milt Josephsberg, Jack Rose, Norman Panama, Melvin Frank, Albert Schwartz, Norman Sullivan, Jack Douglas, Paul Laven, Dr. Samuel Kurtzman, Fred S. Fox, Hal Block, and Larry Marks.

Here are some samples of the Hope wit over the years:
(1953) "I like to be here in case one of these years they'll have one left over."
(1960, during an actors' strike) "This audience is the most glamorous strike meeting in the history of organized labor. . . . I never expected to see

the day when agents would be starving in the streets. . . . If this keeps up, Ronald Reagan will be the only actor working. . . . Who else but actors would give up working for Lent?"

(1961) "This evening's awards would decide which actors and actresses had the best press agents. . . . Some motion pictures make money even *with* the Production Code's seal of approval."

(1962) "Welcome to 'Judgment at Santa Monica'. . . . We left the side door open so the cast of *Mutiny on the Bounty* could wade ashore. . . . The Academy Awards were of such universal interest, the Kennedys have given their travel agents the night off. . . . Everyone's here except George C. Scott—he's home with his back to the set. . . . This show is being taped for our actors overseas. . . . But things are looking up for the United States overseas now that Zanuck has given our Army back. . . . Some of the nominations are noteworthy, especially Sophia Loren's *Two Women*, which I indeed think she is . . . and this is the year Charles Boyer could win for his *Fanny*. . . . *The Hustler*—that's the biography of Bing Crosby's obstetrician. . . . *La Dolce Vita*—that's a documentary on what to do until the spaghetti is ready. . . . *Cleopatra* proved Mrs. Stone was not the only one who had a Roman Spring. . . . One of the most poignant sights of recent years was Spyros Skouras in Rome intoning, 'Friends, Romans, countrymen, lend me.' "

(1965) "Welcome to Santa Monica on the Thames. . . . This is envy time in the valley and I'm the Jolly Green Emcee. . . . This year Hollywood is handing out foreign aid. . . . Before picking up Oscar tonight, an actor must show his passport. . . . Crosby's show was pre-empted, so he's home—he thinks there's an award for the *most* short subject. . . . There'll always be an England, even if it is in Hollywood. . . . But the United States still leads the world in the production of popcorn. . . . Richard Burton has been nominated for *Becket*—that's the movie in which he's friends with a man—he still doesn't know he's been nominated—his phone is still off the hook."

(1966) "Welcome to *The Agony and the Ecstasy*. . . . Here you have the stars of today and the Senators of tomorrow. . . . If George Hamilton plays his cards right, he might be the second Hamilton to get into the White House. . . . I never had a chance this year—I can't drink like Lee Marvin, grunt like Rod Steiger, can't ennunciate like Sir Laurence Olivier—and when it comes to Richard Burton, I'm really in trouble. . . . This set looks like Lloyd Bridge's rumpus room."

(1967) "Welcome to Hollywood, the birthplace of politicians. . . . Really, the Academy should give an Oscar for the best performance as a Governor [camera shot of Reagan in audience]. . . . Let's get down to the business of awarding the people responsible for making motion pictures what they are today—for adults only."

(1968) "Welcome to Award night—in my house it's known as Passover . . . This two-day delay [postponed because of the funeral of Dr. Martin Luther King] has been tough on the nominees—how would you like to spend two days in a crouch? . . . I will not seek nor will I accept an Oscar—if anyone believes that, I'll kill myself. . . . I've never seen such jewels and furs and beads and curls—and that's only the men. . . . Really, all these jewels and furs remind me of the unemployment office at Palm Springs. . . . This was a great year for Hollywood—some of the pictures nominated for Academy Awards were even made here. . . . Hollywood has now proven it can make as good dirty movies as Europe."

(1970) "Welcome to a show dedicated to the proposition that jealousy and envy shall not perish from the earth. . . . I know Elizabeth Taylor has arrived because I just saw an armored car parked outside. . . . After some of last year's films, it's a pleasure to see actors and actresses with their clothes on. . . . Do you remember when a naive Hollywood sought new *faces?* . . . So many X-rated movies are now being made, actors won't put their hands and feet outside Graumann's anymore—from here on there'll be sit-ins there. . . . Crime may not pay but today's films prove there's a fortune in exploiting incest and homosexuality. . . . It's gotten so we're now putting on the screen things the French wouldn't put on postcards . . . If actors in Swedish films leave the bedroom, they feel they're going on location. . . . Were *High Noon* to be made today it would probably be set during the lunch hour in a junior high school. . . . What used to be the end of a film—the hero walking with his horse into the sunset—is now the beginning of a 'beautiful friendship.' "

Some of Bob Hope's concluding remarks have been memorable:

(1960) "Well, that about knocks it—it's all over but the sniveling."

(1962) "It's all over but the snarling. At the celebration dinner in the Beverly-Hilton which follows, I shall be found at a table with Sid Luft and Eddie Fisher."

(1965) "The losers will all join hands and march on the British Embassy."

(1966) "The Academy Award ceremony is the apotheosis of the movies which have helped me to support my government in the style to which it has become accustomed. . . . This meeting of the Great Society stands adjourned."

(1967) "I don't mind losing but I hate to go home and explain to my kids how the actors I've been sneering at all year beat me out."

(1968) "That's it. The losers can now go back to their gurus and their beds of nails. [Seriously, referring to Dr. King:] Remember, rioting and indifference are equal sins."

(1970) "Remember, the losers can always run for Governor."

In 1971, Hope, as one of the "Friends," appeared midway and sparked the evening with his monologue:

"I'm sure I just saw George C. Scott in the parking lot carrying a Patton swagger stick and letting air out of tires. . . . I'm pleased Howard Hughes is present [pointing to an empty chair in a corner]. . . . There has been a lot of propaganda about sexual perversion in recent films—but Love Story is distinguished by the fact that the hero falls in love with a girl. . . . Regarding the recent pornography, the line "I love you" is no longer a declaration but a demonstration. . . . These days you can win an Oscar without getting out of bed. . . . The motion picture industry's major problem at the moment is finding an Italian to play in The Godfather and in making it plain that that film is about Cub Scouts. . . . I'll be around in case George C. Scott really doesn't want an Oscar."

In 1969, Bob was not one of the ten "Friends," but he was brought on toward the end of the program to present Martha Raye with the Jean Hersholt Humanitarian Award and joked about his small part in the festivities: "I finally made it. This has been a brilliant show. It's had almost everything. I've been feeling like the third Smothers Brother. I've been waiting in one of the dressing rooms where I could sneer in private. . . . You know, they're doing things on the screen today I wouldn't do in bed—even if I had the chance."

Other good Hope lines coming from Oscar shows were:

In introducing Joan Crawford in 1965 to present the best director's award: "Would you mind stopping off at my house after the show—I have a garage full of empties!" (Miss Crawford did not deign a reply.)

"To present the award for 1961's best picture, I give you the man who has done as much for the top hat and white tie as Brando has done for mumbling—Fred Astaire."

To introduce the presenter for best film of 1965: "We had thought to get Mr. and Mrs. Cary Grant to present this award. What an inspiration it is when a man like Grant so quickly shows results in a new line of work! But the Grants couldn't get a baby-sitter. So we've settled for Jack Lemmon." Said Lemmon: "I volunteered to baby-sit but the Grants considered me unreliable."

But Bob was caught twice with no lines to say. In 1960 when he was presented with the Jean Hersholt Humanitarian Award, he first quipped, "I often thought there must be a way [to get an Oscar]," but then he said, "I don't know what to say—I don't have writers for this type of work." And when he was given his gold medal in 1966, he could only mumble thank you a few times then said, "I'm caught with my idiot boards down."

CREAM OF THE CROP
(AWARD WINNING MOVIES 1927–1980)

Year	Photoplay Readers	Oscars	New York Film Critics	National Board of Review (English Language)	Hollywood Foreign Press Association Golden Globe (Drama)
1927	Seventh Heaven				
1928	Four Sons	Wings			
1929	Disraeli	Broadway Melody			
1930	All Quiet on the Western Front	All Quiet on the Western Front			
1931	Cimarron	Cimarron			
1932	Smilin' Through	Grand Hotel			
1933	Little Women	Cavalcade			
1934	The Barretts of Wimpole Street	It Happened One Night			
1935	Naughty Marietta	Mutiny on the Bounty	The Informer		
1936	San Francisco	The Great Ziegfeld	Mr. Deeds Goes to Town		
1937	Captains Courageous	The Life of Emile Zola	The Life of Emile Zola		
1938	Sweethearts	You Can't Take It with You	The Citadel		
1939	Gone With the Wind	Gone With the Wind	Wuthering Heights		
1940	(no awards)	The Grapes of Wrath	Rebecca		

Year	Photoplay Readers	Oscars	New York Film Critics	National Board of Review (English Language)	Hollywood Foreign Press Association Golden Globe (Drama)
1941	(no awards)	How Green Was My Valley	Citizen Kane		
1942	(no awards)	Mrs. Miniver	In Which We Serve		
1943	(no awards)	Casablanca	Watch on the Rhine		The Song of Bernadette
1944	Going My Way	Going My Way	Going My Way		Going My Way
1945	The Valley of Decision	The Lost Weekend	The Lost Weekend	The True Glory	The Lost Weekend
1946	The Bells of St. Mary's	The Best Years of Our Lives	The Best Years of Our Lives	Henry V	The Best Years of Our Lives
1947	The Jolson Story	Gentleman's Agreement	Gentleman's Agreement	Monsieur Verdoux	Gentleman's Agreement
1948	Sitting Pretty	Hamlet	Treasure of Sierra Madre	Paisan	Tie: Treasure of Sierra Madre & Johnny Belinda
1949	The Stratton Story	All the King's Men	All the King's Men	The Bicycle	All the King's Men
1950	Battleground	All About Eve	All About Eve	Sunset Boulevard	Sunset Boulevard

CREAM OF THE CROP
(AWARD WINNING MOVIES 1927–1980)

Year	Photoplay Readers	Oscars	New York Film Critics	National Board of Review (English Language)	Hollywood Foreign Press Association Golden Globe (Drama)
1951	Show Boat	An American in Paris	A Streetcar Named Desire	A Place in the Sun	A Place in the Sun
1952	With a Song in My Heart	The Greatest Show on Earth	High Noon	The Quiet Man	The Greatest Show on Earth
1953	From Here to Eternity	From Here to Eternity	From Here to Eternity	Julius Caesar	The Robe
1954	Magnificent Obsession	On the Waterfront	On the Waterfront	On the Waterfront	On the Waterfront
1955	Love is a Many-Splendored Thing	Marty	Marty	Marty	East of Eden
1956	Giant	Around the World in 80 Days	Around the World in 80 Days	Around the World in 80 Days	Around the World in 80 Days
1957	An Affair to Remember	The Bridge on the River Kwai	The Bridge on the River Kwai	The Bridge on the River Kwai	The Bridge on the River Kwai
1958	Gigi	Gigi	The Defiant Ones	The Old Man and the Sea	The Defiant Ones
1959	Pillow Talk	Ben-Hur	Ben-Hur	The Nun's Story	Ben-Hur
1960	(no awards)	The Apartment	Tie: Sons and Lovers & The Apartment	Sons and Lovers	Spartacus

Year	Photoplay Readers	Oscars	New York Film Critics	National Board of Review (English Language)	Hollywood Foreign Press Association Golden Globe (Drama)
1961	Splendor in the Grass	West Side Story	West Side Story	Question 7	The Guns of Navarone
1962	The Miracle Worker	Lawrence of Arabia	(no awards)	The Longest Day	Lawrence of Arabia
1963	How the West Was Won	Tom Jones	Tom Jones	Tom Jones	The Cardinal
1964	The Unsinkable Molly Brown	My Fair Lady	My Fair Lady	Becket	Becket
1965	The Sound of Music	The Sound of Music	Darling	The Eleanor Roosevelt Story	Doctor Zhivago
1966	The Russians Are Coming, the Russians Are Coming	A Man for All Seasons	A Man for All Seasons	A Man for All Seasons	A Man for All Seasons
1967	The Dirty Dozen	In the Heat of the Night	In the Heat of the Night	Far from the Madding Crowd	In the Heat of the Night
1968	(award discontinued)	Oliver!	The Lion in Winter	The Shoes of the Fisherman	The Lion in Winter
1969		Midnight Cowboy	They Shoot Horses, Don't They?	Anne of the Thousand Days	

(continued)

CREAM OF THE CROP
(AWARD WINNING MOVIES 1927–1980)

Year	Oscars	New York Film Critics	National Board of Review (English Language)	Hollywood Foreign Press Association Golden Globe (Drama)
1970	Patton	Five Easy Pieces	Patton	Love Story
1971	The French Connection	A Clockwork Orange	Macbeth	The French Connection
1972	The Godfather	Cries and Whispers	Cabaret	The Godfather
1973	The Sting	Day for Night	The Sting	The Exorcist
1974	The Godfather, Part II	Amarcord	The Conversation	Chinatown
1975	One Flew Over the Cockoo's Nest	Nashville	Tie: Nashville & Barry Lyndon	One Flew Over the Cockoo's Nest
1976	Rocky	All the President's Men	All the President's Men	Rocky
1977	Annie Hall	Annie Hall	The Turning Point	Goodbye Girl
1978	The Deerhunter	The Deerhunter	Days of Heaven	Midnight Express
1979	Kramer vs. Kramer	Kramer vs. Kramer	Manhattan	Kramer vs. Kramer
1980	Ordinary People	Ordinary People	Ordinary People	Ordinary People

Photo 68

Photo 69

Photo 70

Photo 71

Photo 72

Photo 73

THANK YOU NOTES

On accepting their Oscars, here's what some people said:

Edith Head, costume design for *The Sting,* (1970): "Imagine dressing the two handsomest men in the world and then getting this!"

Shelley Winters, best supporting actress for *A Patch of Blue,* (1965): " . . . and I want to thank my director [Guy Green] who understood the role better than I did." (She played a lush and a whore.)

Sammy Cahn and **James Van Heuson** for the song, "High Hopes," (1959): Said Sammy, "Thank." Said Jimmy, "You."

Ben Johnson, best supporting actor for *The Last Picture Show,* (1972): "It couldn't happen to a nicer fella."

John Mills, best supporting actor for *Ryan's Daughter,* (1971): "I had not expected to win—but it was a wonderful choice."

Jerry Greenberg, film editor for *The French Connection,* (1971): " . . . and thanks to the New York City subway system."

Yvonne Blake, costume design for *Nicholas and Alexandra,* (1972): "I suppose I ought to acknowledge that if there hadn't been a Russian Revolution, I wouldn't be here."

Emil Kosa, Jr., special effects for *Cleopatra,* (1963), when accepting the award from presenter Angie Dickinson: "I wish I could take the lady home instead of the statue."

Lee Marvin, best actor for *Cat Ballou,* (1965): "Half of this belongs to a horse some place out in the valley."

Julie Andrews, best actress for *Mary Poppins*, (1964): "You Americans are famous for your hospitality, but this is ridiculous!"

Bing Crosby, best actor for *Going My Way*, (1944): "It's the first time anyone ever called me an actor."

Jane Wyman, best actress for her portrayal of a deaf/mute in *Johnny Belinda*, (1948): "I accept this very gratefully for keeping my mouth shut. I think I'll do it again."

Claudette Colbert, best actress for *It Happened One Night*, (1934): "I'm happy enough to cry but can't take the time to do it. A taxi is waiting outside [for me] with the engine running!"

Eva Marie Saint (pregnant at the time), for best supporting actress in *On The Waterfront*, (1954): "I may have the baby right here."

George Jessel, receiving the Jean Hersholt Humanitarian Award in 1970: "Hearing all that made me think I must be already dead."

BACK TO THEIR ROOTS

Identify the stars from their birthplaces followed by clues.

1. Adelaide, Australia–*Rebecca's* Housekeeper.
2. Valparaiso, Chile–Universal horror films heroine.
3. Darjeeling, India–Scarlett and Blanche.
4. Biaritz, France–Married both Ginger Rogers and Dorothy Malone.
5. Trieste, Italy–He lit Bette's cigarette in *Now Voyager*.
6. Stockholm, Sweden–*Bus Riley's* girl.
7. Neath, Wales–Bulldog Drummond later looked for a bottle in a chandelier.
8. Sakhalian Island, U.S.S.R.–Musical king of Siam.
9. Humacao, Puerto Rico–Won supporting Oscar for *West Side Story*.
10. Pontrhydyfen, South Wales–Alexander the Great and Dr. Faustus.
11. Lemburg, Austria–Fugitive who became Pasteur and Zola.
12. Helensburg, Scotland–She dispensed tea and sympathy.
13. St. Petersburg, Russia–The Falcon and his brother.
14. Barcelona, Spain–Mr. "Latin Rhythm."
15. Tokyo, Japan–Academy Award winning sisters.
16. Durango, Mexico–Madam DuBarry, Ramona, and Evangeline.
17. Sheveningen, Holland–Irene Dunne's husband in *I Remember Mama*.
18. Buenos Aires, Argentina–Married both Arlene Dahl and Esther Williams.
19. Cagilari, Sardinia–Twin sisters.
20. Brussels, Belgium–Funny face had breakfast in a jewelry store.

BATTLE SCARRED

Listed below are the stars of films about World War II. Identify the films.

1. Marlon Brando, Montgomery Clift, Dean Martin, May Britt.
2. Cary Grant, John Garfield, Dane Clark, Alan Hale.
3. Charlton Heston, Henry Fonda, James Coburn, Robert Mitchum, Glenn Ford.
4. Rock Hudson, George Peppard, Nigel Greene, Guy Stockwell, Jack Watson.
5. George Segal, James Fox, Patrick O'Neal, Denholm Elliott, John Mills.
6. Anthony Quinn, Anna Magnani, Virna Lisi, Hardy Kruger.
7. Robert Taylor, Robert Walker, George Murphy, Thomas Mitchell, Lloyd Nolan.
8. Dirk Bogarde, Ingrid Thulin, Helmut Greim, Helmut Berger, Charlotte Rampling.
9. George C. Scott, Karl Malden, Stephen Young, Frank Latimore.
10. Brian Donlevy, Robert Preston, Macdonald Carey, William Bendix, Albert Dekker.
11. Claudette Colbert, Paulette Goddard, Veronica Lake, George Reeves, Walter Abel.
12. William Holden, Otto Preminger, Don Taylor, Robert Strauss, Peter Graves.
13. John Wayne, Rod Steiger, Robert Ryan, Peter Lawford, Henry Fonda, Red Buttons.
14. John Wayne, John Agar, Forrest Tucker, Adele Mara, Julie Bishop.
15. William Holden, Alec Guinness, Sessue Hayakawa, Geoffrey Horne.
16. Gregory Peck, Anthony Quinn, David Niven, Stanley Baker, Irene Papas.
17. Lee Marvin, Ernest Borgnine, Jim Brown, John Cassavetes, Robert Ryan.
18. Humphrey Bogart, Ingrid Bergman, Peter Lorre, Claude Rains.
19. Gregory Peck, Ed Flanders, Dan O'Herlihy, Sandy Kenyon.
20. Robert Taylor, Richard Todd, Dana Wynter, Edmond O'Brien.

157

Photo 74

MELODIC MEMORIES (1)

The songs listed on the left were sung in films of the '20s by the stars listed on the right. Match the songs with the singers and identify the films.

1. "Am I Blue"	A. John Boles
2. "A Precious Little Thing Called Love"	B. Gloria Swanson
3. "Just You, Just Me"	C. Hal Skelly
4. "The Breakaway"	D. Janet Gaynor
5. "Pagan Love Song"	E. George Jessel
6. "One Alone"	F. Al Jolson
7. "Louise"	G. Ethel Waters
8. "True Blue Lou"	H. Marilyn Miller
9 "He's So Unusual"	I. Jeanette MacDonald
10. "Love, Your Magic Spell Is Everywhere"	J. Ramon Novarro
11. "If I Had a Talking Picture of You"	K. Fannie Brice
12. "Look for the Silver Lining"	L. Nick Lucas
13. "What Wouldn't I Do for That Man?"	M. Nancy Carroll
14. "My Mother's Eyes"	N. Lupe Velez
15. "Second Hand Rose"	O. Maurice Chevalier
16. "Sonny Boy"	P. Cliff Edwards
17. "Dream Lover"	Q. Pola Negri
18. "Where Is the Song of Songs for Me"	R. Helen Morgan
19. "Paradise"	S. Sue Carol
20. "Tip Toe Through the Tulips"	T. Helen Kane

MELODIC MEMORIES(2)

The songs listed on the left were sung in films of the '30s by the stars listed on the right. Match the songs with the singers and identify the films.

1. "Only a Rose"
2. "My Future Just Passed"
3. "Sing, You Sinners"
4. "Beyond the Blue Horizon"
5. "The Rose of Tralee"
6. "My Baby Just Cares for Me"
7. "Falling in Love Again"
8. "Let Me Sing, I'm Happy"
9. "I Only Have Eyes for You"
10. "Cocktails for Two"
11. "Puttin' on the Ritz"
12. "Let's Fall in Love"
a13. "On the Good Ship Lollipop"
14. "Vagabond Lover"
15. "They Call Me Sister Honky Tonk"
16. "Remember My Forgotten Man"
17. "You Brought a New Kind of Love to Me"
18. "Shanghai Lil"
19. "It Happened in Monterey"
20. "You're Getting to Be a Habit with Me"

A. Rudy Vallee
B. Al Jolson
C. Joan Blondell
D. James Cagney
E. Harry Richman
F. Carl Brisson
G. John Boles
H. Shirley Temple
I. Dennis King
J. Bebe Daniels
K. Lillian Roth
L. Ann Sothern
M. Maurice Chevalier
N. Mae West
O. John McCormack
P. Dick Powell
Q. Marlene Dietrich
R. Charles "Buddy" Rogers
S. Eddie Cantor
T. Jeanette MacDonald

Photo 75

MELODIC MEMORIES(3)

The songs listed on the left were sung in movies of the '40s by the stars listed on the right. Match the stars with the songs and identify the films.

1. "Blue Lovebird"
2. "That Old Black Magic"
3. "Say a Prayer for the Boys Over There"
4. "As Time Goes By"
5. "Happiness Is Just a Thing Called Joe"
6. "I Couldn't Sleep a Wink Last Night"
7. "South American Way"
8. "(All of a Sudden) My Heart Sings"
9. "One for My Baby"
10. "Boogie Woogie Bugle Boy from Company C"
11. "Honeysuckle Rose"
12. "Zigeuner"
13. "The Last Time I Saw Paris"
14. "They're Either Too Young or Too Old"
15. "Murder He Says"
16. "Minnie from Trinidad"
17. "Accentuate the Positive"
18. "I'll Walk Alone"
19. "You'd Be So Nice to Come Home To"
20. "Long Ago and Far Away"

A. Andrews Sisters
B. Gene Kelly
C. Bette Davis
D. Ann Sothern
E. Bing Crosby and Sonny Tufts
F. Betty Grable
G. Judy Garland
H. Betty Hutton
I. Dinah Shore
J. Janet Blair
K. Deanna Durbin
L. Alice Faye
M. Jeanette MacDonald
N. Johnny Johnston
O. Fred Astaire
P. Dooley Wilson
Q. Kathryn Grayson
R. Frank Sinatra
S. Carmen Miranda
T. Ethel Waters

MELODIC MEMORIES (4)

The songs listed on the left were sung in films of the '50s by the stars listed on the right. Match the songs with the stars and identify the films.

1. "Be My Love"
2. "Too Late Now"
3. "Secret Love"
4. "All the Way"
5. "A Stairway to Pardise"
6. "In the Cool, Cool, Cool of the Evening"
7. "Oh, What a Beautiful Morning"
8. "Tammy"
9. "That's Amore"
10. "Heat Wave"
11. "You Wonderful You"
12. "The Man That Got Away"
13. "Love Letters in the Sand"
14. "A Person Could Develop a Cold"
15. "Something's Gotta Give"
16. "Bless Your Beautiful Hide"
17. "I'm Gonna Wash That Man Right Outa My Hair"
18. "Thank Heaven for Little Girls"
19. "Make 'em Laugh"
20. "Too Darn Hot"

A. Judy Garland
B. Fred Astaire
C. Ann Miller
D. Pat Boone
E. Maurice Chevalier
F. Marilyn Monroe
G. Vivian Blaine
H. Mitzi Gaynor
I. Howard Keel
J. Bing Crosby and Jane Wyman
K. Donald O'Connor
L. Gordon MacRae
M. Mario Lanza
N. Georges Guetary
O. Gene Kelly
P. Jane Powell
Q. Debbie Reynolds
R. Frank Sinatra
S. Dean Martin
T. Doris Day

AND THE LOSER WAS . . . (1)

The stars on the left were nominated for Oscars in the films listed on the right. Match the stars and films.

1. Shelley Winters
2. Robert Redford
3. Barbra Streisand
4. Robert De Niro
5. Michael Caine
6. Sissy Spacek
7. Jon Voight
8. Alan Bates
9. Ellen Burstyn
10. Jean Simmons
11. Peter Finch
12. Peter O'Toole
13. Steve McQueen
14. Carol Channing
15. Ryan O'Neal
16. Ann-Margret
17. Chief Dan George
18. Jack Nicholson
19. Paul Winfield
20. Geraldine Page

A. *Pete 'n' Tillie*
B. *Tommy*
C. *The Ruling Class*
D. *Little Big Man*
E. *Five Easy Pieces*
F. *Love Story*
G. *Thoroughly Modern Millie*
H. *Sounder*
I. *The Happy Ending*
J. *The Sand Pebbles*
K. *The Last Picture Show*
L. *The Fixer*
M. *Taxi Driver*
N. *Midnight Cowboy*
O. *The Poseidon Adventure*
P. *Carrie*
Q. *The Sting*
R. *The Way We Were*
S. *Sunday Bloody Sunday*
T. *Sleuth*

Photo 76

AND THE LOSER WAS . . . (2)

The stars on the left were nominated for Oscars in the films listed on the right. Match the stars and films.

1.	Valerie Perrine	A.	*The Producers*
2.	Marsha Mason	B.	*Taxi Driver*
3.	Al Pacino	C.	*Rachel, Rachel*
4.	Burgess Meredith	D.	*The Towering Inferno*
5.	Vanessa Redgrave	E.	*Star!*
6.	Glenda Jackson	F.	*The Emigrants*
7.	Gene Wilder	G.	*The Exorcist*
8.	Fred Astaire	H.	*The Sterile Cuckoo*
9.	Cicely Tyson	I.	*Anne of the Thousand Days*
10.	Piper Laurie	J.	*Easy Rider*
11.	Anne Bancroft	K.	*The Hospital*
12.	Jodie Foster	L.	*The Graduate*
13.	George C. Scott	M.	*Carrie*
14.	Joanne Woodward	N.	*Sunday Bloody Sunday*
15.	Daniel Massey	O.	*The Godfather, Part II*
16.	Jack Nicholson	P.	*Isadora*
17.	Liv Ullman	Q.	*The Day of the Locust*
18.	Genevieve Bujold	R.	*Lenny*
19.	Liza Minnelli	S.	*Sounder*
20.	Ellen Burstyn	T.	*Cinderella Liberty*

Photo 77

AND THE LOSER WAS (AGAIN) . . .

The five actresses listed on the left have all been nominated for Best Actress but never won an Oscar in that category. Their award-nominated films are listed on the right. Match the stars with their films.

1. Irene Dunne (5 times)
2. Barbara Stanwyck (4 times)
3. Deborah Kerr (6 times)
4. Vanessa Redgrave (3 times)
5. Leslie Caron (2 times)

A. *Ball of Fire*
B. *Edward, My Son*
C. *Mary, Queen of Scots*
D. *Double Indemnity*
E. *Theodora Runs Wild*
F. *The L-Shaped Room*
G. *From Here to Eternity*
H. *Stella Dallas*
I. *The Awful Truth*
J. *The King and I*
K. *Isadora*
L. *Love Affair*
M. *Heaven Knows Mr. Allison*
N. *Lili*
O. *I Remember Mama*
P. *Separate Tables*
Q. *Morgan!*
R. *Sorry, Wrong Number*
S. *The Sundowners*
T. *Cimarron*

AND THE WINNER WAS . . . DIRECTORS

The directors listed on the left won Oscars for the films listed on the right. Match the directors and their films.

1. Francis Ford Coppola		A.	*Midnight Cowboy*
2. George Roy Hill		B.	*The Graduate*
3. William Friedkin		C.	*Patton*
4. Bob Fosse		D.	*A Man for All Seasons*
5. John Avildsen		E.	*My Fair Lady*
6. Carol Reed		F.	*Lawrence of Arabia*
7. Robert Wise		G.	*Ben-Hur*
8. Tony Richardson		H.	*The French Connection*
9 Milos Forman		I.	*Gigi*
10. Billy Wilder		J.	*Giant*
11. Fred Zinneman		K.	*Casablanca*
12. William Wyler		L.	*The Godfather, Part II*
13. John Schlesinger		M.	*The Sting*
14. George Cukor		N.	*Oliver!*
15. David Lean		O.	*Rocky*
16. George Stevens		P.	*Tom Jones*
17. Mike Nichols		Q.	*The Apartment*
18. Vincente Minnelli		R.	*The Sound of Music*
19. Michael Curtiz		S.	*Cabaret*
		T.	*One Flew Over the Cuckoo's Nest*
20. Franklin J. Schaffner			

AND THE WINNER WAS . . . (1920s)

There were only two years in the '20s when the Oscars were awarded: 1927/28 and 1928/29. The stars listed on the left were nominated for the films listed on the right. (In the first year, stars were nominated for more than one film, a ruling which was promptly changed.) Asterisks denote winners. Match the stars with the films.

1. Gloria Swanson	A. *Seventh Heaven*
2. Warner Baxter*	B. *The Noose*
3. Janet Gaynor*	C. *A Ship Comes In*
4. Charles Chaplin* (Special)	D. *The Valiant*
5. Ruth Chatterton	E. *The Last Command*
6. Emil Jannings*	F. *Street Angel*
7. Betty Compson	G. *Thunderbolt*
8. Bessie Love	H. *The Patent Leather Kid*
9. Lewis Stone	I. *Sadie Thompson*
10. Richard Barthelmess	J. *Coquette*
11. George Bancroft	K. *The Letter*
12. Paul Muni	L. *The Patriot*
13. Mary Pickford*	M. *Alibi*
14. Jeanne Eagels	N. *The Broadway Melody*
15. Louise Dresser	O. *In Old Arizona*
16. Chester Morris	P. *Madame X*
	Q. *The Barker*
	R. *Sunrise*
	S. *The Way of All Flesh*
	T. *The Circus*

AND THE WINNER WAS . . . (1930s)

The stars listed on the left won their Oscars during the '30s for Best Actor or Best Actress in the films listed on the right. Match the stars with the films.

1. Marie Dressler	A.	*The Sin of Madelon Claudet*
2. Katharine Hepburn	B.	*Dangerous*
3. Fredric March	C.	*Disraeli*
4. Charles Laughton	D.	*The Story of Louis Pasteur*
5. Claudette Colbert	E.	*The Champ*
6. Norma Shearer	F.	*The Good Earth*
7. Bette Davis	G.	*The Great Ziegfeld*
8. Luise Rainer	H.	*Jezebel*
9. Lionel Barrymore	I.	*Gone With the Wind*
10. Clark Gable	J.	*The Private Life of Henry VIII*
11. Paul Muni	K.	*Captains Courageous*
12. George Arliss	L.	*It Happened One Night*
13. Victor McLaglen	M.	*The Divorcee*
14. Wallace Beery	N.	*Goodbye, Mr. Chips*
15. Vivien Leigh	O.	*Morning Glory*
16. Robert Donat	P.	*Dr. Jekyll and Mr. Hyde*
17. Spencer Tracy	Q.	*Min and Bill*
18. Helen Hayes	R.	*The Informer*
	S.	*A Free Soul*
	T.	*Boys Town*

LOSERS AND WINNERS (1930s)

The supporting Oscars were first given out in 1936. The stars listed on the left were nominated for the films listed on the right. Asterisks denote winners. Match the stars and the films.

1. Hattie McDaniel*
2. Bonita Granville
3. Edna May Oliver
4. Gale Sondergaard*
5. Geraldine Fitzgerald
6. Thomas Mitchell*
7. Anne Shirley
8. John Garfield
9. Maria Ouspenskaya
10. Fay Bainter*
11. Beulah Bondi
12. Claire Trevor
13. H. B. Warner
14. Walter Brennan*
15. Billie Burke
16. Alice Brady*
17. Brian Donlevy
18. Basil Rathbone
19. Joseph Schildkraut*

A. *Jezebel*
B. *Stella Dallas*
C. *In Old Chicago*
D. *Dodsworth*
E. *Come and Get It!*
F. *Kentucky*
G. *Merrily We Live*
H. *Romeo and Juliet*
I. *Dead End*
J. *Beau Geste*
K. *Gone With the Wind*
L. *Four Daughters*
M. *The Life of Emile Zola*
N. *Wuthering Heights*
O. *These Three*
P. *Lost Horizon*
Q. *Drums Along the Mohawk*
R. *The Gorgeous Hussy*
S. *Anthony Adverse*
T. *Stagecoach*

AND THE LOSER WAS . . . (1930s) (1)

The actors listed on the left were nominated for Best Actor Oscars for the films listed on the right during the '30s. Match the stars and the films.

1. Clark Gable		A.	*The Front Page*
2. Wallace Beery		B.	*Cimarron*
3. Jackie Cooper		C.	*Mr. Smith Goes to Washington*
4. Charles Boyer		D.	*A Star Is Born*
5 James Cagney		E.	*Dodsworth*
6. Laurence Olivier		F.	*Babes in Arms*
7. Robert Montgomery		G.	*Affairs of Cellini*
8. Spencer Tracy		H.	*The Citadel*
9. James Stewart		I.	*My Man Godfrey*
10. Alfred Lunt		J.	*I am a Fugitive from a Chain Gang*
11. Leslie Howard		K.	*Skippy*
12. Paul Muni		L.	*The Guardsman*
13. Walter Huston		M.	*Gone With the Wind*
14. Mickey Rooney		N.	*San Francisco*
15. Frank Morgan		O.	*Night Must Fall*
16. William Powell		P.	*The Big House*
17. Adolphe Menjou		Q.	*Angels with Dirty Faces*
18. Fredric March		R.	*Algiers*
19. Robert Donat		S.	*Pygmalion*
20. Richard Dix		T.	*Wuthering Heights*

Photo 78

AND THE LOSER WAS . . . (1930s) (2)

The actresses listed on the left were nominated for Best Actress in the films listed on the right during the '30s. Match the stars with the films.

1. Irene Dunne		A.	Stella Dallas
2. Marlene Dietrich		B.	Goodbye, Mr. Chips
3. Bette Davis		C.	Becky Sharp
4. Greta Garbo		D.	Holiday
5. May Robson		E.	Pygmalion
6. Janet Gaynor		F.	Marie Antoinette
7. Claudette Colbert		G.	Three Comrades
8. Ann Harding		H.	Alice Adams
9. Miriam Hopkins		I.	Camille
10. Norma Shearer		J.	The Dark Angel
11. Lynn Fontanne		K.	The Awful Truth
12. Barbara Stanwyck		L.	My Man Godfrey
13. Elizabeth Bergner		M.	One Night of Love
14. Margaret Sullavan		N.	The Guardsman
15. Merle Oberon		O.	Morocco
16. Greer Garson		P.	Escape Me Never
17. Katharine Hepburn		Q.	Dark Victory
18. Wendy Hiller		R.	Private Worlds
19. Carole Lombard		S.	Lady for a Day
20. Grace Moore		T.	A Star Is Born

AND THE WINNER WAS . . . (1940s) (1)

The stars listed on the left won their Oscars during the '40s for Best Actor or Best Actress in the films listed on the right. Match the stars with the films.

1.	Joan Fontaine	A.	Sargeant York
2.	Paul Lukas	B.	Mrs. Miniver
3.	Ginger Rogers	C.	The Song of Bernadette
4.	James Cagney	D.	Going My Way
5.	Ingrid Bergman	E.	To Each His Own
6.	James Stewart	F.	The Lost Weekend
7.	Joan Crawford	G.	Johnny Belinda
8.	Ronald Colman	H.	The Farmer's Daughter
9.	Gary Cooper	I.	Kitty Foyle
10.	Olivia de Havilland	J.	Hamlet
11.	Greer Garson	K.	The Best Years of Our Lives
12.	Broderick Crawford	L.	The Heiress
13.	Jennifer Jones	M.	Mildred Pierce
14.	Laurence Olivier	N.	Watch on the Rhine
15.	Fredric March	O.	Suspicion
16.	Bing Crosby	P.	All the King's Men
17.	Jane Wyman	Q.	Gaslight
18.	Loretta Young	R.	A Double Life
19.	Ray Milland	S.	Yankee Doodle Dandy
		T.	The Philadelphia Story

Photo 79

AND THE WINNER WAS . . . (1940s) (2)

The stars listed on the left won their Oscars during the '40s for Best Supporting Actor or Actress in the films listed on the right. Match the stars with the films.

1. Mercedes McCambridge	A. *Treasure of Sierra Madre*
2. Anne Revere	B. *The Best Years of Our Lives*
3. Celeste Holm	C. *A Tree Grows in Brooklyn*
4. Charles Coburn	D. *Mrs. Miniver*
5. Ethel Barrymore	E. *Key Largo*
6. Anne Baxter	F. *For Whom the Bell Tolls*
7. Edmund Gwenn	G. *The Great Lie*
8. Teresa Wright	H. *Going My Way*
9. Dean Jagger	I. *The Grapes of Wrath*
10. Van Heflin	J. *The More the Merrier*
11. Donald Crisp	K. *The Westerner*
12. James Dunn	L. *The Razor's Edge*
13. Jane Darwell	M. *All the King's Men*
14. Walter Huston	N. *None But the Lonely Heart*
15. Walter Brennan	O. *Gentleman's Agreement*
16. Mary Astor	P. *How Green Was My Valley*
17. Harold Russell	Q. *National Velvet*
18. Katina Paxinou	R. *Johnny Eager*
19. Barry Fitzgerald	S. *Miracle on 34th Street*
20. Claire Trevor	T. *Twelve O'Clock High*

AND THE LOSER WAS . . . (1940s)(1)

The actors listed on the left were nominated for Best Actor Oscars in the films listed on the right. Match the stars with the films.

1. Kirk Douglas	A. *Rebecca*
2. Clifton Webb	B. *Citizen Kane*
3. Henry Fonda	C. *The Sands of Iwo Jima*
4. John Garfield	D. *The Great Dictator*
5. Cary Grant	E. *Casablanca*
6. Richard Todd	F. *The Search*
7. Dan Dailey	G. *Gaslight*
8. William Powell	H. *Anchors Aweigh*
9. Robert Montgomery	I. *The Jolson Story*
10. Cornel Wilde	J. *Body and Soul*
11. John Wayne	K. *Penny Serenade*
12. Charles Boyer	L. *Gentleman's Agreement*
13. Montgomery Clift	M. *Champion*
14. Laurence Olivier	N. *A Song to Remember*
15. Humphrey Bogart	O. *When My Baby Smiles at Me*
16. Larry Parks	P. *Life with Father*
17. Orson Welles	Q. *The Hasty Heart*
18. Gene Kelly	R. *Sitting Pretty*
19. Gregory Peck	S. *The Grapes of Wrath*
20. Charles Chaplin	T. *Here Comes Mr. Jordan*

Photo 80   176

AND THE LOSER WAS . . . (1940s)(2)

The actresses listed on the left were nominated for Best Actress Oscars in the films listed on the right. Match the stars and the films.

1.	Joan Crawford	A.	*Duel in the Sun*
2.	Jeanne Crain	B.	*The Yearling*
3.	Greer Garson	C.	*Edward, My Son*
4.	Rosalind Russell	D.	*The Letter*
5.	Susan Hayward	E.	*Brief Encounter*
6.	Gene Tierney	F.	*The Snake Pit*
7.	Jean Arthur	G.	*The Philadelphia Story*
8.	Ingrid Bergman	H.	*Rebecca*
9.	Martha Scott	I.	*Since You Went Away*
10.	Barbara Stanwyck	J.	*Leave Her to Heaven*
11.	Bette Davis	K.	*Possessed*
12.	Teresa Wright	L.	*The More the Merrier*
13.	Katharine Hepburn	M.	*Our Town*
14.	Olivia de Havilland	N.	*Pinky*
15.	Jane Wyman	O.	*Pride of the Yankees*
16.	Joan Fontaine	P.	*Joan of Arc*
17.	Claudette Colbert	Q.	*Madame Curie*
18.	Jennifer Jones	R.	*Sorry Wrong Number*
19.	Celia Johnson	S.	*My Foolish Heart*
20.	Deborah Kerr	T.	*Sister Kenny*

AND THE LOSER WAS ... (1940s)(3)

The actors listed on the left were nominated for Supporting Oscars in the films listed on the right. Match the stars with the films.

1. John Ireland	A.	*The Heiress*
2. Richard Widmark	B.	*The Luck of the Irish*
3. John Dall	C.	*Crossfire*
4. Arthur Kennedy	D.	*For Whom the Bell Tolls*
5. Monty Woolley	E.	*The Jolson Story*
6. Claude Rains	F.	*Yankee Doodle Dandy*
7. William Bendix	G.	*I Remember Mama*
8. James Stephenson	H.	*Laura*
9. Ralph Richardson	I.	*Mrs. Miniver*
10. Walter Huston	J.	*The Maltese Falcon*
11. Frank Morgan	K.	*The Corn Is Green*
12. Jose Ferrer	L.	*The Letter*
13. Sydney Greenstreet	M.	*All the King's Men*
14. Robert Ryan	N.	*Wake Island*
15. Akim Tamiroff	O.	*Tortilla Flat*
16. Cecil Kellaway	P.	*Kiss of Death*
17. Henry Travers	Q.	*Since You Went Away*
18. William Demarest	R.	*Notorious*
19. Clifton Webb	S.	*Champion*
20. Oscar Homolka	T.	*Joan of Arc*

AND THE LOSER WAS . . . (1940s)(4)

The actresses listed on the left were nominated for Supporting Oscars in the films listed on the right. Match the stars with the films.

1. Judith Anderson		A.	All This and Heaven Too
2. Ethel Waters		B.	Anna and the King of Siam
3. Marjorie Main		C.	The Picture of Dorian Gray
4. Eve Arden		D.	Come to the Stable
5. Flora Robson		E.	Since You Went Away
6. Aline MacMahon		F.	Duel in the Sun
7. Ruth Hussey		G.	Now Voyager
8. Angela Lansbury		H.	So Proudly We Hail
9. Paulette Goddard		I.	I Remember Mama
10. Agnes Moorehead		J.	Sergeant York
11. Jean Simmons		K.	Mildred Pierce
12. Barbara O'Neil		L.	Watch on the Rhine
13. Gale Sondergaard		M.	Rebecca
14. Margaret Wycherly		N.	Dragon Seed
15. Elsa Lanchester		O.	The Egg and I
16. Lucile Watson		P.	Hamlet
17. Lillian Gish		Q.	Mrs. Parkington
18. Gladys Cooper		R.	Pinky
19. Jennifer Jones		S.	Saratoga Trunk
20. Ellen Corby		T.	The Philadelphia Story

AND THE WINNER WAS . . . (1950s)(1)

The stars listed on the left won Oscars for Best Actor or Best Actress in the films listed on the right. Match the stars with the films.

1.	Vivien Leigh	A.	*Cyrano de Bergerac*
2.	Grace Kelly	B.	*Come Back, Little Sheba*
3.	Ernest Borgnine	C.	*Stalag 17*
4.	Judy Holliday	D.	*The African Queen*
5.	Yul Brynner	E.	*The Rose Tattoo*
6.	Marlon Brando	F.	*Room at the Top*
7.	Humphrey Bogart	G.	*High Noon*
8.	Alec Guinness	H.	*I Want to Live*
9.	Ingrid Bergman	I.	*The Bridge on the River Kwai*
10.	Jose Ferrer	J.	*Roman Holiday*
11.	Susan Hayward	K.	*The Three Faces of Eve*
12.	Anna Magnani	L.	*Ben-Hur*
13.	Shirley Booth	M.	*The Country Girl*
14.	Joanne Woodward	N.	*Separate Tables*
15.	Simone Signoret	O.	*On the Waterfront*
16.	Gary Cooper	P.	*The King and I*
17.	Charlton Heston	Q.	*Born Yesterday*
18.	Audrey Hepburn	R.	*Anastasia*
19.	David Niven	S.	*A Streetcar Named Desire*
20.	William Holden	T.	*Marty*

Photo 81

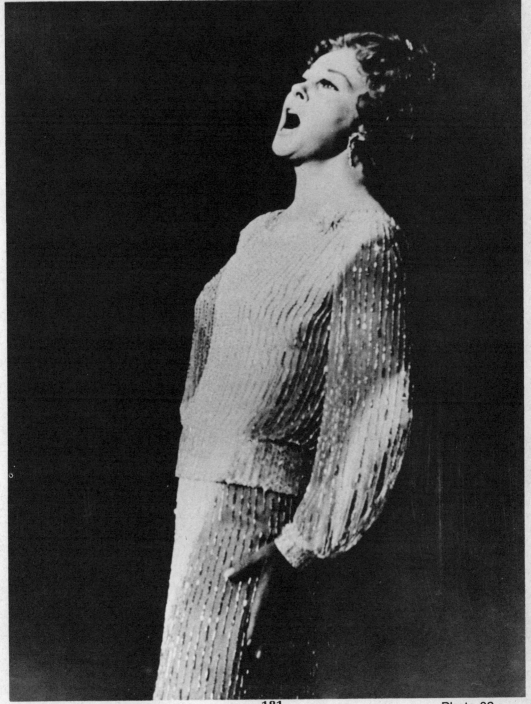

181 Photo 82

AND THE WINNER WAS . . . (1950s) (2)

The stars listed on the left won Oscars for Best Supporting Actor or Actress in the films listed on the right. Match the stars with the films.

1. Shelley Winters
2. Red Buttons
3. Dorothy Malone
4. Edmond O'Brien
5. Gloria Grahame
6. Myoshi Umeki
7. Hugh Griffith
8. Jo Van Fleet
9. Anthony Quinn
10. Wendy Hiller
11. Frank Sinatra
12. Josephine Hull
13. Burl Ives
14. Eva Marie Saint
15. Kim Hunter
16. Donna Reed
17. Karl Malden
18. George Sanders
19. Jack Lemmon

A. *Ben-Hur*
B. *The Big Country*
C. *Separate Tables*
D. *Lust for Life*
E. *From Here to Eternity*
F. *Mister Roberts*
G. *On the Waterfront*
H. *Viva Zapata!*
I. *A Streetcar Named Desire*
J. *The Diary of Anne Frank*
K. *All About Eve*
L. *The Barefoot Contessa*
M. *Written on the Wind*
N. *Harvey*
O. *The Bad and the Beautiful*
P. *East of Eden*
Q. *Sayonara*

Photo 83

AND THE LOSER WAS . . . (1950s) (1)

The actors listed on the left were nominated for Best Actor Oscars in the films listed on the right. Match the stars with the films.

1. Anthony Franciosa	A. *Richard III*
2. Rock Hudson	B. *A Star Is Born*
3. James Cagney	C. *Some Like It Hot*
4. Laurence Harvey	D. *From Here to Eternity*
5. Bing Crosby	E. *The Caine Mutiny*
6. Richard Burton	F. *Witness for the Prosecution*
7. Kirk Douglas	G. *Bright Victory*
8. Alec Guinness	H. *The Man with the Golden Arm*
9. Jack Lemmon	I. *Giant*
10. James Stewart	J. *Moulin Rouge*
11. Montgomery Clift	K. *A Hatful of Rain*
12. Spencer Tracy	L. *The Country Girl*
13. James Mason	M. *Julius Caesar*
14. Jose Ferrer	N. *Harvey*
15. Laurence Olivier	O. *Room at the Top*
16. Humphrey Bogart	P. *Love Me or Leave Me*
17. Arthur Kennedy	Q. *The Robe*
18. Marlon Brando	R. *The Lavender Hill Mob*
19. Frank Sinatra	S. *Lust for Life*
20. Charles Laughton	T. *The Old Man and the Sea*

AND THE LOSER WAS . . . (1950s) (2)

The actresses listed on the left were nominated for Best Actress Oscars in the films listed on the right. Match the stars with the films.

1. Eleanor Parker
2. Susan Hayward
3. Doris Day
4. Dorothy Dandridge
5. Judy Garland
6. Audrey Hepburn
7. Julie Harris
8. Nancy Kelly
9. Gloria Swanson
10. Lana Turner
11. Deborah Kerr
12. Katharine Hepburn
13. Jennifer Jones
14. Bette Davis
15. Leslie Caron
16. Jane Wyman
17. Rosalind Russell
18. Shirley MacLaine
19. Joan Crawford
20. Ava Gardner

A. *Sudden Fear*
B. *From Here to Eternity*
C. *Sunset Boulevard*
D. *The Bad Seed*
E. *The African Queen*
F. *Auntie Mame*
G. *The Star*
H. *The Blue Veil*
I. *Lili*
J. *Mogambo*
K. *Some Came Running*
L. *Carmen Jones*
M. *Member of the Wedding*
N. *The Nun's Story*
O. *Peyton Place*
P. *Pillow Talk*
Q. *I'll Cry Tomorrow*
R. *A Star Is Born*
S. *Caged*
T. *Love Is a Many-Splendored Thing*

AND THE LOSER WAS . . . (1950s) (3)

The actors listed on the left were nominated for Best Supporting Actor in the films listed on the right. Match the stars with the films.

1.	Arthur Kennedy	A.	*My Cousin Rachel*
2.	Kevin McCarthy	B.	*Rebel Without a Cause*
3.	Don Murray	C.	*The Bold and the Brave*
4.	Robert Stack	D.	*Sudden Fear*
5.	Gig Young	E.	*The Defiant Ones*
6.	Sessue Hayakawa	F.	*Picnic*
7.	Robert Vaughn	G.	*Broken Arrow*
8.	Richard Burton	H.	*Stalag 17*
9.	Anthony Perkins	I.	*The Diary of Anne Frank*
10.	Erich von Stroheim	J.	*The Young Philadelphians*
11.	Victor McLaglen	K.	*The Caine Mutiny*
12.	Jeff Chandler	L.	*Written on the Wind*
13.	Arthur O'Connell	M.	*Death of a Salesman*
14.	Jack Palance	N.	*Sunset Boulevard*
15.	Ed Wynn	O.	*Trial*
16.	Robert Strauss	P.	*The Bridge on the River Kwai*
17.	Theodore Bikel	Q.	*Come Fill the Cup*
18.	Sal Mineo	R.	*Friendly Persuasion*
19.	Mickey Rooney	S.	*Bus Stop*
20.	Tom Tully	T.	*The Quiet Man*

AND THE LOSER WAS . . . (1950s) (4)

The actresses listed on the left were nominated for Best Supporting Actress in the films listed on the right. Match the stars with the films.

1. Grace Kelly	A.	*Pillow Talk*
2. Peggy Lee	B.	*Torch Song*
3. Nina Foch	C.	*The Bad Seed*
4. Elsa Lanchester	D.	*Sunset Boulevard*
5. Peggy Cass	E.	*Room at the Top*
6. Geraldine Page	F.	*The High and the Mighty*
7. Hope Emerson	G.	*Detective Story*
8. Hermione Baddeley	H.	*Some Came Running*
9. Marjorie Rambeau	I.	*Rebel Without a Cause*
10. Joan Blondell	J.	*Imitation of Life*
11. Betsy Blair	K.	*Peyton Place*
12. Lee Grant	L.	*The Blue Veil*
13. Martha Hyer	M.	*Mogambo*
14. Nancy Olson	N.	*Caged*
15. Thelma Ritter	O.	*Auntie Mame*
16. Juanita Moore	P.	*Pete Kelly's Blues*
17. Eileen Heckart	Q.	*Executive Suite*
18. Natalie Wood	R.	*Witness for the Prosecution*
19. Hope Lange	S.	*Hondo*
20. Claire Trevor	T.	*Marty*

Photo 84

AND THE WINNER WAS . . . (1960s) (1)

The stars listed on the left won Oscars for Best Actor or Best Actress in the films listed on the right. Match the stars with the films.

1.	Elizabeth Taylor	A.	*Judgment at Nuremburg*
2.	Gregory Peck	B.	*The Miracle Worker*
3.	Barbra Streisand	C.	*Lilies of the Field*
4.	Patricia Neal	D.	*The Prime of Miss Jean Brodie*
5.	Burt Lancaster	E.	*My Fair Lady*
6.	Julie Andrews	F.	*True Grit*
7.	Julie Christie	G.	*Cat Ballou*
8.	Sophia Loren	H.	*Charly*
9.	Sidney Poitier	I.	*Darling*
10.	Katharine Hepburn	J.	*Funny Girl*
11.	Maggie Smith	K.	*A Man for All Seasons*
12.	Maximilian Schell	L.	*Mary Poppins*
13.	John Wayne	M.	*In the Heat of the Night*
14.	Rex Harrison	N.	*Two Women*
15.	Rod Steiger	O.	*Guess Who's Coming to Dinner*
16.	Anne Bancroft	P.	*Butterfield 8*
17.	Cliff Robertson	Q.	*Hud*
18.	Paul Scofield	R.	*Who's Afraid of Virginia Woolf?*
19.	Lee Marvin	S.	*To Kill a Mockingbird*
		T.	*Elmer Gantry*

AND THE WINNER WAS . . . (1960s) (2)

The stars listed on the left won Oscars for Best Supporting Actor or Actress in the films listed on the right. Match the stars with the films.

1.	Ruth Gordon	A.	*The Subject Was Roses*
2.	Walter Matthau	B.	*Cactus Flower*
3.	Estelle Parsons	C.	*Cool Hand Luke*
4.	Patty Duke	D.	*Topkapi*
5.	Gig Young	E.	*West Side Story*
6.	Sandy Dennis	F.	*A Thousand Clowns*
7.	Ed Begley	G.	*Elmer Gantry*
8.	Lila Kedrova	H.	*The V.I.P.s*
9.	Melvyn Douglas	I.	*A Patch of Blue*
10.	Goldie Hawn	J.	*Who's Afraid of Virginia Woolf?*
11.	Rita Moreno	K.	*The Miracle Worker*
12.	Peter Ustinov	L.	*Spartacus*
13.	Shirley Jones	M.	*Sweet Bird of Youth*
14.	Jack Albertson	N.	*Hud*
15.	Martin Balsam	O.	*They Shoot Horses, Don't They?*
16.	George Chakiris	P.	*The Fortune Cookie*
17.	Margaret Rutherford	Q.	*Zorba the Greek*
18.	Shelley Winters	R.	*Rosemary's Baby*
19.	George Kennedy	S.	*Bonnie and Clyde*

Photo 85

AND THE LOSER WAS . . . (1960s) (1)

The actors listed on the left were nominated for Best Actor Oscars for the films listed on the right. Match the stars with the films.

1. Peter O'Toole		A.	Anne of the Thousand Days
2. Michael Caine		B.	Cool Hand Luke
3. Warren Beatty		C.	Dr. Strangelove
4. Laurence Olivier		D.	Birdman of Alcatraz
5. Spencer Tracy		E.	The Apartment
6. Anthony Quinn		F.	The Fixer
7. Steve McQueen		G.	Fanny
8. Richard Burton		H.	The Pawnbroker
9. Richard Harris		I.	The Graduate
10. Jack Lemmon		J.	Tom Jones
11. Alan Arkin		K.	Alfie
12. Charles Boyer		L.	Ship of Fools
13. Burt Lancaster		M.	The Sand Pebbles
14. Paul Newman		N.	A Lion in Winter
15. Albert Finney		O.	This Sporting Life
16. Rod Steiger		P.	Bonnie and Clyde
17. Dustin Hoffman		Q.	Othello
18. Peter Sellers		R.	Guess Who's Coming to Dinner
19. Oscar Werner		S.	Zorba the Greek
20. Alan Bates		T.	The Heart Is a Lonely Hunter

AND THE LOSER WAS . . . (1960s) (2)

The actresses listed on the left were nominated for Best Actress Oscars for the films listed on the right. Match the stars with the films.

1. Greer Garson	A. *The Apartment*
2. Bette Davis	B. *The L-Shaped Room*
3. Debbie Reynolds	C. *Splendor in the Grass*
4. Shirley MacLaine	D. *Georgy Girl*
5. Julie Andrews	E. *Wait Until Dark*
6. Lee Remick	F. *Sweet Bird of Youth*
7. Patricia Neal	G. *The Sterile Cuckoo*
8. Anne Bancroft	H. *The Hustler*
9. Melina Mercouri	I. *Rachel, Rachel*
10. Liza Minnelli	J. *Long Day's Journey Into Night*
11. Vanessa Redgrave	K. *Bonnie and Clyde*
12. Piper Laurie	L. *Days of Wine and Roses*
13. Joanne Woodward	M. *The Unsinkable Molly Brown*
14. Katharine Hepburn	N. *Never on Sunday*
15. Faye Dunaway	O. *The Subject Was Roses*
16. Natalie Wood	P. *What Ever Happened to Baby Jane?*
17. Audrey Hepburn	Q. *The Graduate*
18. Leslie Caron	R. *Isadora*
19. Lynn Redgrave	S. *Sunrise at Campobello*
20. Geraldine Page	T. *The Sound of Music*

AND THE LOSER WAS . . . (1960s) (3)

The actors listed on the left were nominated for Best Supporting Actor in the films listed on the right. Match the stars with the films.

1. Jack Nicholson		A.	The Dirty Dozen
2. Michael Dunn		B.	A Man for All Seasons
3. Lee Tracy		C.	The Cardinal
4. Daniel Massey		D.	Georgy Girl
5. John Gielgud		E.	Lawrence of Arabia
6. Nick Adams		F.	My Fair Lady
7. Gene Wilder		G.	Judgment at Nuremberg
8. Omar Sharif		H.	Who's Afraid of Virginia Woolf?
9. Montgomery Clift		I.	Captain Newman, M.D.
10. John Cassavetes		J.	Easy Rider
11. Terence Stamp		K.	Seven Days in May
12. Victor Buono		L.	Billy Budd
13. Gene Hackman		M.	Star!
14. John Huston		N.	Ship of Fools
15. Bobby Darin		O.	What Ever Happened to Baby Jane?
16. James Mason		P.	The Producers
17. Edmond O'Brien		Q.	Twilight of Honor
18. Robert Shaw		R.	Becket
19. Stanley Holloway		S.	The Best Man
20. George Segal		T.	Bonnie and Clyde

Photo 86

AND THE LOSER WAS . . . (1960s) (4)

The actresses listed on the left were nominated for Supporting Actress
Oscars in the films listed on the right. Match the stars with the films.

1. Sylvia Miles	A.	*Funny Girl*
2. Katharine Ross	B.	*Barefoot in the Park*
3. Wendy Hiller	C.	*Judgment at Nuremberg*
4. Agnes Moorehead	D.	*The Manchurian Candidate*
5. Maggie Smith	E.	*Rachel, Rachel*
6. Edith Evans	F.	*Birdman of Alcatraz*
7. Susannah York	G.	*You're a Big Boy, Now*
8. Una Merkel	H.	*My Fair Lady*
9. Angela Lansbury	I.	*Thoroughly Modern Millie*
10. Janet Leigh	J.	*Inside Daisy Clover*
11. Kay Medford	K.	*Sweet Bird of Youth*
12. Judy Garland	L.	*A Man for All Seasons*
13. Mildred Natwick	M.	*Midnight Cowboy*
14. Thelma Ritter	N.	*Summer and Smoke*
15. Gladys Cooper	O.	*Tom Jones*
16. Estelle Parsons	P.	*The Graduate*
17. Shirley Knight	Q.	*Psycho*
18. Geraldine Page	R.	*Othello*
19. Ruth Gordon	S.	*Hush Hush, Sweet Charlotte*
20. Carol Channing	T.	*They Shoot Horses, Don't They?*

Photo 87

WINNERS AND LOSERS (1970s) (1)

The stars listed on the left were all nominated for Best Actor in the films listed on the right. Asterisks denote winners. Match the stars with the films.

1. Jack Nicholson*		A.	The Godfather
2. Sylvester Stallone		B.	Taxi Driver
3. Robert Redford		C.	Serpico
4. Albert Finney		D.	Sleuth
5. Jack Lemmon*		E.	Lenny
6. Michael Caine		F.	The French Connection
7. Art Carney*		G.	The Sunshine Boys
8. Paul Winfield		H.	Love Story
9. Topol		I.	The Ruling Class
10. Peter Finch*		J.	Patton
11. Al Pacino		K.	The Great White Hope
12. Dustin Hoffman		L.	One Flew Over the Cuckoo's Nest
13. Marlon Brando*		M.	Murder on the Orient Express
14. Ryan O'Neal		N.	Harry and Tonto
15. Peter O'Toole		O.	Fiddler on the Roof
16. James Earl Jones		P.	Save the Tiger
17. Gene Hackman*		Q.	Sounder
18. Walter Matthau		R.	Rocky
19. Robert DeNiro		S.	The Sting
20. George C. Scott*		T.	Network

WINNERS AND LOSERS (1970s) (2)

The stars listed on the left were nominated for Best Actress in the films listed on the right. Asterisks denote winners. Match the stars with the films.

1. Jane Alexander	A. *The Way We Were*
2. Faye Dunaway*	B. *Klute*
3. Glenda Jackson*	C. *Mahogany*
4. Cicely Tyson	D. *Carrie*
5. Gena Rowlands	E. *Cabaret*
6. Janet Suzman	F. *Ryan's Daughter*
7. Sarah Miles	G. *Lenny*
8. Carol Kane	H. *The Emigrants*
9. Vanessa Redgrave	I. *One Flew Over the Cuckoo's Nest*
10. Liza Minnelli*	J. *Hester Street*
11. Talia Shire	K. *Tommy*
12. Barbra Streisand	L. *A Touch of Class*
13. Louise Fletcher*	M. *Rocky*
14. Liv Ullmann	N. *Network*
15. Ellen Burstyn*	O. *A Woman Under the Influence*
16. Valerie Perrine	P. *The Great White Hope*
17. Diana Ross	Q. *Nicholas and Alexandra*
18. Ann-Margret	R. *Sounder*
19. Sissy Spacek	S. *Mary, Queen of Scots*
20. Jane Fonda*	T. *Alice Doesn't Live Here Anymore*

WINNERS AND LOSERS (1970s) (3)

The actors listed on the left were nominated for Best Supporting Actor Oscars for the films listed on the right. Asterisks denote winners. Match the stars with the films.

1. Gene Hackman		A.	Sometimes a Great Notion
2. Jason Miller		B.	Cabaret
3. John Houseman*		C.	Network
4. Burgess Meredith		D.	The Godfather
5. Chris Sarandon		E.	Shampoo
6. Chief Dan George		F.	The French Connection
7. Randy Quaid		G.	The Godfather, Part II
8. Jack Warden		H.	Save the Tiger
9. Ned Beatty		I.	I Never Sang for My Father
10. Jeff Bridges		J.	The Towering Inferno
11. Joel Grey*		K.	The Last Detail
12. Robert DeNiro*		L.	Little Big Man
13. George Burns*		M.	Ryan's Daughter
14. Roy Scheider		N.	Rocky
15. Jack Gilford		O.	The Paper Chase
16. Jason Robards*		P.	Dog Day Afternoon
17. James Caan		Q.	The Exorcist
18. Fred Astaire		R.	The Sunshine Boys
19. John Mills*		S.	All the President's Men
20. Richard Jaekel		T.	The Last Picture Show

Photo 88

WINNERS AND LOSERS (1970s) (4)

The actresses listed on the left were all nominated for Best Supporting Actress Oscars for the films listed on the right. Asterisks denote winners. Match the stars with the films.

1. Piper Laurie	A. *Five Easy Pieces*
2. Maureen Stapleton	B. *Shampoo*
3. Cloris Leachman*	C. *Paper Moon*
4. Ann-Margret	D. *Butterflies Are Free*
5. Beatrice Straight*	E. *Nashville*
6. Geraldine Page	F. *The Exorcist*
7. Candy Clark	G. *M*A*S*H*
8. Sylvia Sidney	H. *The Poseidon Adventure*
9. Lee Grant*	I. *Murder on the Orient Express*
10. Linda Blair	J. *The Go-Between*
11. Talia Shire	K. *The Last Picture Show*
12. Sylvia Miles	L. *Pete 'n' Tillie*
13. Eileen Heckart*	M. *Network*
14. Karen Black	N. *Airport*
15. Margaret Leighton	O. *Carnal Knowledge*
16. Lily Tomlin	P. *Carrie*
17. Tatum O'Neal*	Q. *American Graffiti*
18. Sally Kellerman	R. *The Godfather, Part II*
19. Shelley Winters	S. *Summer Wishes, Winter Dreams*
20. Ingrid Bergman*	T. *Farewell, My Lovely*

197

Photo 90

Photo 91

199

Photo 92

Photo 93

201

Photo 94

Photo 95

203

Photo 96

ACADEMY AWARD
WINNERS AND NOMINEES
IN MAJOR CATEGORIES
(1927–1980)

ACADEMY AWARD WINNERS AND NOMINEES IN MAJOR CATEGORIES (1927–1980)

1927/28

Best Picture
Wings, The Last Command, The Racket, Seventh Heaven, The Way of All Flesh

Best Director
*Frank Borzage, *Seventh Heaven*; Herbert Brenon, Sorrell and Son; King Vidor, The Crowd

Best Comedy Director
*Lewis Milestone, *Two Arabian Knights*; Ted Wilde, Speedy; Charles Chaplin, The Circus

Best Actor
*Emil Jannings, *The Last Command, The Way of All Flesh*; Richard Barthelmess, The Noose, The Patent Leather Kid; Charles Chaplin, The Circus

Best Actress
*Janet Gaynor, *Seventh Heaven, Street Angel, Sunrise*; Gloria Swanson, Sadie Thompson; Louise Dresser, A Ship Comes In

1928/29

Best Picture
The Broadway Melody, Alibi, Hollywood Revue, In Old Arizona, The Patriot

Best Director
*Frank Lloyd, *The Divine Lady*; Lionel Barrymore, Madame X; Harry Beaumont, Broadway Melody; Irving Cummings, In Old Arizona; Frank Lloyd, Weary River, Drag; Ernst Lubitsch, The Patriot

*denotes winner

207

Best Actor

*Warner Baxter, *In Old Arizona*; Chester Morris, *Alibi*; Paul Muni, *The Valiant*; George Bancroft, *Thunderbolt*; Lewis Stone, *The Patriot*

Best Actress

*Mary Pickford, *Coquette*; Ruth Chatterton, *Madame X*; Betty Compson, *The Barker*; Jeanne Eagles, *The Letter*; Bessie Love, *Broadway Melody*

1929/30

Best Picture

**All Quiet on the Western Front*, The Big House, Disraeli, The Divorcee, The Love Parade

Best Director

*Lewis Mileston, *All Quiet on the Western Front*; Clarence Brown, *Anna Christie, Romance*; Robert Leonard, *The Divorcee*; Ernst Lubitsch, *The Love Parade*; King Vidor, *Hallelujah*

Best Actor

*George Arliss, *Disraeli*; George Arliss, *The Green Goddess*; Wallace Beery, *The Big House*; Maurice Chevalier, *The Big Pond, The Love Parade*; Ronald Colman, *Bulldog Drummond, Condemned*; Lawrence Tibbett, *The Rogue Song*

Best Actress

*Norma Shearer, *The Divorcee*; Nancy Carroll, *The Devil's Holiday*; Ruth Chatterton, *Sarah and Son*; Greta Garbo, *Anna Christie, Romance*; Norma Shearer, *Their Own Desire*; Gloria Swanson, *The Trespasser*

1930/31

Best Picture

**Cimarron*, East Lynne, The Front Page, Skippy, Trader Horn

Best Director

*Norman Taurog, *Skippy*; Clarence Brown, *A Free Soul*; Lewis Milestone, *The Front Page*; Wesley Ruggles, *Cimarron*; Josef von Sternberg, *Morocco*

Best Actor

*Lionel Barrymore, *A Free Soul*; Jackie Cooper, *Skippy*; Richard Dix, *Cimarron*; Fredric March, *The Royal Family of Broadway*; Adolphe Menjou, *The Front Page*

Best Actress

*Marie Dressler, *Min and Bill*; Marlene Dietrich, *Morocco*; Irenne Dunne, *Cimarron*; Ann Harding, *Holiday*; Norma Shearer, *A Free Soul*

1931/32

Best Picture

**Grand Hotel*, Arrowsmith, Bad Girl, The Champ, Five Star Final, One Hour with You, Shanghai Express, Smiling Lieutenant

*denotes winner

Best Director
*Frank Borzage, **Bad Girl**; King Vidor, The Champ; Josef von Sternberg, Shanghai Express
Best Actor
*Wallace Beery, **The Champ**; *Fredric March, **Dr. Jekyll and Mr. Hyde;** Alfred Lunt, The Guardsman
Best Actress
*Helen Hayes, **The Sin of Madelon Claudet**; Marie Dressler, Emma; Lynn Fontanne, The Guardsman

1932/33
Best Picture
***Cavalcade**, A Farewell to Arms, Forty-Second Street, I am a Fugitive from a Chain Gang, Lady for a Day, Little Women, The Private Life of Henry VIII, She Done Him Wrong, Smilin' Through, State Fair
Best Director
*Frank Lloyd, **Cavalcade**; Frank Capra, Lady for a Day; George Cukor, Little Women
Best Actor
*Charles Laughton, **Private Life of Henry VIII**; Leslie Howard, Berkeley Square; Paul Muni, I am a Fugitive from a Chain Gang
Best Actress
*Katharine Hepburn, **Morning Glory**; May Robson, Lady for a Day; Diana Wynward, Cavalcade

1934
Best Picture
***It Happened One Night**, The Barretts of Wimpole Street, Cleopatra, Flirtation Walk, The Gay Divorcee, Here Comes the Navy, The House of Rothschild, Imitation of Life, One Night of Love, The Thin Man, Viva Villa, The White Parade
Best Director
*Frank Capra, **It Happened One Night**; Victor Schertzinger, One Night of Love; W. S. Van Dyke, The Thin Man
Best Actor
*Clark Gable, **It Happened One Night**; Frank Morgan, Affairs of Cellini; William Powell, The Thin Man
Best Actress
*Claudette Colbert, **It Happened One Night**; Grace Moore, One Night of Love; Norma Shearer, The Barretts of Wimpole Street

*denotes winner

1935

Best Picture
Mutiny on the Bounty, Alice Adams, Broadway Melody of 1936, Captain Blood, David Copperfield, The Informer, Les Miserables, The Lives of a Bengal Lancer, A Midsummer Night's Dream, Naughty Marietta, Ruggles of Red Gap, Top Hat

Best Director
*John Ford, *The Informer*; Henry Hathaway, The Lives of a Bengal Lancer; Frank Lloyd, Mutiny on the Bounty

Best Actor
*Victor McLaglen, *The Informer*; Clark Gable, Mutiny on the Bounty; Charles Laughton, Mutiny on the Bounty; Franchot Tone, Mutiny on the Bounty

Best Actress
*Bette Davis, *Dangerous*; Elisabeth Bergner, Escape Me Never; Claudette Colbert, Private Worlds; Katharine Hepburn, Alice Adams

1936

Best Picture
The Great Ziegfeld, Anthony Adverse, Dodsworth, Libeled Lady, Mr. Deeds Goes to Town, Romeo and Juliet, San Francisco, The Story of Louis Pasteur, A Tale of Two Cities, Three Smart Girls

Best Director
Frank Capra, *Mr. Deeds Goes to Town*; Gregory La Cava, My Man Godfrey; Robert Z. Leonard, The Great Ziegfeld; W. S. Van Dyke, San Francisco; William Wyler, Dodsworth

Best Actor
*Paul Muni, *The Story of Louis Pasteur*; Gary Cooper, Mr. Deeds Goes to Town; William Powell, My Man Godfrey; Walter Huston, Dodsworth; Spencer Tracy, San Francisco

Best Actress
*Luise Rainer, *The Great Ziegfeld*; Irene Dunne, Theodora Goes Wild; Gladys George, Valiant is the Word for Carrie; Carole Lombard, My Man Godfrey; Norma Shearer, Romeo and Juliet

Best Supporting Actor
*Walter Brennan, *Come and Get It*; Mischa Auer, My Man Godfrey; Stuart Erwin, Pigskin Parade; Basil Rathbone, Romeo and Juliet; Akim Tamiroff, The General Died at Dawn

Best Supporting Actress
*Gale Sondergaard, *Anthony Adverse*; Beulah Bondi, The Gorgeous Hussy; Alice Brady, My Man Godfrey; Bonita Granville, These Three; Maria Ouspenskaya, Dodsworth

*denotes winner

1937

Best Picture
The Life of Emile Zola, The Awful Truth, Captains Courageous, Dead End, The Good Earth, In Old Chicago, Lost Horizon, 100 Men and a Girl, Stage Door, A Star is Born

Best Director
*Leo McCarey, *The Awful Truth*; Sidney Franklin, The Good Earth; William Dieterie, The Life of Emile Zola; Gregory LaCava, Stage Door; William Wellman, A Star is Born

Best Actor
*Spencer Tracy, *Captains Courageous*; Charles Boyer, Conquest; Fredric March, A Star is Born; Robert Montgomery, Night Must Fall; Paul Muni, The Life of Emile Zola

Best Actress
*Luise Rainer, *The Good Earth*; Irene Dunne, The Awful Truth; Greta Garbo, Camille; Janet Gaynor, A Star is Born; Barbara Stanwyck, Stella Dallas

Best Supporting Actor
*Joseph Schildkraut, *The Life of Emile Zola*; Ralph Bellamy, The Awful Truth; Thomas Mitchell, Hurricane; H. B. Warner, Lost Horizon; Roland Young, Topper

Best Supporting Actress
*Alice Brady, *In Old Chicago*; Andrea Leeds, Stage Door; Anne Shirley, Stella Dallas; Claire Trevor, Dead End; May Whitty, Night Must Fall

1938

Best Picture
You Can't Take It With You, The Adventures of Robin Hood, Alexander's Ragtime Band, Boys Town, The Citadel, Four Daughters, Grand Illusions, Jezebel, Pygmalion, Test Pilot

Best Director
Frank Capra, *You Can't Take It With You*; Michael Curtiz, Angels with Dirty Faces, Four Daughters; Norman Taurog, Boys Town; King Vidor, The Citadel

Best Actor
*Spencer Tracy, *Boys Town*; Charles Boyer, Algiers; James Cagney, Angels with Dirty Faces; Robert Donat, The Citadel; Leslie Howard, Pygmalion

Best Actress
*Bette Davis, *Jezebel*; Faye Bainter, White Banners; Wendy Hiller, Pygmalion; Norma Shearer, Marie Antoinette; Margaret Sullavan, Three Comrades

Best Supporting Actor
*Walter Brennan, *Kentucky*; John Garfield, Four Daughters; Gene Lockhart, Algiers; Robert Morley, Marie Antoinette; Basil Rathbone, If I Were King

*denotes winner

211

Best Supporting Actress

*Fay Bainter, *Jezebel*; Beulah Bondi, *Of Human Hearts*; Billie Burke, *Merrily We Live*; Spring Byington, *You Can't Take It With You*; Miliza Korjus, *The Great Waltz*

1939
Best Picture

Gone with the Wind, Dark Victory, Goodbye, Mr. Chips, Love Affair, Mr. Smith Goes to Washington, Ninotchka, Of Mice and Men, Stagecoach, The Wizard of Oz, Wuthering Heights

Best Director

*Victor Fleming, *Gone with the Wind*; Frank Capra, Mr. Smith Goes to Washington; John Ford, Stagecoach; Sam Wood, Goodbye, Mr. Chips; William Wyler, Wuthering Heights

Best Actor

*Robert Donat, *Goodbye, Mr. Chips*; Clark Gable, Gone with the Wind; Laurence Olivier, Wuthering Heights; Mickey Rooney, Babes in Arms; James Stewart, Mr. Smith Goes to Washington

Best Actress

*Vivien Leigh, *Gone with the Wind*; Bette Davis, Dark Victory; Irene Dunne, Love Affair; Greta Garbo, Ninotchka; Greer Garson, Goodbye, Mr. Chips

Best Supporting Actor

*Thomas Mitchell, *Stagecoach*; Brian Aherne, Juarez; Harry Carey, Mr. Smith Goes to Washington; Brian Donlevy, Beau Geste; Claude Rains, Mr. Smith Goes to Washington

Best Supporting Actress

*Hattie McDaniel, *Gone with the Wind*; Olivia de Havilland, Gone with the Wind; Geraldine Fitzgerald, Wuthering Heights; Edna May Oliver, Drums Along the Mohawk; Maria Ouspenskaya, Love Affair

1940
Best Picture

Rebecca, All This, and Heaven Too, Foreign Correspondent, The Grapes of Wrath, The Great Dictator, Kitty Foyle, The Letter, The Long Voyage Home, Our Town, The Philadelphia Story

Best Director

*John Ford, *The Grapes of Wrath*; George Cukor, The Philadelphia Story; Alfred Hitchcock, Rebecca; Sam Wood, Kitty Foyle; William Wyler, The Letter

Best Actor

*James Stewart, *The Philadelphia Story*; Charles Chaplin, The Great Dictator; Henry Fonda, The Grapes of Wrath; Raymond Massey, Abe Lincoln in Illinois; Laurence Olivier, Rebecca

*denotes winner

Best Actress
  *Ginger Rogers, *Kitty Foyle*; Bette Davis, The Letter; Joan Fontaine, Rebecca; Katharine Hepburn, The Philadelphia Story; Martha Scott, Our Town

Best Supporting Actor
  *Walter Brennan, *The Westerner*; Albert Basserman, Foreign Correspondent; William Gargan, They Knew What They Wanted; Jack Oakie, The Great Dictator; James Stephenson, The Letter

Best Supporting Actress
  *Jane Darwell, *The Grapes of Wrath*; Judith Anderson, Rebecca; Ruth Hussey, The Philadelphia Story; Barbara O'Neil, All This, and Heaven Too; Marjorie Rambeau, Primrose Path

1941

Best Picture
  How Green Was My Valley, Blossoms in the Dust, Citizen Kane, Here Comes Mr. Jordan, Hold Back the Dawn, The Little Foxes, The Maltese Falcon, One Foot in Heaven, Sergeant York, Suspicion

Best Director
  *John Ford, *How Green Was My Valley*; Alexander Hall, Here Comes Mr. Jordan; Howard Hawks, Sergeant York; Orson Welles, Citizen Kane; William Wyler, The Little Foxes

Best Actor
  *Gary Cooper, *Sergeant York*; Cary Grant, Penny Serenade; Walter Huston, All That Money Can Buy; Robert Montgomery, Here Comes Mr. Jordan; Orson Welles, Citizen Kane

Best Actress
  *Joan Fontaine, *Suspicion*; Bette Davis, The Little Foxes; Greer Garson, Blossoms in the Dust; Olivia de Havilland, Hold Back the Dawn; Barbara Stanwyck, Ball of Fire

Best Supporting Actor
  *Donald Crisp, *How Green Was My Valley*; Walter Brennan, Sergeant York; Charles Coburn, The Devil and Miss Jones; James Gleason, Here Comes Mr. Jordan; Sydney Greenstreet, The Maltese Falcon

Best Supporting Actress
  *Mary Astor, *The Great Lie*; Sara Allgood, How Green Was My Valley; Patricia Collinge, The Little Foxes; Teresa Wright, The Little Foxes; Margaret Wycherly, Sergeant York

1942

Best Picture
  Mrs. Miniver, The Invaders, The Magnificent Ambersons, The Pied Piper, Pride of the Yankees, Random Harvest, Talk of the Town, Wake Island, Yankee Doodle Dandy, Kings Row

*denotes winner

Best Director
*William Wyler, *Mrs. Miniver*; Michael Curtiz, *Yankee Doodle Dandy*; John Farrow, *Wake Island*; Mervyn LeRoy, *Random Harvest*; Sam Wood, *Kings Row*

Best Actor
*James Cagney, *Yankee Doodle Dandy*; Ronald Colman, *Random Harvest*; Gary Cooper, *Pride of the Yankees*; Walter Pidgeon, *Mrs. Miniver*; Monty Woolley, *The Pied Piper*

Best Actress
*Greer Garson, *Mrs. Miniver*; Bette Davis, *Now Voyager*; Katharine Hepburn, *Woman of the Year*; Rosalind Russell, *My Sister Eileen*; Teresa Wright, *Pride of the Yankees*

Best Supporting Actor
*Van Heflin, *Johnny Eager*; William Bendix, *Wake Island*; Walter Huston, *Yankee Doodle Dandy*; Frank Morgan, *Tortilla Flat*; Henry Travers, *Mrs. Miniver*

Best Supporting Actress
*Teresa Wright, *Mrs. Miniver*; Gladys Cooper, *Now Voyager*; Agnes Moorehead, *The Magnificent Ambersons*; Susan Peters, *Random Harvest*; May Whitty, *Mrs. Miniver*

1943
Best Picture
Casablanca, For Whom the Bell Tolls, Heaven Can Wait, The Human Comedy, In Which We Serve, Madame Curie, The More the Merrier, The Ox-Bow Incident, The Song of Bernadette, Watch on the Rhine

Best Director
*Michael Curtiz, *Casablanca*; Clarence Brown, *The Human Comedy*; Henry King, *The Song of Bernadette*; Ernst Lubitsch, *Heaven Can Wait*; George Stevens, *The More the Merrier*

Best Actor
*Paul Lukas, *Watch on the Rhine*; Humphrey Bogart, *Casablanca*; Gary Cooper, *For Whom the Bell Tolls*; Walter Pidgeon, *Madame Curie*; Mickey Rooney, *The Human Comedy*

Best Actress
*Jennifer Jones, *The Song of Bernadette*; Jean Arthur, *The More the Merrier*; Ingrid Bergman, *For Whom the Bell Tolls*; Joan Fontaine, *The Constant Nymph*; Greer Garson, *Madame Curie*

Best Supporting Actor
*Charles Coburn, *The More the Merrier*; Charles Bickford, *The Song of Bernadette*; J. Carroll Naish, *Sahara*; Claude Rains, *Casablanca*; Akim Tamiroff, *For Whom the Bell Tolls*

*denotes winner

Best Supporting Actress
*Katina Paxinou, *For Whom the Bell Tolls*; Gladys Cooper, The Song of Bernadette; Paulette Goddard, So Proudly We Hail; Anne Revere, The Song of Bernadette; Lucille Watson, Watch on the Rhine

1944
Best Picture
**Going My Way*, Double Indemnity, Gaslight, Since You Went Away, Wilson
Best Director
*Leo McCarey, *Going My Way*; Alfred Hitchcock, Lifeboat; Henry King, Wilson; Otto Preminger, Laura; Billy Wilder, Double Indemnity
Best Actor
*Bing Crosby, *Going My Way*; Charles Boyer, Gaslight; Barry Fitzgerald, Going My Way; Cary Grant, None But the Lonely Heart; Alexander Knox, Wilson
Best Actress
*Ingrid Bergman, *Gaslight*; Claudette Colbert, Since You Went Away; Bette Davis, Mr. Skeffington; Greer Garson, Mrs. Parkington; Barbara Stanwyck, Double Indemnity
Best Supporting Actor
*Barry Fitzgerald, *Going My Way*; Hume Cronyn, The Seventh Cross; Claude Rains, Mr. Skeffington; Clifton Webb, Laura; Monty Woolley, Since You Went Away
Best Supporting Actress
*Ethel Barrymore, *None But the Lonely Heart*; Jennifer Jones, Since You Went Away; Angela Lansbury, Gaslight; Aline MacMahon, Dragon Seed; Agnes Moorehead, Mrs. Parkington

1945
Best Picture
**The Lost Weekend*, Anchors Aweigh, The Bells of St. Mary's, Mildred Pierce, Spellbound
Best Director
*Billy Wilder, *The Lost Weekend*; Clarence Brown, National Velvet; Alfred Hitchcock, Spellbound; Leo McCarey, The Bells of St. Mary's; Jean Renoir, The Southerner
Best Actor
*Ray Milland, *The Lost Weekend*; Bing Crosby, The Bells of St. Mary's; Gene Kelly, Anchors Aweigh; Gregory Peck, The Keys of the Kingdom; Cornel Wilde, A Song to Remember
Best Actress
*Joan Crawford, *Mildred Pierce*; Ingrid Bergman, The Bells of St. Mary's;

denotes winner

Greer Garson, *The Valley of Decision*; Jennifer Jones, *Love Letters*; Gene Tierney, *Leave Her to Heaven*

Best Supporting Actor

*James Dunn, *A Tree Grows in Brooklyn*; Michael Chekhov, *Spellbound*; John Dall, *The Corn is Green*; Robert Mitchum, *G. I. Joe*; J. Carroll Naish, *A Medal for Benny*

Best Supporting Actress

*Anne Revere, *National Velvet*; Eve Arden, *Mildred Pierce*; Ann Blyth, *Mildred Pierce*; Angela Lansbury, *The Picture of Dorian Gray*; Joan Lorring, *The Corn is Green*

1946

Best Picture

The Best Years of Our Lives, Henry V, It's a Wonderful Life, The Razor's Edge, The Yearling

Best Director

*William Wyler, *The Best Years of Our Lives*; Clarence Brown, *The Yearling*; Frank Capra, *It's a Wonderful Life*; David Lean, *Brief Encounter*; Robert Siodmak, *The Killers*

Best Actor

*Fredric March, *The Best Years of Our Lives*; Laurence Olivier, *Henry V*; Larry Parks, *The Jolson Story*; Gregory Peck, *The Yearling*; James Stewart, *It's a Wonderful Life*

Best Actress

*Olivia de Havilland, *To Each His Own*; Celia Johnson, *Brief Encounter*; Jennifer Jones, *Duel in the Sun*; Rosalind Russell, *Sister Kenny*; Jane Wyman, *The Yearling*

Best Supporting Actor

*Harold Russell, *The Best Years of Our Lives*; Charles Coburn, *The Green Years*; William Demarest, *The Jolson Story*; Claude Rains, *Notorious*; Clifton Webb, *The Razor's Edge*

Best Supporting Actress

*Anne Baxter, *The Razor's Edge*; Ethel Barrymore, *The Spiral Staircase*; Lillian Gish, *Duel in the Sun*; Flora Robson, *Saratoga Trunk*; Gale Sondergaard, *Anna and the King of Siam*

1947

Best Picture

Gentleman's Agreement, The Bishop's Wife, Crossfire, Great Expectations, Miracle on 34th Street

Best Director

*Elia Kazan, *Gentleman's Agreement*; George Cukor, *A Double Life*; Edward Dmytryk, *Crossfire*; Henry Koster, *The Bishop's Wife*; David Lean, *Great Expectations*

**denotes winner*

216

Best Actor
   *Ronald Colman, *A Double Life*; John Garfield, *Body and Soul*; Gregory Peck, *Gentleman's Agreement*; William Powell, *Life with Father*; Michael Redgrave, *Mourning Becomes Electra*

Best Actress
   *Loretta Young, *The Farmer's Daughter*; Joan Crawford, *Possessed*; Susan Hayward, *Smash Up—The Story of a Woman*; Dorothy McGuire, *Gentleman's Agreement*; Rosalind Russell, *Mourning Becomes Electra*

Best Supporting Actor
   *Edmund Gwenn, *Miracle on 34th Street*; Charles Bickford, *The Farmer's Daughter*; Thomas Gomez, *Ride the Pink Horse*; Robert Ryan, *Crossfire*; Richard Widmark, *Kiss of Death*

Best Supporting Actress
   *Celeste Holm, *Gentleman's Agreement*; Ethel Barrymore, *The Paradine Case*; Gloria Grahame, *Crossfire*; Marjorie Main, *The Egg and I*; Anne Revere, *Gentleman's Agreement*

1948

Best Picture
   Hamlet, Johnny Belinda, The Red Shoes, The Snake Pit, Treasure of Sierra Madre

Best Director
   *John Huston, *Treasure of Sierra Madre*; Anatole Litvak, *The Snake Pit*; Jean Negulesco, *Johnny Belinda*; Laurence Olivier, *Hamlet*; Fred Zinnemann, *The Search*

Best Actor
   *Laurence Olivier, *Hamlet*; Lew Ayres, *Johnny Belinda*; Montgomery Clift, *The Search*; Dan Dailey, *When My Baby Smiles at Me*; Clifton Webb, *Sitting Pretty*

Best Actress
   *Jane Wyman, *Johnny Belinda*; Ingrid Bergman, *Joan of Arc*; Olivia de Havilland, *The Snake Pit*; Irene Dunne, *I Remember Mama*; Barbara Stanwyck, *Sorry, Wrong Number*

Best Support Actor
   *Walter Huston, *Treasure of Sierra Madre*; Charles Bickford, *Johnny Belinda*; Jose Ferrer, *Joan of Arc*; Oscar Homolka, *I Remember Mama*; Cecil Kellaway, *The Luck of the Irish*

Best Supporting Actress
   *Claire Trevor, *Key Largo*; Barbara Bel Geddes, *I Remember Mama*; Ellen Corby, *I Remember Mama*; Agnes Moorehead, *Johnny Belinda*; Jean Simmons, *Hamlet*

*denotes winner

1949

Best Picture

*All the King's Men, Battleground, The Heiress, A Letter to Three Wives, Twelve O'Clock High

Best Director

*Joseph L. Mankiewicz, A Letter to Three Wives; Carol Reed, The Fallen Idol; Robert Rossen, All the King's Men; William A. Wellman, Battleground; William Wyler, The Heiress

Best Actor

*Broderick Crawford, All the King's Men; Kirk Douglas, Champion; Gregory Peck, Twelve O'Clock High; Richard Todd, The Hasty Heart; John Wayne, Sands of Iwo Jima

Best Actress

*Olivia de Havilland, The Heiress; Jeanne Crain, Pinky; Susan Hayward, My Foolish Heart; Deborah Kerr, Edward My Son; Loretta Young, Come to the Stable

Best Supporting Actor

*Dean Jagger, Twelve O'Clock High; John Ireland, All the King's Men; Arthur Kennedy, Champion; Ralph Richardson, The Heiress; James Whitmore, Battleground

Best Supporting Actress

*Mercedes McCambridge, All the King's Men; Ethel Barrymore, Pinky; Celeste Holm, Come to the Stable; Elsa Lanchester, Come to the Stable; Ethel Waters, Pinky

1950

Best Picture

*All About Eve, Born Yesterday, Father of the Bride, King Solomon's Mines, Sunset Boulevard

Best Director

*Joseph L. Mankiewicz, All About Eve; George Cukor, Born Yesterday; John Huston, Asphalt Jungle; Carol Reed, The Third Man; Billy Wilder, Sunset Boulevard

Best Actor

*Jose Ferrer, Cyrano de Bergerac; Louis Calhern, The Magnificent Yankee; William Holden, Sunset Boulevard; James Stewart, Harvey; Spencer Tracy, Father of the Bride

Best Actress

*Judy Holliday, Born Yesterday; Anne Baxter, All About Eve; Bette Davis, All About Eve; Eleanor Parker, Caged; Gloria Swanson, Sunset Boulevard

Best Supporting Actor

*George Sanders, All About Eve; Jeff Chandler, Broken Arrow; Edmund Gwenn, Mister 880; Sam Jaffe, The Asphalt Jungle; Eric von Stroheim, Sunset Boulevard

*denotes winner

Best Supporting Actress

*Josephine Hull, *Harvey*; Hope Emerson, *Caged*; Celeste Holm, *All About Eve*; Nancy Olson, *Sunset Boulevard*; Thelma Ritter, *All About Eve*

1951
Best Picture
**An American in Paris*, Decision Before Dawn, A Place in the Sun, Quo Vadis, A Streetcar Named Desire

Best Director
*George Stevens, *A Place in the Sun*; John Huston, The African Queen; Elia Kazan, A Streetcar Named Desire; Vincente Minnelli, An American in Paris; William Wyler, Detective Story

Best Actor
*Humphrey Bogart, *The African Queen*; Marlon Brando, A Streetcar Named Desire; Montgomery Clift, A Place in the Sun; Arthur Kennedy, Bright Victory; Fredric March, Death of a Salesman

Best Actress
*Vivien Leigh, *A Streetcar Named Desire*; Katharine Hepburn, The African Queen; Eleanor Parker, Detective Story; Shelley Winters, A Place in the Sun; Jane Wyman, The Blue Veil

Best Supporting Actor
*Karl Malden, *A Streetcar Named Desire*; Leo Genn, Quo Vadis; Kevin McCarthy, Death of a Salesman; Peter Ustinov, Quo Vadis; Gig Young, Come Fill the Cup

Best Supporting Actress
*Kim Hunter, *A Streetcar Named Desire*; Joan Blondell, The Blue Veil; Mildred Dunnock, Death of a Salesman; Lee Grant, Detective Story; Thelma Ritter, The Mating Season

1952
Best Picture
**The Greatest Show on Earth*, High Noon, Ivanhoe, Moulin Rouge, The Quiet Man

Best Director
*John Ford, *The Quiet Man*; Cecil B. DeMille, The Greatest Show on Earth; John Huston, Moulin Rouge; Joseph L. Mankiewicz, Five Fingers; Fred Zinnemann, High Noon

Best Actor
*Gary Cooper, *High Noon*; Marlon Brando, Viva Zapata! Kirk Douglas, The Bad and the Beautiful; Jose Ferrer, Moulin Rouge; Alec Guinness, The Lavender Hill Mob

Best Actress
*Shirley Booth, *Come Back, Little Sheba*; Joan Crawford, Sudden Fear; Bette

**denotes winner*

Davis, *The Star*; Julie Harris, *The Member of the Wedding*

Best Supporting Actor

*Anthony Quinn, ***Viva Zapata!***; Richard Burton, *My Cousin Rachel*; Arthur Hunnicutt, *The Blue Sky*; Victor McLaglen, *The Quiet Man*; Jack Palance, *Sudden Fear*

Best Supporting Actress

*Gloria Grahame, ***The Bad and the Beautiful***; Jean Hagen, *Singin' in the Rain*; Colette Marchand, *Moulin Rouge*; Terry Moore, *Come Back, Little Sheba*; Thelma Ritter, *With a Song in My Heart*

1953

Best Picture

*****From Here to Eternity***, Julius Caesar, The Robe, Roman Holiday, Shane

Best Director

*****Fred Zinnemann, *From Here to Eternity***; George Stevens, *Shane*; Charles Walters, *Lili*; Billy Wilder, *Stalag 17*; William Wyler, *Roman Holiday*

Best Actor

*****William Holden, *Stalag 17***; Marlon Brando, *Julius Caesar*; Richard Burton, *The Robe*; Montgomery Clift, *From Here to Eternity*; Burt Lancaster, *From Here to Eternity*

Best Actress

*****Audrey Hepburn, *Roman Holiday***; Leslie Caron, *Lili*; Ava Gardner, *Mogambo*; Deborah Kerr, *From Here to Eternity*; Maggie McNamara, *The Moon is Blue*

Best Supporting Actor

*****Frank Sinatra, *From Here to Eternity***; Eddie Albert, *Roman Holiday*; Brandon De Wilde; *Shane*; Robert Strauss, *Stalag 17*

Best Supporting Actress

*****Donna Reed, *From Here to Eternity***; Grace Kelly, *Mogambo*; Geraldine Page, *Hondo*; Marjorie Rambeau, *Torch Song*; Thelma Ritter, *Pickup on South Street*

1954

Best Picture

*****On the Waterfront***, The Caine Mutiny, The Country Girl, Seven Brides for Seven Brothers, Three Coins in the Fountain

Best Director

*****Elia Kazan, *On the Waterfront***; Alfred Hitchcock, *Rear Window*; George Seaton, *The Country Girl*; William Wellman, *The High and the Mighty*; Billy Wilder, *Sabrina*

Best Actor

*****Marlon Brando, *On the Waterfront***; Humphrey Bogart, *The Caine Mutiny*; Bing Crosby, *The Country Girl*; James Mason, *A Star is Born*; Dan O'Herlihy, *Adventures of Robinson Crusoe*

*denotes winner

220

Best Actress

*Grace Kelly, *The Country Girl*; Dorothy Dandridge, *Carmen Jones*; Judy Garland, *A Star is Born*; Audrey Hepburn, *Sabrina*; Jane Wyman, *Magnificent Obsession*

Best Supporting Actor

*Edmond O'Brien, *The Barefoot Contessa*; Lee J. Cobb, *On the Waterfront*; Karl Malden, *On the Waterfront*; Rod Steiger, *On the Waterfront*; Tom Tully, *The Caine Mutiny*

Best Supporting Actress

*Eva Marie Saint, *On the Waterfront*; Nina Foch, *Executive Suite*; Katy Jurado, *Broken Lance*; Jan Sterling, *The High and the Mighty*; Claire Trevor, *The High and the Mighty*

1955

Best Picture

*Marty, *Love is a Many-Splendored Thing*, *Mister Roberts*, *Picnic*, *The Rose Tattoo*

Best Director

*Delbert Mann, *Marty*; Elia Kazan, *East of Eden*; David Lean, *Summertime*; Joshua Logan, *Picnic*; John Sturges, *Bad Day at Black Rock*

Best Actor

*Ernest Borgnine, *Marty*; James Cagney, *Love Me or Leave Me*; James Dean, *East of Eden*; Frank Sinatra, *The Man with the Golden Arm*; Spencer Tracy, *Bad Day at Black Rock*

Best Actress

*Anna Magnani, *The Rose Tattoo*; Susan Hayward, *I'll Cry Tomorrow*; Katharine Hepburn, *Summertime*; Jennifer Jones, *Love is a Many-Splendored Thing*; Eleanor Parker, *Interrupted Melody*

Best Supporting Actor

*Jack Lemmon, *Mister Roberts*; Arthur Kennedy, *Trial*; Joe Mantell, *Marty*; Sal Mineo, *Rebel Without a Cause*; Arthur O'Connell, *Picnic*

Best Supporting Actress

*Jo Van Fleet, *East of Eden*; Betsy Blair, *Marty*; Peggy Lee, *Pete Kelly's Blues*; Marisa Pavan, *The Rose Tattoo*; Natalie Wood, *Rebel Without a Cause*

1956

Best Picture

*Around the World in 80 Days, *Friendly Persuasion*, *Giant*, *The King and I*, *The Ten Commandments*

Best Director

*George Stevens, *Giant*; Michael Anderson, *Around the World in 80 Days*; Walter Lang, *The King and I*; King Vidor, *War and Peace*; William Wyler, *Friendly Persuasion*

*denotes winner

Best Actor

*Yul Brynner, *The King and I*; James Dean, *Giant*; Kirk Douglas, *Lust for Life*; Rock Hudson, *Giant*; Laurence Olivier, *Richard III*

Best Actress

*Ingrid Bergman, *Anastasia*; Carroll Baker, *Baby Doll*; Katharine Hepburn, *The Rainmaker*; Nancy Kelly, *The Bad Seed*; Deborah Kerr, *The King and I*

Best Supporting Actor

*Anthony Quinn, *Lust for Life*; Don Murray, *Bus Stop*; Anthony Perkins, *Friendly Persuasion*; Mickey Rooney, *The Bold and the Brave*; Robert Stack, *Written on the Wind*

Best Supporting Actress

*Dorothy Malone, *Written on the Wind*; Mildred Dunnock, *Baby Doll*; Eileen Heckart, *The Bad Seed*; Mercedes McCambridge, *Giant*; Patty McCormack, *The Bad Seed*

1957

Best Picture

The Bridge on the River Kwai, Peyton Place, Sayonara, Twelve Angry Men, Witness for the Prosecution

Best Director

*David Lean, *The Bridge on the River Kwai*; Joshua Logan, *Sayonara*; Sidney Lumet, *Twelve Angry Men*; Mark Robson, *Peyton Place*; Billy Wilder, *Witness for the Prosecution*

Best Actor

*Alec Guinness, *The Bridge on the River Kwai*; Marlon Brando, *Sayonara*; Anthony Franciosa, *A Hatful of Rain*; Charles Laughton, *Witness for the Prosecution*; Anthony Quinn, *Wild Is the Wind*

Best Actress

*Joanne Woodward, *The Three Faces of Eve*; Deborah Kerr, *Heaven Knows Mr. Allison*; Anna Magnani, *Wild Is the Wind*; Elizabeth Taylor, *Raintree County*; Lana Turner, *Peyton Place*

Best Supporting Actor

*Red Buttons, *Sayonara*; Vittorio De Sica, *A Farewell to Arms*; Sessue Hayakawa, *The Bridge on the River Kwai*; Arthur Kennedy, *Peyton Place*; Russ Tamblyn, *Peyton Place*

Best Supporting Actress

*Miyoshi Umeki, *Sayonara*; Carolyn Jones, *The Bachelor Party*; Elsa Lanchester, *Witness for the Prosecution*; Hope Lange, *Peyton Place*; Diane Varsi, *Peyton Place*

1958

Best Picture

Gigi, Auntie Mame, Cat on a Hot Tin Roof, The Defiant Ones, Separate Tables

*denotes winner

Best Director

*Vincente Minnelli, *Gigi*; Richard Brooks, Cat on a Hot Tin Roof; Stanley Kramer, The Defiant Ones; Mark Robson, The Inn of the Sixth Happiness; Robert Wise, I Want to Live!

Best Actor

*David Niven, *Separate Tables*; Tony Curtis, The Defiant Ones; Paul Newman, Cat on a Hot Tin Roof; Sidney Poitier, The Defiant Ones; Spencer Tracy, The Old Man and the Sea

Best Actress

*Susan Hayward, *I Want to Live!*; Deborah Kerr, Separate Tables; Shirley MacLaine, Some Came Running; Rosalind Russell, Auntie Mame; Elizabeth Taylor, Cat on a Hot Tin Roof

Best Supporting Actor

*Burl Ives, *The Big Country*; Theodore Bikel, The Defiant Ones; Lee J. Cobb, The Brothers Karamazov; Arthur Kennedy, Some Came Running; Gig Young, Teacher's Pet

Best Supporting Actress

*Wendy Hiller, *Separate Tables*; Peggy Cass, Auntie Mame; Martha Hyer, Some Came Running; Maureen Stapleton, Lonelyhearts; Cara Williams, The Defiant Ones

1959

Best Picture

**Ben-Hur*, Anatomy of a Murder, The Diary of Anne Frank, The Nun's Story, Room at the Top

Best Director

*William Wyler, *Ben-Hur*; Jack Clayton, Room at the Top, George Stevens, The Diary of Anne Frank, Billy Wilder, Some Like It Hot, Fred Zinnemann, The Nun's Story

Best Actor

*Charlton Heston, *Ben-Hur*; Laurence Harvey, Room at the Top; Jack Lemmon, Some Like It Hot; Paul Muni, The Last Angry Man; James Stewart, Anatomy of a Murder

Best Actress

*Simone Signoret, *Room at the Top*; Doris Day, Pillow Talk; Audrey Hepburn, The Nun's Story; Katharine Hepburn, Suddenly Last Summer; Elizabeth Taylor, Suddenly Last Summer

Best Supporting Actor

*Hugh Griffith, *Ben-Hur*; Arthur O'Connell, Anatomy of a Murder; George C. Scott, Anatomy of a Murder; Robert Vaughn, The Young Philadelphians; Ed Wynn, The Diary of Anne Frank

Best Supporting Actress

*Shelley Winters, *The Diary of Anne Frank*; Hermione Baddeley, Room at

*denotes winner

223

the Top; Susan Kohner, *Imitation of Life*; Juanita Moore, *Imitation of Life*; Thelma Ritter, *Pillow Talk*

1960

Best Picture
*The Apartment, The Alamo, Elmer Gantry, Sons and Lovers, The Sundowners

Best Director
Billy Wilder, **The Apartment; Jack Cardiff, *Sons and Lovers*; Jules Dassin, *Never on Sunday*; Alfred Hitchcock, *Psycho*; Fred Zinnemann, *The Sundowners*

Best Actor
Burt Lancaster, **Elmer Gantry; Trevor Howard, *Sons and Lovers*; Jack Lemmon, *The Apartment*; Laurence Olivier, *The Entertainer*; Spencer Tracy, *Inherit the Wind*

Best Actress
Elizabeth Taylor, **Butterfield 8; Greer Garson, *Sunrise at Campobello*; Deborah Kerr, *The Sundowners*; Shirley MacLaine, *The Apartment*; Melina Mercouri, *Never on Sunday*

Best Supporting Actor
Peter Ustinov, **Spartacus; Peter Falk, *Murder, Inc.*; Jack Kruschen, *The Apartment*; Sal Mineo, *Exodus*; Chill Wills, *The Alamo*

Best Supporting Actress
Shirley Jones, **Elmer Gantry; Glynis Johns, *The Sundowners*; Shirley Knight, *The Dark at the Top of the Stairs*; Janet Leigh, *Psycho*; Mary Ure, *Sons and Lovers*

1961

Best Picture
*West Side Story, Fanny, The Guns of Navarone, The Hustler, Judgment at Nuremberg

Best Director
Robert Wise, **Jerome Robbins, *West Side Story*; Federico Fellini, *La Dolce Vita*; Stanley Kramer, *Judgment at Nuremberg*; Robert Rossen, *The Hustler*; J. Lee Thompson, *The Guns of Navarone*

Best Actor
Maximilian Schell, **Judgment at Nuremberg; Charles Boyer, *Fanny*; Paul Newman, *The Hustler*; Spencer Tracy, *Judgment at Nuremberg*; Stuart Whitman, *The Mark*

Best Actress
Sophia Loren, **Two Women; Audrey Hepburn, *Breakfast at Tiffany's*; Piper Laurie, *The Hustler*; Geraldine Page, *Summer and Smoke*; Natalie Wood, *Splendor in the Grass*

*denotes winner

Best Supporting Actor

*George Chakiris, *West Side Story*; Montgomery Clift, *Judgment at Nuremberg*; Peter Falk, *Pocketful of Miracles*; Jackie Gleason, *The Hustler*; George C. Scott, *The Hustler*

Best Supporting Actress

*Rita Moreno, *West Side Story*; Fay Bainter, *The Children's Hour*; Judy Garland, *Judgment at Nuremberg*; Lotte Lenya, *The Roman Spring of Mrs. Stone*; Una Merkel, *Summer and Smoke*

1962
Best Picture

Lawrence of Arabia, The Longest Day, The Music Man, Mutiny on the Bounty, To Kill a Mockingbird

Best Director

*David Lean, *Lawrence of Arabia*; Pietro Germi, *Divorce—Italian Style*; Robert Mulligan, *To Kill a Mockingbird*; Arthur Penn, *The Miracle Worker*; Frank Perry, *David and Lisa*

Best Actor

*Gregory Peck, *To Kill a Mockingbird*; Burt Lancaster, *Birdman of Alcatraz*; Jack Lemmon, *Days of Wine and Roses*; Marcello Mastroianni, *Divorce—Italian Style*; Peter O'Toole, *Lawrence of Arabia*

Best Actress

*Anne Bancroft, *The Miracle Worker*; Bette Davis, *What Ever Happened to Baby Jane?*; Katharine Hepburn, *Long Day's Journey Into Night*; Geraldine Page, *Sweet Bird of Youth*; Lee Remick, *Days of Wine and Roses*

Best Supporting Actor

*Ed Begley, *Sweet Bird of Youth*; Victor Buono, *What Ever Happened to Baby Jane?*; Telly Savalas, *Birdman of Alcatraz*; Omar Sharif, *Lawrence of Arabia*; Terence Stamp, *Billy Budd*

Best Supporting Actress

*Patty Duke, *The Miracle Worker*; Mary Badham, *To Kill a Mockingbird*; Shirley Knight, *Sweet Bird of Youth*; Angela Lansbury, *The Manchurian Candidate*; Thelma Ritter, *Birdman of Alcatraz*

1963
Best Picture

Tom Jones, America, America, Cleopatra, How the West Was Won, Lilies of the Field

Best Director

*Tony Richardson, *Tom Jones*; Federico Fellini, *8½*; Elia Kazan, *America, America*; Otto Preminger, *The Cardinal*; Martin Ritt, *Hud*

*denotes winner

Best Actor
  *Sidney Poitier, *Lilies of the Field*; Albert Finney, *Tom Jones*; Richard Harris, *The Sporting Life*; Rex Harrison, *Cleopatra*; Paul Newman, *Hud*
Best Actress
  *Patricia Neal, *Hud*; Leslie Caron, *The L-Shaped Room*; Shirley MacLaine, *Irma La Douce*; Rachel Roberts, *This Sporting Life*; Natalie Wood, *Love With the Proper Stranger*
Best Supporting Actor
  *Melvyn Douglas, *Hud*; Nick Adams, *Twilight of Honor*; Bobby Darin, *Captain Newman, M.D.*; Hugh Griffith, *Tom Jones*; John Huston, *The Cardinal*
Best Supporting Actress
  *Margaret Rutherford, *The V.I.P.s*; Diane Cilento, *Tom Jones*; Edith Evans, *Tom Jones*; Joyce Redman, *Tom Jones*; Lilia Skala, *Lilies of the Field*

1964
Best Picture
  My Fair Lady, Becket, Dr. Strangelove, Mary Poppins, Zorba the Greek
Best Director
  *George Cukor, *My Fair Lady*; Michael Cacoyannis, *Zorba the Greek*; Peter Glenville, *Becket*; Stanley Kubrick, *Dr. Strangelove*; Robert Stevenson, *Mary Poppins*
Best Actor
  *Rex Harrison, *My Fair Lady*; Richard Burton, *Becket*; Peter O'Toole, *Becket*; Anthony Quinn, *Zorba the Greek*; Peter Sellers, *Dr. Strangelove*
Best Actress
  *Julie Andrews, *Mary Poppins*; Anne Bancroft, *The Pumpkin Eater*; Sophia Loren, *Marriage—Italian Style*; Debbie Reynolds, *The Unsinkable Molly Brown*; Kim Stanley, *Seance on a Wet Afternoon*
Best Supporting Actor
  *Peter Ustinov, *Topkapi*; John Gielgud, *Becket*; Stanley Holloway, *My Fair Lady*; Edmond O'Brien, *Seven Days in May*; Lee Tracy, *The Best Man*
Best Supporting Actress
  *Lila Kedrova, *Zorba the Greek*; Gladys Cooper, *My Fair Lady*; Edith Evans, *The Chalk Garden*; Grayson Hall, *The Night of the Iguana*; Agnes Moorehead, *Hush Hush, Sweet Charlotte*

1965
Best Picture
  The Sound of Music, Darling, Doctor Zhivago, Ship of Fools, A Thousand Clowns
Best Director
  *Robert Wise, *The Sound of Music*; David Lean, *Doctor Zhivago*; Hiroshi

*denotes winner

Teshigahara, *Woman in the Dunes*; John Schlesinger, *Darling*; William Wyler, *The Collector*

Best Actor
*Lee Marvin, *Cat Ballou*; Richard Burton, *The Spy Who Came in from the Cold*; Laurence Olivier, *Othello*; Rod Steiger, *The Pawnbroker*; Oskar Werner, *Ship of Fools*

Best Actress
*Julie Christie, *Darling*; Julie Andrews, *The Sound of Music*; Samantha Eggar, *The Collector*; Elizabeth Hartman, *A Patch of Blue*; Simone Signoret, *Ship of Fools*

Best Supporting Actor
*Martin Balsam, *A Thousand Clowns*; Ian Bannen, *The Flight of the Phoenix*; Tom Courtenay, *Doctor Zhivago*; Michael Dunn, *Ship of Fools*; Frank Finlay, *Othello*

Best Supporting Actress
*Shelley Winters, *A Patch of Blue*; Ruth Gordon, *Inside Daisy Clover*; Joyce Redman, *Othello*; Maggie Smith, *Othello*; Peggy Wood, *The Sound of Music*

1966

Best Picture
**A Man For All Seasons*, Alfie, The Russians Are Coming, The Russians Are Coming, The Sand Pebbles, Who's Afraid of Virginia Woolf?

Best Director
*Fred Zinnemann, *A Man For All Seasons*; Michelangelo Antonioni, *Blow-Up*; Richard Brooks, *The Professionals*; Claude Lelouch, *A Man and a Woman*; Mike Nichols, *Who's Afraid of Virginia Woolf?*

Best Actor
*Paul Scofield, *A Man For All Seasons*; Alan Arkin, *The Russians Are Coming, The Russians Are Coming*; Richard Burton, *Who's Afraid of Virginia Woolf?*; Michael Caine, *Alfie*; Steve McQueen, *The Sand Pebbles*

Best Actress
*Elizabeth Taylor, *Who's Afraid of Virginia Woolf?*; Anouk Aimee, *A Man and a Woman*; Ida Kaminska, *The Shop on Main Street*; Lynn Redgrave, *Georgy Girl*; Vanessa Redgrave, *Morgan!*

Best Supporting Actor
*Walter Matthau, *The Fortune Cookie*; Mako, *The Sand Pebbles*; James Mason, *Georgy Girl*; George Segal, *Who's Afraid of Virginia Woolf?*; Robert Shaw, *A Man For All Seasons*

Best Supporting Actress
*Sandy Dennis, *Who's Afraid of Virginia Woolf?*; Wendy Hiller, *A Man For All Seasons*; Jocelyn Lagarde, *Hawaii*; Vivien Merchant, *Alfie*; Geraldine Page, *You're a Big Boy Now*

denotes winner

1967

Best Picture

In the Heat of the Night, Bonnie and Clyde, Doctor Doolittle, The Graduate, Guess Who's Coming to Dinner

Best Director

*Mike Nichols, **The Graduate**; Richard Brooks, In Cold Blood; Norman Jewison, In the Heat of the Night; Stanley Kramer, Guess Who's Coming to Dinner; Arthur Penn, Bonnie and Clyde

Best Actor

*Rod Steiger, **In the Heat of the Night**; Warren Beatty, Bonnie and Clyde; Dustin Hoffman, The Graduate; Paul Newman, Cool Hand Luke; Spencer Tracy, Guess Who's Coming to Dinner

Best Actress

*Katharine Hepburn, **Guess Who's Coming to Dinner**; Anne Bancroft, The Graduate; Faye Dunaway, Bonnie and Clyde; Edith Evans, The Whisperers; Audrey Hepburn, Wait Until Dark

Best Supporting Actor

*George Kennedy, **Cool Hand Luke**; John Cassavetes, The Dirty Dozen; Gene Hackman, Bonnie and Clyde; Cecil Kellaway, Guess Who's Coming to Dinner; Michael J. Pollard, Bonnie and Clyde

Best Supporting Actress

*Estelle Parsons, **Bonnie and Clyde**; Carol Channing, Thoroughly Modern Millie; Mildred Natwick, Barefoot in the Park; Beah Richards, Guess Who's Coming to Dinner; Katharine Ross, The Graduate

1968

Best Picture

Oliver!, Funny Girl, The Lion in Winter, Rachel, Rachel, Romeo and Juliet

Best Director

*Carol Reed, **Oliver!**; Anthony Harvey, The Lion in Winter; Stanley Kubrick, 2001: A Space Odyssey; Gillo Pontecorvo, The Battle of Algiers; Franco Zeffirelli, Romeo and Juliet

Best Actor

*Cliff Robertson, **Charly**; Alan Arkin, The Heart is a Lonely Hunter; Alan Bates, The Fixer; Ron Moody, Oliver!; Peter O'Toole, The Lion in Winter

Best Actress

*Barbra Streisand, **Funny Girl**; *Katharine Hepburn, **The Lion in Winter**; Patricia Neal, The Subject Was Roses; Vanessa Redgrave, Isadora; Joanne Woodward, Rachel, Rachel

Best Supporting Actor

*Jack Albertson, **The Subject Was Roses**; Seymour Cassel, Faces; Daniel Massey, Star!; Jack Wild, Oliver!; Gene Wilder, The Producers

**denotes winner*

Best Supporting Actress

*Ruth Gordon, *Rosemary's Baby*; Lynn Carlin, *Faces*; Sondra Locke, *The Heart is a Lonely Hunter*; Kay Medford, *Funny Girl*; Estelle Parsons, *Rachel, Rachel*

1969

Best Picture

**Midnight Cowboy*, Anne of the Thousand Days, Butch Cassidy and the Sundance Kid, Hello, Dolly!, Z

Best Director

*John Schlesinger, *Midnight Cowboy*; Costa Gavras, *Z*; Arthur Penn, *Alice's Restaurant*; Sydney Pollack, *They Shoot Horses, Don't They?*; George Roy Hill, *Butch Cassidy and the Sundance Kid*

Best Actor

*John Wayne, *True Grit*; Richard Burton, *Anne of the Thousand Days*; Dustin Hoffman, *Midnight Cowboy*; Peter O'Toole, *Goodbye, Mr. Chips*; John Voight, *Midnight Cowboy*

Best Actress

*Maggie Smith, *The Prime of Miss Jean Brodie*; Genevieve Bujold, *Anne of the Thousand Days*; Jane Fonda, *They Shoot Horses, Don't They?*; Liza Minnelli, *The Sterile Cuckoo*; Jean Simmons, *The Happy Ending*

Best Supporting Actor

*Gig Young, *They Shoot Horses, Don't They?*; Rupert Crosse, *The Reivers*; Elliott Gould, *Bob & Carol & Ted & Alice*; Jack Nicholson, *Easy Rider*; Anthony Quayle, *Anne of the Thousand Days*

Best Supporting Actress

*Goldie Hawn, *Cactus Flower*; Catherine Burns, *Last Summer*; Dyan Cannon, *Bob & Carol & Ted & Alice*; Sylvia Miles, *Midnight Cowboy*; Susannah York, *They Shoot Horses, Don't They?*

1970

Best Picture

**Patton*, Airport, Five Easy Pieces, Love Story, M*A*S*H

Best Director

*Franklin J. Schaffner, *Patton*; Robert Altman, *M*A*S*H*; Federico Fellini, *Satyricon*; Arthur Hiller, *Love Story*; Ken Russell, *Women in Love*

Best Actor

*George C. Scott, *Patton* (award declined); Melvyn Douglas, *I Never Sang for my Father*; James Earl Jones, *The Great White Hope*; Jack Nicholson, *Five Easy Pieces*; Ryan O'Neal, *Love Story*

Best Actress

*Glenda Jackson, *Women in Love*; Jane Alexander, *The Great White Hope*;

*denotes winner

Ali MacGraw, *Love Story*; Sarah Miles, *Ryan's Daughter*; Carrie Snodgrass, *Diary of a Mad Housewife*

Best Supporting Actor

*John Mills, **Ryan's Daughter**; Richard Castellano, *Lovers and Other Strangers*; Chief Dan George, *Little Big Man*; Gene Hackman, *I Never Sang for my Father*; John Marley, *Love Story*

Best Supporting Actress

*Helen Hayes, **Airport**; Karen Black, *Five Easy Pieces*; Lee Grant, *The Landlord*; Sally Kellerman, *M*A*S*H*; Maureen Stapleton, *Airport*

1971

Best Picture

The French Connection, A Clockwork Orange, Fiddler on the Roof, The Last Picture Show, Nicholas and Alexandra

Best Director

*William Freidkin, **The French Connection**; Peter Bogdanovich, *The Last Picture Show*; Norman Jewison, *Fiddler on the Roof*; Stanley Kubrick, *A Clockwork Orange*; John Schlesinger, *Sunday Bloody Sunday*

Best Actor

*Gene Hackman, **The French Connection**; Peter Finch, *Sunday Bloody Sunday*; Walter Matthau, *Kotch*; George C. Scott, *The Hospital*; Topol, *Fiddler on the Roof*

Best Actress

*Jane Fonda, **Klute**; Julie Christie, *McCabe and Mrs. Miller*; Glenda Jackson, *Sunday Bloody Sunday*; Vanessa Redgrave, *Mary, Queen of Scots*; Janet Suzman, *Nicholas and Alexandra*

Best Supporting Actor

*Ben Johnson, **The Last Picture Show**; Jeff Bridges, *The Last Picture Show*; Leonard Frey, *Fiddler on the Roof*; Richard Jaekel, *Sometimes a Great Notion*; Roy Scheider, *The French Connection*

Best Supporting Actress

*Cloris Leachman, **The Last Picture Show**; Ellen Burstyn, *The Last Picture Show*; Barbara Harris, *Who Is Harry Kellerman and Why Is He Saying All Those Terrible Things About Me?*; Margaret Leighton, *The Go-Between*; Ann-Margret, *Carnal Knowledge*

1972

Best Picture

The Godfather, Cabaret, Deliverance, The Emigrants, Sounder

Best Director

*Bob Fosse, **Cabaret**; John Boorman, *Deliverance*; Francis Ford Coppola, *The Godfather*; Joseph L. Mankiewicz, *Sleuth*; Jan Troell, *The Emigrants*

*denotes winner

Best Actor
*Marlon Brando, *The Godfather* (award declined); Michael, *Sleuth*; Laurence Olivier, *Sleuth*; Peter O'Toole, *The Ruling Class*; Paul Winfield, *Sounder*

Best Actress
*Liza Minnelli, *Cabaret*; Diana Ross, *Lady Sings the Blues*; Maggie Smith, *Travels with My Aunt*; Cicely Tyson, *Sounder*; Liv Ullmann, *The Emigrants*

Best Supporting Actor
*Joel Grey, *Cabaret*; Eddie Albert, *The Heartbreak Kid*; James Caan, *The Godfather*; Robert Duvall, *The Godfather*; Al Pacino, *The Godfather*

Best Supporting Actress
*Eileen Heckart, *Butterflies Are Free*; Jeannie Berlin, *The Heartbreak Kid*; Geraldine Page, *Pete 'n' Tillie*; Susan Tyrell, *Fat City*; Shelley Winters, *The Poseidon Adventure*

1973
Best Picture
The Sting, American Graffiti, Cries and Whispers, The Exorcist, A Touch of Class

Best Director
*George Roy Hill, *The Sting*; Ingmar Bergman, *Cries and Whispers*; Bernardo Bertolucci, *Last Tango in Paris*; William Freidkin, *The Exorcist*; George Lucas, *American Graffiti*

Best Actor
*Jack Lemmon, *Save the Tiger*; Marlon Brando, *Last Tango in Paris*; Jack Nicholson, *The Last Detail*; Al Pacino, *Serpico*; Robert Redford, *The Sting*

Best Actress
*Glenda Jackson, *A Touch of Class*; Ellen Burstyn, *The Exorcist*; Marsha Mason, *Cinderella Liberty*; Barbra Streisand, *The Way We Were*; Joanne Woodward, *Summer Wishes, Winter Dreams*

Best Supporting Actor
*John Houseman, *The Paper Chase*; Vincent Gardenia, *Bang the Drum Slowly*; Jack Gilford, *Save the Tiger*; Jason Miller, *The Exorcist*; Randy Quaid, *The Last Detail*

Best Supporting Actress
*Tatum O'Neal, *Paper Moon*; Linda Blair, *The Exorcist*; Candy Clark, *American Graffiti*; Madeline Kahn, *Paper Moon*; Sylvia Sidney, *Summer Wishes, Winter Dreams*

1974
Best Picture
The Godfather, Part II, Chinatown, The Conversation, Lenny, The Towering Inferno

*denotes winner

Best Director

*Francis Ford Coppola, *The Godfather, Part II*; John Cassavetes, *A Woman Under the Influence*; Bob Fosse, *Lenny*; Roman Polanski, *Chinatown*; Francois Truffaut, *Day for Night*

Best Actor

*Art Carney, *Harry and Tonto*; Albert Finney, *Murder on the Orient Express*; Dustin Hoffman, *Lenny*; Jack Nicholson, *Chinatown*; Al Pacino, *The Godfather, Part II*

Best Actress

*Ellen Burstyn, *Alice Doesn't Live Here Anymore*; Diahann Carroll, *Claudine*; Faye Dunaway, *Chinatown*; Valerie Perrine, *Lenny*; Gena Rowlands, *A Woman Under the Influence*

Best Supporting Actor

*Robert DeNiro, *The Godfather, Part II*; Fred Astaire, *The Towering Inferno*; Jeff Bridges, *Thunderbolt and Lightfoot*; Michael V. Gazo, *The Godfather, Part II*; Lee Strasberg, *The Godfather, Part II*

Best Supporting Actress

*Ingrid Bergman, *Murder on the Orient Express*; Valentina Cortese, *Day for Night*; Madeline Kahn, *Blazing Saddles*; Diane Ladd, *Alice Doesn't Live Here Anymore*; Talia Shire, *The Godfather, Part II*

1975

Best Picture

**One Flew Over the Cuckoo's Nest*, Barry Lyndon, Dog Day Afternoon, Jaws, Nashville

Best Director

*Milos Forman, *One Flew Over the Cuckoo's Nest*; Robert Altman, *Nashville*; Federico Fellini, *Amarcord*; Stanley Kubrick, *Barry Lyndon*; Sidney Lumet, *Dog Day Afternoon*

Best Actor

*Jack Nicholson, *One Flew Over the Cuckoo's Nest*; Walter Matthau, *The Sunshine Boys*; Al Pacino, *Dog Day Afternoon*; Maximilian Schell, *The Man in the Glass Booth*; James Whitmore, *Give 'em Hell, Harry*

Best Actress

*Louise Fletcher, *One Flew Over the Cuckoo's Nest*; Isabelle Adjani, *The Story of Adele H.*; Ann-Margret, *Tommy*; Glenda Jackson, *Hedda*; Carol Kane, *Hester Street*

Best Supporting Actor

*George Burns, *The Sunshine Boys*, Brad Dourif, *One Flew Over the Cuckoo's Nest*; Burgess Meredith, *The Day of the Locust*; Chris Sarandan, *Dog Day Afternoon*; Jack Warden, *Shampoo*

Best Supporting Actress

*Lee Grant, *Shampoo*; Ronee Blakley, *Nashville*; Sylvia Miles, *Farewell, My Lovely*; Lily Tomlin, *Nashville*; Brenda Vaccaro, *Once Is Not Enough*

*denotes winner

1976
Best Picture
Rocky, All the President's Men, Bound For Glory, Network, Taxi Driver
Best Director
*John G. Avildsen, *Rocky*; Ingmar Bergman, Face to Face; Sidney Lumet, Network; Alan J. Pakula, All the President's Men; Lina Wertmuller, Seven Beauties
Best Actor
*Peter Finch, *Network*; Robert DeNiro, Taxi Driver; Giancarlo Giannini, Seven Beauties; William Holden, Network; Sylvester Stallone, Rocky
Best Actress
*Faye Dunaway, *Network*; Marie-Christine Barrault, Cousin, Cousine; Talia Shire, Rocky; Sissy Spacek, Carrie; Liv Ullmann, Face to Face
Best Supporting Actor
*Jason Robards, *All the President's Men*. Ned Beatty, Network; Burgess Meredith, Rocky; Laurence Olivier, Marathon Man; Burt Young, Rocky
Best Supporting Actress
*Beatrice Straight, *Network*; Jane Alexander, All the President's Men; Jodie Foster, Taxi Driver; Lee Grant, Voyage of the Damned; Piper Laurie, Carrie

1977
Best Picture
Annie Hall, The Goodbye Girl, Julia, Star Wars, The Turning Point
Best Director
*Woody Allen, *Annie Hall*; George Lucas, Star Wars; Herbert Ross, The Turning Point; Steven Spielberg, Close Encounters of the Third Kind; Fred Zinneman, Julia
Best Actor
*Richard Dreyfuss, *The Goodbye Girl*; Woody Allen, Annie Hall; Richard Burton, Equus; Marcello Mastroianni, A Special Day; John Travolta, Saturday Night Fever
Best Actress
*Diane Keaton, *Annie Hall*, Anne Bancroft, The Turning Point; Jane Fonda, Julia; Shirley MacLaine, The Turning Point; Marsha Mason, The Goodbye Girl
Best Supporting Actor
*Jason Robards, *Julia*; Mikhail Baryshnikov, The Turning Point; Peter Firth, Equus; Alec Guinness, Star Wars; Maximilian Schell, Julia
Best Supporting Actress
*Vanessa Redgrave, *Julia*; Leslie Browne, The Turning Point; Quinn Cummings, The Goodbye Girl; Melinda Dillon, Close Encounters of the Third Kind; Tuesday Weld, Looking for Mr. Goodbar

*denotes winner

233

1978

Best Picture

The Deer Hunter, Coming Home, Heaven Can Wait, Midnight Express, An Unmarried Woman

Best Director

*Michael Cimino, **The Deer Hunter**; Woody Allen, Interiors; Hal Ashby, Coming Home; Warren Beatty and Buck Henry, Heaven Can Wait; Alan Parke, Midnight Express

Best Actor

*Jon Voight, **Coming Home**; Warren Beatty, Heaven Can Wait; Gary Busey, The Buddy Holly Story; Robert DeNiro, The Deer Hunter; Laurence Olivier, The Boys from Brazil

Best Actress

*Jane Fonda, **Coming Home**; Ingrid Bergman, Autumn Sonata; Ellen Burstyn, Same Time, Next Year; Jill Clayburgh, An Unmarried Woman; Geraldine Page, Interiors

Best Supporting Actor

*Christopher Walken, **The Deer Hunter**; Bruce Dern, Coming Home; Richard Farnsworth, Comes a Horseman; John Hurt, Midnight Express; Jack Warden, Heaven Can Wait

Best Supporting Actress

*Maggie Smith, **California Suite**; Dyan Cannon, Heaven Can Wait; Penelope Mitford, Coming Home; Maureen Stapleton, Interiors; Meryl Streep, The Deer Hunter

1979

Best Picture

Kramer vs. Kramer, All That Jazz, Apocalypse Now, Breaking Away, Norma Rae

Best Director

*Robert Benton, **Kramer vs. Kramer**; Francis Ford Coppola, Apocalypse Now; Bob Fosse, All That Jazz; Edouard Molinaro, La Cage Aux Folles; Peter Yates, Breaking Away

Best Actor

*Dustin Hoffman, **Kramer vs. Kramer**; Jack Lemmon, The China Syndrome; Al Pacino, . . . And Justice for All; Roy Scheider, All That Jazz; Peter Sellers, Being There

Best Actress

*Sally Field, **Norma Rae**; Jill Clayburgh, Starting Over; Jane Fonda, The China Syndrome; Marsha Mason, Chapter Two; Bette Midler, The Rose

Best Supporting Actor

*Melvyn Douglas, **Being There**; Robert Duvall, Apocalypse Now; Frederic

*denotes winner

234

Forrest, *The Rose*; Justin Henry, *Kramer vs. Kramer*; Mickey Rooney, *The Black Stallion*

Best Supporting Actress

*Meryl Streep, **Kramer vs. Kramer**; Jane Alexander, *Kramer vs. Kramer*; Barbara Barrie, *Breaking Away*; Candice Bergen, *Starting Over*; Mariel Hemingway, *Manhattan*

1980

Best Picture

**Ordinary People*, Coal Miner's Daughter, The Elephant Man, Raging Bull, Tess*

Best Director

*Robert Redford, **Ordinary People**; David Lynch, *The Elephant Man*; Roman Polanski, *Tess*; Richard Rush, *The Stunt Man*; Martin Scorsese, *Raging Bull*

Best Actor

*Robert De Niro, **Raging Bull**; Robert Duvall, *The Great Santini*; John Hurt, *The Elephant Man*; Jack Lemmon, *Tribute*; Peter O'Toole, *The Stunt Man*

Best Actress

*Sissy Spacek, **Coal Miner's Daughter**; Ellen Burstyn, *Resurrection*; Goldie Hawn, *Private Benjamin*; Mary Tyler Moore, *Ordinary People*; Gena Rowlands, *Gloria*

Best Supporting Actor

*Timothy Hutton, **Ordinary People**; Judd Hirsch, *Ordinary People*; Michael O'Keefe, *The Great Santini*; Joe Pesci, *Raging Bull*; Jason Robards, *Melvin and Howard*

Best Supporting Actress

*Mary Steenburgen, **Melvin and Howard**; Eileen Brennan, *Private Benjamin*; Eva Le Gallienne, *Resurrection*; Cathy Moriarty, *Raging Bull*; Diana Scarwid, *Inside Moves*

*denotes winner

ANSWER SECTION

Answers for photo quiz

1. Anne Bancroft; *The Turning Point*
2. Mario Lanza; *The Student Prince*
3. Katharine Hepburn; *Long Day's Journey Into Night*
4. Bette Davis; *Bad Sister* (1931)
5. Orson Welles; Bernstein
6. Joan Crawford; *Trog* (1970)
7. Marilyn Monroe; *The Misfits* (1961)
8. Ginger Rogers; ten
9. Spencer Tracy; Clarence Darrow in *Inherit the Wind* (Welles played Darrow in *Compulsion*)
10. The Beatles; *Yellow Submarine*
11. Clint Eastwood; Harry Callahan
12. Janet Leigh and Tony Curtis; Jamie Lee Curtis
13. Robert Mitchum and Shirley MacLaine; *Two for the Seesaw*
14. George Reeves; Brent Tarleton
15. Bela Lugosi; *Ninotchka*
16. Fred MacMurray; *Pushover*
17. Adolphe Menjou; *Pollyanna* (1960)
18. Jean Simmons; *Hamlet*; Ophelia
19. Rory Calhoun; *Something for the Boys* (1944)
20. Peter Finch; *Network* (1976)
21. Bruce Dern and Marthe Keller; *Black Sunday*
22. Mae Clarke and James Cagney; *The Public Enemy*
23. Maureen O'Hara; *Rio Grande, The Quiet Man, The Wings of Eagles, McLintock!, Big Jake*
24. Shelley Winters; *A Double Life*
25. Julie Christie and Laurence Harvey; *Darling*
26. Frank Sinatra; *Higher and Higher*
27. Tommy Dorsey; *The Fabulous Dorseys*
28. Ron Ely; Elmo Lincoln was the first screen Tarzan.
29. Fred Astaire; Leslie Caron
30. Edward Arnold; *You Can't Take it With You*
31. Greta Garbo; Mauritz Stiller
32. Mae West; *Night After Night* (1932)
33. Marlene Dietrich; Lola Lola
34. Kay Francis; *The White Angel*
35. Bing Crosby; *Mississippi*
36. John Huston; *The Maltese Falcon*
37. Shirley Knight; George C. Scott
38. Al Pacino; *Dog Day Afternoon*
39. Marlon Brando and Vivien Leigh; *A Streetcar Named Desire*
40. Peter Lawford; *Good News*
41. June Allyson; James Stewart
42. Phil Silvers; *Hit Parade of 1941*
43. Ethel Merman; *Follow the Leader* (1930)
44. Judy Garland; George Cukor
45. Dean Martin; Matt Helm
46. Liza Minnelli; *Silent Movie*
47. Lynn Bari; *Sun Valley Serenade*

48. Celeste Holm; Karen Richards
49. Marlon Brando; Marc Antony in *Julius Caesar*
50. Elizabeth Taylor; *There's One Born Every Minute* (1942)
51. Cary Grant; George Cukor
52. Ingrid Bergman; Ilsa Lund
53. Judy Garland; *The Wizard of Oz*; Frank Baum
54. James Cagney; *A Midsummer Night's Dream*
55. Marlene Dietrich; *Touch of Evil*
56. Gary Cooper; *Man of the West*
57. Ethel Waters; *Pinky*
58. Clark Gable and Vivien Leigh; Margaret Mitchell (*Gone With the Wind*)
59. Joan Bennett; *Bulldog Drummond*
60. Donna Reed; Alma in *From Here to Eternity*
61. Ann Sheridan; *Kings Row*
62. Jack Nicholson and Faye Dunaway; *Chinatown*
63. Jon Voight and Dustin Hoffman; *Midnight Cowboy*
64. Walter Brennan; *Rio Bravo*
65. Shirley Maclaine: *Irma La Douce*
66. Fredric March; two; *Dr. Jekyll and Mr. Hyde, The Best Years of Our Lives*
67. Bob Hope; Lucille Ball
68. *Gone With the Wind*; George Cukor
69. Joan Crawford; *Grand Hotel*
70. Charlton Heston; *Ben-Hur*
71. *Clockwork Orange*
72. Jack Nicholson and Faye Dunaway; *Chinatown*
73. Sylvester Stallone and Burgess Meredith; *Rocky*
74. David Niven; Phileas Fogg (*Around the World in 80 Days*)
75. Ann Sothern; *Maisie*
76. Jodie Foster and Robert DeNiro; *Taxi Driver*
77. Glenda Jackson and Murray Head; *Sunday Bloody Sunday*
78. Robert Montgomery; Dwight D. Eisenhower
79. Jennifer Jones; Phyllis Isley
80. Richard Todd; *Stage Fright*
81. Yul Brynner (at the head of the table) and Deborah Kerr; *The King and I*
82. Susan Hayward; *Valley of the Dolls*
83. Kim Hunter; Stella Kowalski (*A Streetcar Named Desire*)
84. Nina Foch; *Return of the Vampire* (1943)
85. Betty Field and Burt Lancaster; *Birdman of Alcatraz*
86. Stanley Holloway; *My Fair Lady*
87. Frank Sinatra and Janet Leigh; *The Manchurian Candidate*
88. John Houseman; *Seven Days in May*
89. Robert Redford; *War Hunt* (1962)
90. Larry Blyden and Barbra Streisand; *On a Clear Day You Can See Forever*
91. Gene Wilder and Bob Newhart; *Bonnie and Clyde* (1967)
92. Faye Dunaway; Milady de Winter; *The Three Musketeers, The Four Musketeers*
93. Strother Martin and James Stewart; Charles A. Lindbergh
94. James Dean; *East of Eden, Rebel Without a Cause, Giant*
95. Laurence Harvey; *Summer and Smoke*
96. Hope Lange; *Peyton Place*

Answers – NAME DROPPERS (1)

1 – F	6 – B	11 – D	16 – S
2 – O	7 – L	12 – T	17 – G
3 – H	8 – A	13 – I	18 – K
4 – E	9 – M	14 – C	19 – Q
5 – J	10 – N	15 – R	20 – P

Answers – NAME DROPPERS (2)

1 – H	6 – L	11 – B	16 – M
2 – Q	7 – A	12 – D	17 – E
3 – T	8 – S	13 – G	18 – K
4 – N	9 – F	14 – I	19 – P
5 – J	10 – R	15 – C	20 – O

Answers – MALE CALL

1. Robert Taylor
2. Michael Sarrazin
3. Dick Van Dyke
4. Gary Cooper
5. Fredric March
6. Ernest Borgnine
7. Frank Sinatra
8. Paul Newman
9. Sam Jaffe
10. Tyrone Power
11. Alan Arkin
12. Burt Lancaster
13. Dudley Moore
14. Stacey Keach
15. Alan Bates
16. Bob Hope
17. Craig Stevens
18. Marlon Brando
19. Tom Tryon
20. Dustin Hoffman

Answers – WHO WAS THAT LADY? (1)

1. Rosalind Russell
2. Raquel Welch
3. Sara Miles
4. Jean Peters
5. Natalie Wood
6. Loretta Young
7. Angie Dickinson
8. Sophia Loren
9. Monica Vitti
10. Pam Grier
11. Lucille Ball
12. Joanne Woodward
13. Lynn Redgrave
14. Shirley MacLaine
15. Olivia de Havilland
16. Natalie Wood
17. Susan Hayward
18. Gina Lollabrigida
19. Ginger Rogers
20. Greer Garson

Answers – WHO WAS THAT LADY? (2)

1. Shirley MacLaine
2. Debbie Reynolds
3. Liza Minnelli
4. Shirley Temple
5. Carol Baker
6. Sheree North
7. Anne Bancroft
8. Ingrid Bergman
9. Ann Baxter
10. Glenda Jackson
11. Carrie Snodgrass
12. Sophia Loren
13. Ginger Rogers
14. Joanne Woodward
15. Claudette Colbert
16. Joan Crawford
17. Barbara Stanwyck
18. Rita Hayworth
19. Barbara Stanwyck
20. Julie Andrews

Answers – THE ROYAL TREATMENT (1)

1. Florence Eldredge
2. Charles Laughton
3. Laurence Olivier
4. Henry Wilcoxon
5. Jean Simmons
6. Katharine Hepburn
7. Pamela Brown
8. Bette Davis
9. Laurence Olivier
10. Basil Rathbone
11. Flora Robson
12. Richard Burton
13. Genevieve Bujold
14. Merle Oberon
15. Peter O'Toole
16. Peter O'Toole
17. Robert Shaw
18. Flora Robson
19. Bette Davis
20. Charles Laughton

Answers – THE ROYAL TREATMENT (2)

1. Liv Ullman
2. Katharine Hepburn
3. John Gielgud
4. John Barrymore
5. Ethel Barrymore
6. Greta Garbo
7. Marlene Dietrich
8. Tallulah Bankhead
9. Claude Rains
10. Richard Burton
11. Peter Ustinov
12. Norma Shearer
13. Robert Morley
14. Louis Calhern
15. Vanessa Redgrave
16. Janet Suzman
17. Marlon Brando
18. Charles Boyer
19. Charles Laughton
20. Merle Oberon

Answers – KATE

1. *Alice Adams*
2. *The Rainmaker*
3. *Summertime*
4. *Little Women*
5. *Morning Glory*
6. *The Little Minister*
7. *Sylvia Scarlet*
8. *Bringing Up Baby*
9. *Holiday*
10. *A Bill of Divorcement*
11. *The African Queen*
12. *Woman of the Year*
13. *Without Love*
14. *Suddenly Last Summer*
15. *The Madwoman of Chaillot*
16. *A Lion in Winter*
17. *A Long Day's Journey Into Night*
18. *The Desk Set*
19. *The Philadelphia Story*
20. *Guess Who's Coming to Dinner?*

Answers – BETTE

1. *What Ever Happened to Baby Jane?*
2. *Dead Ringer*
3. *A Double Life*
4. *Bunny O'Hare*
5. *Hush, Hush, Sweet Charlotte*
6. *The Corn Is Green*
7. *Now Voyager*
8. *The Little Foxes*
9. *Jezebel*
10. *Old Acquaintance*
11. *The Old Maid*
12. *Mr. Skeffington*
13. *The Bride Came C.O.D.*
14. *In This Our Life*
15. *All About Eve*
16. *The Star*
17. *Beyond the Forest*
18. *The Catered Affair*
19. *Dark Victory*
20. *The Letter*

Answers – ORSON

1. *Journey into Fear*
2. *The Stranger*
3. *Tomorrow Is Forever*
4. *Lady From Shanghai*
5. *The Third Man*
6. *Touch of Evil*
7. *Black Magic*
8. *Jane Eyre*
9. *The Black Rose*
10. *Confidential Report (Mr. Arkadin)*
11. *The Long Hot Summer*
12. *The Roots of Heaven*
13. *Compulsion*
14. *Man in the Shadow*
15. *Citizen Kane*
16. *Ferry to Hong Kong*
17. *The Trial*
18. *The V.I.P.s*
19. *House of Cards*
20. *Marco the Magnificent*

Answers – JOAN

1. *Autumn Leaves*
2. *A Woman's Face*
3. *Queen Bee*
4. *Mildred Pierce*
5. *Daisy Kenyon*
6. *Susan and God*
7. *The Women*
8. *Johnny Guitar*
9. *Flamingo Road*
10. *Humoresque*
11. *Harriet Craig*
12. *Strange Cargo*

13. Torch Song
14. Dancing Lady
15. Rain
16. Reunion in France
17. Above Suspicion
18. Sudden Fear
19. When Ladies Meet
20. Grand Hotel

Answers – MARILYN
1. Some Like It Hot
2. The Prince and the Showgirl
3. Let's Make Love
4. The Misfits
5. There's No Business Like Show Business
6. River of No Return
7. How to Marry a Millionaire
8. Gentlemen Prefer Blondes
9. Niagara
10. O. Henry's Full House
11. Monkey Business
12. Bus Stop
13. The Seven Year Itch
14. The Asphalt Jungle
15. Love Nest
16. Don't Bother to Knock
17. We're Not Married
18. Clash By Night
19. Let's Do It Again
20. Ladies of the Chorus

Answers – GINGER
1. Oh, Men! Oh, Women!
2. Teenage Rebel
3. The First Traveling Saleslady
4. Tight Spot
5. Weekend at the Waldorf
6. The Magnificent Doll
7. Lady in the Dark
8. I'll Be Seeing You
9. It Had to Be You
10. Forever Female
11. The Groom Wore Spurs
12. The Barkleys of Broadway
13. Perfect Strangers
14. Storm Warning
15. Dreamboat
16. Stage Door
17. Kitty Foyle
18. Roxie Hart
19. The Major and the Minor
20. Bachelor Mother

Answers – SPENCER
1. It's a Mad, Mad, Mad, Mad World
2. Guess Who's Coming to Dinner
3. Judgment at Nuremberg
4. Inherit the Wind
5. The Last Hurrah
6. The Old Man and the Sea
7. Bad Day at Black Rock
8. Broken Lance
9. Sea of Grass
10. Cass Timberlane
11. State of the Union
12. Edward My Son
13. Adam's Rib
14. A Guy Named Joe
15. The Actress
16. Father of the Bride
17. Tortilla Flat
18. Keeper of the Flame
19. Mannequin
20. Fury

Answers – GOOD TIMING
1. Night of the Generals
2. Day for Night
3. Night of the Hunter
4. Bad Day at Black Rock
5. A Hard Day's Night
6. Night and Day
7. The Night Fighters
8. Long Day's Journey into Night
9. Night Must Fall
10. Dog Day Afternoon
11. The Night They Raided Minskey's
12. Days of Wine and Roses
13. Nightmare Alley
14. A Day at the Races
15. A Night at the Opera
16. Night of the Iguana
17. The Night Porter
18. The Night Walker
19. One Night of Love
20. The Day the Earth Stood Still

Answers – VERBATIM
1. Little Caesar
2. Born Yesterday
3. Yankee Doodle Dandy
4. Gunga Din
5. The King and I
6. The Grapes of Wrath
7. I Am a Fugitive from a Chain Gang

241

8. Mutiny on the Bounty
9. Treasure of Sierra Madre
10. Sunset Boulevard
11. Funny Girl
12. It Happened One Night
13. Night After Night
14. Kings Row
15. A Place in the Sun
16. To Have and Have Not
17. The Bad Seed
18. The Man Who Came to Dinner
19. On the Waterfront
20. King Kong

Answers – BORN AGAIN

1 – I	6 – H	11 – P	16 – S
2 – F	7 – R	12 – A	17 – N
3 – M	8 – B	13 – C	18 – D
4 – J	9 – T	14 – E	19 – L
5 – K	10 – O	15 – Q	20 – G

Answers – MIXED DOUBLES

1. Richard Burton and Elizabeth Taylor
2. Audie Murphy and Wanda Hendrix
3. Tony Curtis and Janet Leigh
4. Dick Powell and June Allyson
5. Dick Powell and Joan Blondell
6. Rod Steiger and Claire Bloom
7. George C. Scott and Trish Van Devere
8. Charles Bronson and Jill Ireland
9. Robert Wagner and Natalie Wood
10. Paul Newman and Joanne Woodward
11. Eli Wallach and Anne Jackson
12. Eddie Fisher and Debbie Reynolds
13. Cary Grant and Betsy Drake
14. John Cassavetes and Gene Rowlands
15. Troy Donahue and Suzanne Pleshette
16. Louis Hayward and Ida Lupino
17. Howard Duff and Ida Lupino
18. John Hodiak and Anne Baxter
19. Franchot Tone and Joan Crawford
20. Stewart Granger and Jean Simmons

Answers – COUNT DOWN

1. One Potato, Two Potato
2. The Taking of Pelham 1, 2, 3,

3. Five Finger Exercises
4. The Three Musketeers
5. One Two Three
6. Three Secrets
7. The Ten Commandments
8. Two for the Seesaw
9. The Seven-Ups
10. Seven Days in May
11. Five Easy Pieces
12. Two for the Road
13. Three Days of the Condor
14. Butterfield 8
15. Two Weeks with Love
16. Cheaper by the Dozen
17. One Flew Over the Cuckoo's Nest
18. The Seven-Percent Solution
19. 13 Rue Madeleine
20. Three Women

Answers – TO BE CONTINUED

1 – E	6 – K	11 – H	16 – R
2 – G	7 – P	12 – S	17 – M
3 – L	8 – O	13 – Q	18 – D
4 – N	9 – C	14 – B	19 – J
5 – T	10 – A	15 – I	20 – F

Answers – HAIR RAISERS

1. Frankenstein
2. The Wolf Man
3. Mark of the Vampire
4. Dracula
5. House of Frankenstein
6. Murders in the Rue Morgue
7. Frankenstein Meets the Wolf Man
8. Creature from the Black Lagoon
9. The Thing
10. Bride of Frankenstein
11. I Was a Teenage Werewolf
12. Phantom of the Opera
13. Dr. Jekyll and Mr. Hyde
14. The Fly
15. The Mummy
16. The Island of Dr. Moreau
17. House of Wax
18. Isle of the Dead
19. House of Usher
20. The Black Cat

Answers – S.O.S.

1. Earthquake
2. The Towering Inferno

3. The Poseidon Adventure
4. San Francisco
5. In Old Chicago
6. Hurricane
7. Typhoon
8. The Hindenburg
9. Titanic
10. The Last Days of Pompeii
11. The Bedford Incident
12. Dr. Strangelove
13. The Rains Came
14. The Sisters
15. A Night to Remember
16. Forest Rangers
17. The Day the Earth Caught Fire
18. The World, the Flesh and the Devil
19. Black Sunday
20. Lifeboat

Answers – OVER THE RAINBOW (1)
1. The Green Goddess
2. Abie's Irish Rose
3. The Scarlet Letter
4. White Shadows on the South Seas
5. The Black Pirate
6. Gold Diggers of Broadway
7. Lilac Time
8. White Gold
9. Ruggles of Red Gap
10. Bluebeard's Eighth Wife
11. The White Moth
12. The Red Lily
13. The Great White Way
14. The Gold Rush
15. Brown of Harvard
16. The Golden Bed
17. The White Black Sheep
18. Tarzan and the Golden Lion
19. Under the Red Robe
20. Scarlet Seas

Answers – OVER THE RAINBOW (2)
1. The Blue Angel
2. Red Headed Woman
3. Bluebeard's Eighth Wife
4. The Scarlet Empress
5. Red Salute
6. The Black Camel
7. The Scarlet Pimpernel
8. The White Angel
9. Red Dust
10. The Black Cat
11. White Banners

12. Yellow Jack
13. Black Fury
14. The White Sister
15. The Bride Wore Red
16. Anne of Green Gables
17. So Red the Rose
18. Golden Boy
19. Silver Dollar
20. The Green Pastures

Answers – OVER THE RAINBOW (3)
1. The Blue Bird
2. The Red Danube
3. White Heat
4. Yellow Sky
5. Green Dolphin Street
6. White Tie and Tails
7. Three Little Girls in Blue
8. Black Narcissus
9. Blue Skies
10. Silver River
11. Scarlet Street
12. Red River
13. The Blue Dahlia
14. Red Light
15. The White Cliffs of Dover
16. Green Hell
17. Black Magic
18. Golden Earrings
19. The Red Shoes
20. Ride the Pink Horse

Answers – OVER THE RAINBOW (4)
1. The Black Orchid
2. The Blue Angel
3. Red Badge of Courage
4. The Scarlet Coat
5. The Rose Tattoo
6. White Christmas
7. The Yellow Cab Man
8. The Silver Whip
9. The Golden Blade
10. The Purple Mask
11. Green Fire
12. The Blue Veil
13. The Black Rose
14. Blue Denim
15. Red Garters
16. White Witch Doctor
17. The Yellow Tomahawk
18. The Purple Plain
19. Golden Girl
20. Green Mansions

Answers – OVER THE RAINBOW (5)

1. The Green Berets
2. A Patch of Blue
3. Big Red
4. Portrait in Black
5. Dr. Goldfoot and the Bikini Machine
6. Girl with Green Eyes
7. The Grass Is Greener
8. Heller in Pink Tights
9. Blue
10. The Yellow Rolls Royce
11. Blue Hawaii
12. Yellow Canary
13. Red Line
14. The Blue Max
15. Blackbeard's Ghost
16. Gold of the Seven Saints
17. Goldfinger
18. The Angel Wore Red
19. The Pink Panther
20. Reflections in a Golden Eye

Answers – OVER THE RAINBOW (6)

1. A Clockwork Orange
2. The Pink Panther Strikes Again
3. Black Sunday
4. Baby Blue Marine
5. The Black Bird
6. Soldier Blue
7. Kid Blue
8. Lady Sings the Blues
9. Last of the Red Hot Lovers
10. The Man with the Golden Gun
11. Steelyard Blues
12. Soylent Green
13. River of Gold
14. Blacula
15. The Black Windmill
16. Gold
17. Golden Needles
18. Red Sky at Morning
19. The Great White Hope
20. Black Beauty

Answers – UNFORGETTABLES (1)

1. The Heiress
2. King Kong
3. The Informer
4. Dark Victory
5. The Gay Divorcee
6. Stagecoach
7. Stella Dallas
8. Little Caesar
9. Easter Parade
10. High Noon
11. Hurricane
12. Boys Town
13. Mildred Pierce
14. Red River
15. The Public Enemy
16. Citizen Kane
17. A Letter to Three Wives
18. A Star Is Born
19. Double Indemnity
20. Dead End

Answers – UNFORGETTABLES (2)

1. From Here to Eternity
2. The Quiet Man
3. Of Human Bondage
4. The Great Dictator
5. Little Women
6. The Philadelphia Story
7. The Good Earth
8. The Thin Man
9. All Quiet on the Western Front
10. Ninotchka
11. Frankenstein
12. The Ox-Bow Incident
13. David Copperfield
14. Grand Hotel
15. Dracula
16. Mutiny on the Bounty
17. Ben-Hur
18. Lost Horizon
19. Mr. Deeds Goes to Town
20. Mr. Smith Goes to Washington

Answers – UNFORGETABLES (3)

1. My Little Chickadee
2. Destry Rides Again
3. Captains Courageous
4. Meet John Doe
5. Queen Christina
6. Naughty Marietta
7. She Done Him Wrong
8. The Letter
9. Psycho
10. Dinner at Eight
11. A Place in the Sun
12. The Great McGinty
13. Hud
14. Stage Door

15. The Long Voyage Home
16. The Lady Eve
17. The Magnificent Ambersons
18. Meet Me in St. Louis
19. Hail the Conquering Hero
20. The Bank Dick

Answers – THE BRITISH ARE COMING

1. Great Expectations
2. Brief Encounter
3. Henry V
4. Goodbye, Mr. Chips
5. The Fallen Idol
6. The Thirty-Nine Steps
7. The Third Man
8. In Which We Serve
9. Tom Jones
10. Darling
11. The Man in the White Suit
12. Pygmalion
13. Hamlet
14. The Red Shoes
15. Victoria the Great
16. Things to Come
17. Odd Man Out
18. Kind Hearts and Coronets
19. Major Barbara
20. Private Life of Henry VIII

Answers – FOREIGN LEGION

1. Grand Illusion
2. The Bicycle Thief
3. Jules and Jim
4. The Virgin Spring
5. Rashomon
6. Mayerling
7. The Blue Angel
8. Paisan
9. Potemkin
10. The Cabinet of Dr. Caligari
11. The Seventh Seal
12. La Strada
13. La Dolce Vita
14. M
15. Rome: Open City
16. Rocco and His Brothers
17. Black Orpheus
18. Children of Paradise
19. Divorce—Italian Style
20. Shoeshine

Answers – REGARDS TO BROADWAY

1. The Petrified Forest
2. Romeo and Juliet
3. The Green Pastures
4. A Midsummer Night's Dream
5. Anna Christie
6. Golden Boy
7. The Women
8. Boy Meets Girl
9. You Can't Take It With You
10. Stage Door
11. Babes in Arms
12. Brother Rat
13. Jezebel
14. Death Takes a Holiday
15. The Shining Hour
16. These Three (The Children's Hour)
17. Dinner at Eight
18. The Barretts of Wimpole Street
19. Design for Living
20. Private Lives

Answers – SOBRIQUETS

1 – H	6 – P	11 – E	16 – O
2 – Q	7 – A	12 – T	17 – I
3 – K	8 – S	13 – F	18 – J
4 – R	9 – L	14 – C	19 – M
5 – B	10 – N	15 – G	20 – D

Answers – MUSICAL LIVES

1 – F	6 – I	11 – R	16 – D
2 – H	7 – N	12 – P	17 – G
3 – K	8 – L	13 – S	18 – C
4 – M	9 – O	14 – B	19 – J
5 – Q	10 – A	15 – T	20 – E

Answers – ME TARZAN

1. Gordon Scott
2. Elmo Lincoln
3. Ron Ely
4. Johnny Weissmuller
5. Gordon Scott
6. Denny Miller
7. Lex Barker
8. Jock Mahoney
9. Mike Henry
10. Lex Barker
11. James Pierce
12. Frank Merrill
13. Buster Crabbe

14. Bruce Bennett (Herman Brix)
15. Glenn Morris
16. Johnny Weissmuller
17. Ron Ely
18. Gene Pollar
19. Miles O'Keeffe
20. Mike Henry

Answers – DON'T I KNOW YOU? (1)

1 – G	6 – A	11 – F	16 – N
2 – P	7 – S	12 – D	17 – I
3 – T	8 – B	13 – H	18 – O
4 – J	9 – R	14 – E	19 – K
5 – M	10 – C	15 – L	20 – Q

Answers – DON'T I KNOW YOU? (2)

1 – J	6 – A	11 – G	16 – E
2 – T	7 – Q	12 – D	17 – N
3 – M	8 – P	13 – C	18 – H
4 – R	9 – S	14 – I	19 – O
5 – L	10 – B	15 – K	20 – F

Answers – THE ANIMAL KINGDOM

1. *The Sterile Cuckoo*
2. *Save the Tiger*
3. *The Man Who Loved Cat Dancing*
4. *Day of the Dolphins*
5. *Bulldog Drummond*
6. *Planet of the Apes*
7. *Cat Ballou*
8. *Dog Day Afternoon*
9. *Enter the Dragon*
10. *Rooster Cogburn*
11. *Straw Dogs*
12. *The Lion in Winter*
13. *One Flew Over the Cuckoo's Nest*
14. *The Pink Panther*
15. *The Owl and the Pussycat*
16. *The Fox*
17. *A Man Called Horse*
18. *The Brave Bulls*
19. *The Maltese Falcon*
20. *What's New, Pussycat?*

Answers – THE PLAY'S THE THING

1. Gertrude Lawrence
2. Paul Newman
3. Geraldine Page
4. Montgomery Clift
5. Katharine Hepburn
6. Richard Burton
7. Geraldine Page
8. Paul Newman

9. Kim Hunter
10. Warren Beatty
11. Elizabeth Taylor
12. Marlon Brando
13. Anna Magnani
14. Arthur Kennedy
15. Elizabeth Taylor
16. Burl Ives
17. Ava Gardner
18. Laurence Harvey
19. Elizabeth Taylor
20. Marlon Brando

Answers – TALL IN THE SADDLE

1. Fess Parker
2. Paul Newman
3. Burt Reynolds
4. Jason Robards
5. John Wayne
6. Desi Arnaz, Jr.
7. Frank Sinatra
8. Burt Reynolds
9. John Wayne
10. George Montgomery
11. Glenn Ford
12. Bob Hope
13. Jack Buetel
14. Steve McQueen
15. Joel McCrea
16. Jeffrey Hunter
17. William Holden
18. Alan Ladd
19. James Coburn
20. Kris Kristoffersen

Answers – LITTLE BROTHERS

1 – E, *City for Conquest*
2 – H, *Night Passage*
3 – I, *Riffraff*
4 – K, *My Brother Talks to Horses*
5 – M, *Sometimes a Great Notion*
6 – A, *Sea of Grass*
7 – L, *Holiday*
8 – S, *The Irish in 'Em*
9 – R, *Gone with the Wind*
10 – Q, *Broken Lance*
11 – P, *Four Sons*
12 – C, *A Long Day's Journey into Night*
13 – J, *Death of a Salesman*
14 – T, *Toys in the Attic*

15 – F, There's No Business Like
      Show Business
16 – B, Ziegfeld Girl
17 – O, Jesse James
18 – N, Beau Geste
19 – G, House of Strangers
20 – D, Adventure in Baltimore

Answers – KID SISTERS
1 – G, Meet Me in St. Louis
2 – M, The Philadelphia Story
3 – J, The Hard Way
4 – N, Yankee Doodle Dandy
5 – O, The Major and the Minor
6 – T, Gone with the Wind
7 – D, State Fair
8 – S, I Wake Up Screaming
9 – A, The Constant Nymph
10 – Q, The Young in Heart
11 – P, Vigil in the Night
12 – H, Dr. Kildare's Crisis
13 – F, The Gay Sisters
14 – R, Holiday
15 – L, The Secret Heart
16 – B, My Sister Eileen
17 – K, My Sister Eileen
18 – I, Isn't It Romantic
19 – E, The Glass Menagerie
20 – C, The Four Daughters

Answers – LIGHTS, ACTION . . .
FORD
1. The Quiet Man
2. How Green Was My Valley
3. The Grapes of Wrath
4. My Darling Clementine
5. The Man Who Shot Liberty Valance
6. Mogambo
7. The Long Gray Line
8. The Informer
9. The Lost Patrol
10. Mary of Scotland
11. The Plough and the Stars
12. Hurricane
13. Wee Willie Winkie
14. Drums Along the Mohawk
15. Stagecoach
16. Fort Apache
17. Rio Grande
18. Mister Roberts
19. Tobacco Road
20. Young Mr. Lincoln

Answers – LIGHTS, ACTION . . .
HITCHCOCK
1. The Birds
2. Psycho
3. North by Northwest
4. Vertigo
5. The Wrong Man
6. The Man Who Knew Too Much
7. Family Plot
8. Frenzy
9. Torn Curtain
10. The Trouble with Harry
11. To Catch a Thief
12. Rear Window
13. Dial M for Murder
14. Strangers on a Train
15. Stage Fright
16. Notorious
17. Spellbound
18. Lifeboat
19. Suspicion
20. Rebecca

Answers – LIGHTS, ACTION . . .
HUSTON
1. The Maltese Falcon
2. Reflections in a Golden Eye
3. Treasure of Sierra Madre
4. Night of the Iguana
5. Freud
6. Beat the Devil
7. The List of Adrian Messenger
8. The African Queen
9. In This Our Life
10. The Unforgiven
11. Key Largo
12. The Roots of Heaven
13. Heaven Knows, Mr. Allison
14. Moby Dick
15. Moulin Rouge
16. The Asphalt Jungle
17. The Red Badge of Courage
18. The Misfits
19. The Bible
20. We Were Strangers

Answers – LIGHTS, ACTION . . .
CUKOR
1. My Fair Lady
2. A Star Is Born
3. A Double Life
4. The Women

5. *Les Girls*
6. *Wild Is the Wind*
7. *Adam's Rib*
8. *Two Faced Woman*
9. *Little Women*
10. *A Woman's Face*
11. *Camille*
12. *Dinner at Eight*
13. *David Copperfield*
14. *Romeo and Juliet*
15. *Susan and God*
16. *The Philadelphia Story*
17. *Gaslight*
18. *Born Yesterday*
19. *Pat and Mike*
20. *Holiday*

Answers – GUMSHOES (1)
1. William Powell
2. Dick Powell
3. Robert Mitchum
4. Elliott Gould
5. Humphrey Bogart
6. Robert Montgomery
7. George Montgomery
8. James Garner
9. Gracie Allen
10. Frank Sinatra
11. Humphrey Bogart
12. George Segal
13. James Coburn
14. Dean Martin
15. Sean Connery
16. Roger Moore
17. David Niven
18. Peter Sellers
19. Albert Finney
20. Tony Randall

Answers – GUMSHOES (2)
1. Nichol Williamson
2. Basil Rathbone
3. Peter Cushing
4. Paul Newman
5. Bonita Granville
6. Warner Oland
7. Sidney Toler
8. Roland Winters
9. Peter Lorre
10. Ronald Colman
11. Ray Milland
12. John Howard

13. Warren William
14. Ricardo Cortez
15. Donald Wood
16. William Powell
17. Edmund Lowe
18. Warren William
19. Ralph Bellamy
20. William Gargan

Answers – CHORUS LINES (1)
1. *The Band Wagon*
2. *Holiday Inn*
3. *Alexander's Ragtime Band*
4. *There's No Business Like Show Business*
5. *The Wizard of Oz*
6. *Roberta*
7. *Footlight Parade*
8. *Easter Parade*
9. *Kiss Me, Kate*
10. *Show Boat*
11. *The Dolly Sisters*
12. *Tin Pan Alley*
13. *42nd Street*
14. *Singin' in the Rain*
15. *White Christmas*
16. *Road to Morocco*
17. *Meet Me in St. Louis*
18. *Cover Girl*
19. *Seven Brides for Seven Brothers*
20. *Gigi*

Answers – CHORUS LINES (2)
1. *Mary Poppins*
2. *My Fair Lady*
3. *West Side Story*
4. *Guys and Dolls*
5. *An American in Paris*
6. *The Pajama Game*
7. *Ziegfeld Girl*
8. *Yankee Doodle Dandy*
9. *Carmen Jones*
10. *Love Me or Leave Me*
11. *Can Can*
12. *Oklahoma!*
13. *Carousel*
14. *A Date with Judy*
15. *A Night at the Opera*
16. *State Fair*
17. *South Pacific*
18. *Royal Wedding*

19. Night and Day
20. Mother Wore Tights

Answers – THEY'RE PLAYING THEIR SONGS (1)

1 – H, Holiday Inn
2 – N, Gilda
3 – S, A Hole in the Head
4 – J, Summer Stock
5 – T, Curly Top
6 – A, The Man Who Knew Too Much
7 – P, The Caddy
8 – B, Mary Poppins
9 – R, Oklahoma!
10 – C, Where's Charley?
11 – G, South Pacific
12 – F, The Firefly
13 – D, Damn Yankees
14 – Q, Road House
15 – E, Anchors Aweigh
16 – I, Kiss Me, Kate
17 – K, My Fair Lady
18 – M, Born to Dance
19 – O, Dames
20 – L, San Francisco

Answers – THEY'RE PLAYING THEIR SONGS (2)

1 – R, Perils of Pauline
2 – L, The Sound of Music
3 – T, Doctor Doolittle
4 – B, Breakfast at Tiffany's
5 – K, Born to Dance
6 – A, Meet Me in St. Louis
7 – E, Pal Joey
8 – O, Daddy Long Legs
9 – S, Coney Island
10 – D, Alexander's Ragtime Band
11 – Q, Blue Skies
12 – F, The Paleface
13 – I, Lady Be Good
14 – G, Cabaret
15 – J, Suzy
16 – N, Casablanca
17 – H, Canyon Passage
18 – O, Bernadine
19 – M, Guys and Dolls
20 – P, Gigi

Answers – SPEAK EASY

1. The Roaring Twenties
2. The Spirit of St. Louis
3. Public Enemy
4. Little Man, What Now?
5. Little Caesar
6. Three Comrades
7. The Sting
8. The Great American Broadcast
9. The Great Gatsby
10. Thoroughly Modern Millie
11. Singin' in the Rain
12. Scarface
13. Some Like It Hot
14. Pete Kelly's Blues
15. You're My Everything
16. Hollywood Cavalcade
17. Beau James
18. Margie
19. Roxie Hart
20. Love Me or Leave Me

Answers – BROTHER, CAN YOU SPARE A DIME?

1. The Grapes of Wrath
2. The Mortal Storm
3. Paper Moon
4. Blockade
5. Stand Up and Cheer
6. For Whom the Bell Tolls
7. My Man Godfrey
8. A Man's Castle
9. Bonnie and Clyde
10. All the King's Men
11. This Daily Bread
12. G-Men
13. Tobacco Road
14. Last Train from Madrid
15. Love Finds Andy Hardy
16. Fury
17. Black Legion
18. They Shoot Horses, Don't They?
19. Imitation of Life
20. They Won't Forget

Answers – WAR AND PEACE

1. The Best Years of Our Lives
2. The Men
3. Home of the Brave
4. Bright Victory
5. The Hucksters
6. The Man in the Gray Flannel Suit
7. Guadalcanal Diary
8. Gentleman's Agreement

9. *A Walk in the Sun*
10. *The Purple Heart*
11. *Pride of the Marines*
12. *To Hell and Back*
13. *The War Lover*
14. *Five Graves to Cairo*
15. *Thirty Seconds Over Tokyo*
16. *The Desert Fox*
17. *Anchors Aweigh*
18. *All My Sons*
19. *Mrs. Miniver*
20. *Lifeboat*

**Answers – MARLON, ALSO
    STARRING . . .**

1 – O	6 – M	11 – A	16 – C
2 – L	7 – T	12 – I	17 – K
3 – Q	8 – N	13 – S	18 – D
4 – R	9 – B	14 – G	19 – H
5 – P	10 – E	15 – J	20 – F

**Answers – ELIZABETH, ALSO
    STARRING . . .**

1 – I	6 – T	11 – G	16 – B
2 – R	7 – P	12 – J	17 – F
3 – Q	8 – A	13 – C	18 – L
4 – N	9 – D	14 – K	19 – M
5 – S	10 – O	15 – H	20 – E

**Answers – CARY, ALSO
    STARRING . . .**

1 – M	6 – N	11 – F	16 – B
2 – P	7 – C	12 – I	17 – H
3 – Q	8 – O	13 – S	18 – L
4 – R	9 – D	14 – J	19 – E
5 – T	10 – A	15 – K	20 – G

**Answers – INGRID, ALSO
    STARRING . . .**

1 – N	6 – M	11 – S	16 – D
2 – T	7 – A	12 – H	17 – K
3 – O	8 – P	13 – E	18 – B
4 – R	9 – L	14 – J	19 – C
5 – Q	10 – I	15 – G	20 – F

**Answers – GARLAND, ALSO
    STARRING . . .**

1 – N	6 – S	11 – G	16 – E
2 – R	7 – O	12 – P	17 – K
3 – L	8 – A	13 – H	18 – I
4 – T	9 – D	14 – B	19 – F
5 – Q	10 – C	15 – J	20 – M

**Answers – CAGNEY, ALSO
    STARRING . . .**

1 – L	6 – A	11 – O	16 – F
2 – I	7 – C	12 – E	17 – K
3 – R	8 – B	13 – H	18 – G
4 – T	9 – Q	14 – D	19 – N
5 – P	10 – S	15 – J	20 – M

**Answers – DIETRICH, ALSO
    STARRING . . .**

1 – M	6 – D	11 – P	16 – I
2 – O	7 – A	12 – C	17 – G
3 – T	8 – S	13 – E	18 – L
4 – K	9 – B	14 – J	19 – N
5 – R	10 – Q	15 – H	20 – F

**Answers – COOPER, ALSO
    STARRING . . .**

1 – O	6 – S	11 – G	16 – K
2 – L	7 – A	12 – C	17 – M
3 – T	8 – Q	13 – D	18 – J
4 – R	9 – P	14 – E	19 – F
5 – N	10 – B	15 – I	20 – H

Answers – MUSIC TO OUR EARS
1. *On with the Show*
2. *The Jazz Singer*
3. *The Broadway Melody*
4. *Queen of the Night Clubs*
5. *Show Boat*
6. *The Desert Song*
7. *Close Harmony*
8. *My Man*
9. *Show Girl*
10. *Gold Diggers of Broadway*
11. *Broadway Babies*
12. *Marianne*
13. *Rio Rita*
14. *Married in Hollywood*
15. *Sweetie*
16. *The Love Parade*
17. *Sunny Side Up*
18. *Sally*
19. *The Singing Fool*
20. *Lucky Boy*

Answers – A NOVEL IDEA (1)
1. *The Three Musketeers*
2. *Oliver Twist*
3. *The Scarlet Letter*
4. *Love (Anna Karenina)*
5. *Way Down East*
6. *The Sea Beast (Moby Dick)*

7. Peter Pan
8. Beau Geste
9. Camille
10. Ben Hur
11. The Hunchback of Notre Dame
12. The Last of the Mohicans
13. The Phantom of the Opera
14. The Iron Mask
15. The Enchanted Cottage
16. Show Boat
17. So Big
18. Scaramouche
19. Ramona
20. The Virginian

Answers – A NOVEL IDEA (2)
1. Anthony Adverse
2. Gone With the Wind
3. The Good Earth
4. Stella Dallas
5. Magnificent Obsession
6. A Tale of Two Cities
7. Goodbye, Mr. Chips
8. Lost Horizon
9. Beau Geste
10. Mutiny on the Bounty
11. The Prisoner of Zenda
12. Camille
13. The Rains Came
14. Anna Karenina
15. Captains Courageous
16. Wuthering Heights
17. White Banners
18. Of Human Bondage
19. Show Boat
20. Grand Hotel

Answers – A NOVEL IDEA (3)
1. All Quiet on the Western Front
2. Captain Blood
3. The Old Maid
4. The Prince and the Pauper
5. Three Comrades
6. Dr. Jekyll and Mr. Hyde
7. Kidnapped
8. Imitation of Life
9. A Farewell to Arms
10. Private Worlds
11. Les Miserables
12. Little Women
13. I Married a Doctor (Main Street)
14. Babbitt

15. Dodsworth
16. The Scarlet Pimpernel
17. Satan Met a Lady (The Maltese Falcon)
18. Becky Sharp (Vanity Fair)
19. The Thin Man
20. Drums Along the Mohawk

Answers – A NOVEL IDEA (4)
1. The Sea of Grass
2. The Bridge of San Luis Rey
3. Kitty Foyle
4. For Whom the Bell Tolls
5. Gentleman's Agreement
6. The Fountainhead
7. The Lost Weekend
8. Mildred Pierce
9. Saratoga Trunk
10. How Green Was My Valley
11. The Grapes of Wrath
12. Tobacco Road
13. Pride and Prejudice
14. Jane Eyre
15. A Tree Grows in Brooklyn
16. Cass Timberlane
17. Green Dolphin Street
18. Forever Amber
19. The Hunchback of Notre Dame
20. Rebecca

Answers – A NOVEL IDEA (5)
1. The Hucksters
2. The Miracle of the Bells
3. The Yearling
4. Kings Row
5. Dragon Seed
6. The Human Comedy
7. The Heiress (Washington Square)
8. China Sky
9. The Snake Pit
10. Lady of Burlesque (The G-String Murders)
11. H. M. Pulham, Esq.
12. B. F.'s Daughter
13. Arch of Triumph
14. The Valley of Decision
15. Guadalcanal Diary
16. Daisy Kenyon
17. Double Indemnity
18. Little Women
19. Random Harvest
20. Edge of Darkness

Answers – WHERE IN THE WORLD?

1. In Old Chicago
2. Abe Lincoln in Illinois
3. Chinatown
4. Last Tango in Paris
5. Nashville
6. Next Stop, Greenwich Village
7. California Split
8. Algiers
9. Oklahoma!
10. Lawrence of Arabia
11. An Angel from Texas
12. Appointment in Berlin
13. San Francisco
14. New York, New York
15. Roman Holiday
16. The Lords of Flatbush
17. Escape to Burma
18. Road to Singapore
19. Hawaii
20. Diamond Head

Answers – MISSING LINKS

1. My Foolish Heart; Heart is a Lonely Hunter
2. The Last Time I Saw Paris; Paris Blues
3. Long Day's Journey into Night; Night at the Opera
4. The African Queen; Queen Christina
5. Some Like it Hot; Hot Rock
6. Mr. Deeds Goes to Town; Town Without Pity
7. How Green Was My Valley; Valley of the Dolls
8. The Thin Man; Man with the Golden Gun
9. Anne of the Thousand Days; Days of Wine and Roses
10. The Scarlet Letter; Letter to Three Wives
11. A Doll's House; House of Seven Gables
12. Diamonds are Forever; Forever Amber
13. Five Miles to Midnight; Midnight Cowboy
14. All that Jazz; Jazz Singer
15. Soldier Blue; Blue Hawaii
16. Sunday Bloody Sunday; Sunday in New York

17. My Fair Lady; Lady from Shanghai
18. Life with Father; Father of the Bride
19. Endless Love; Love and Death
20. Imitation of Life; Life at the Top

Answers – MUSICAL MOMENTS

1 – J, Cabaret
2 – P, Gypsy
3 – N, Cat Ballou
4 – T, Sweet Charity
5 – O, Camelot
6 – L, Oliver!
7 – A, Star!
8 – S, Honeysuckle Rose
9 – C, A Star Is Born
10 – B, Mahogany
11 – R, Mame
12 – D, Man of La Mancha
13 – G, Cabaret
14 – E, Thoroughly Modern Millie
15 – M, Some Like It Hot
16 – Q, The Rose
17 – I, Nashville
18 – K, My Fair Lady
19 – H, A Little Night Music
20 – F, I Could Go on Singing

Answers – BACK TO THEIR ROOTS

1. Judith Anderson
2. Maria Montez
3. Vivien Leigh
4. Jacques Bergerac
5. Louis Hayward
6. Ann-Margret
7. Ray Milland
8. Yul Brynner
9. Rita Moreno
10. Richard Burton
11. Paul Muni
12. Deborah Kerr
13. George Sanders and Tom Conway
14. Xavier Cugat
15. Olivia de Havilland and Joan Fontaine
16. Dolores Del Rio
17. Philip Dorn
18. Fernando Lamas
19. Pier Angeli and Marisa Pavan
20. Audrey Hepburn

Answers – BATTLE SCARRED
1. The Young Lions
2. Destination Tokyo
3. Midway
4. Tobruk
5. King Rat
6. Secret of Santa Vittoria
7. Bataan
8. The Damned
9. Patton
10. Wake Island
11. So Proudly We Hail
12. Stalag 17
13. The Longest Day
14. Sands of Iwo Jima
15. Bridge on the River Kwai
16. The Guns of Navarone
17. The Dirty Dozen
18. Casablanca
19. MacArthur
20. D-Day, the 6th of June

Answers – MELODIC MEMORIES (1)
1 – G, On with the Show
2 – M, The Shopworn Angel
3 – P, Marianne
4 – S, Fox Movietone Follies
5 – J, The Pagan
6 – A, The Desert Song
7 – O, Innocents of Paris
8 – C, The Dance of Life
9 – T, Sweetie
10 – B, The Trespasser
11 – D, Sunny Side Up
12 – H, Sally
13 – R, Applause
14 – E, Lucky Boy
15 – K, My Man
16 – F, The Singing Fool
17 – I, The Love Parade
18 – N, Lady of the Pavements
19 – Q, A Woman Commands
20 – L, Gold Diggers of Broadway

Answers – MELODIC MEMORIES (2)
1 – I, The Vagabond King
2 – R, Safety in Numbers
3 – K, Honey
4 – T, Monte Carlo
5 – O, Song O' My Heart
6 – S, Whoopee
7 – Q, The Blue Angel
8 – B, Mammy
9 – P, Dames
10 – F, Murder at the Vanities
11 – E, Puttin' on the Ritz
12 – L, Let's Fall in Love
13 – H, Bright Eyes
14 – A, The Vagabond Lover
15 – N, I'm No Angel
16 – C, Gold Diggers of 1933
17 – M, The Big Pond
18 – D, Footlight Parade
19 – G, The King of Jazz
20 – J, 42nd Street

Answers – MELODIC MEMORIES (3)
1 – L, Lillian Russell
2 – N, Star Spangled Rhythm
3 – K, Hers to Hold
4 – P, Casablanca
5 – T, Cabin in the Sky
6 – R, Higher and Higher
7 – S, Down Argentine Way
8 – Q, Anchors Aweigh
9 – O, The Sky's the Limit
10 – A, Buck Privates
11 – F, Tin Pan Alley
12 – M, Bittersweet
13 – D, Lady Be Good
14 – C, Thank Your Lucky Stars
15 – H, Happy Go Lucky
16 – G, Ziegfeld Girl
17 – E, Here Come the Waves
18 – I, Follow the Boys
19 – J, Something to Shout About
20 – B, Cover Girl

Answers – MELODIC MEMORIES (4)
1 – M, The Toast of New Orleans
2 – P, Royal Wedding
3 – T, Calamity Jane
4 – R, The Joker Is Wild
5 – N, An American in Paris
6 – J, Here Comes the Groom
7 – L, Oklahoma!
8 – Q, Tammy and the Bachelor
9 – S, The Caddy
10 – F, There's No Business Like
Show Business
11 – O, Summer Stock
12 – A, A Star Is Born

13 – D, *Bernadine*
14 – G, *Guys and Dolls*
15 – B, *Daddy Long Legs*
16 – I, *Seven Brides for Seven Brothers*
17 – H, *South Pacific*
18 – E, *Gigi*
19 – K, *Singin' In The Rain*
20 – C, *Kiss Me Kate*

Answers – AND THE LOSER WAS . . . (1)

1 – O	6 – P	11 – S	16 – B
2 – Q	7 – N	12 – C	17 – D
3 – R	8 – L	13 – J	18 – E
4 – M	9 – K	14 – G	19 – H
5 – T	10 – I	15 – F	20 – A

Answers – AND THE LOSER WAS . . . (2)

1 – R	6 – N	11 – L	16 – J
2 – T	7 – A	12 – B	17 – F
3 – O	8 – D	13 – K	18 – I
4 – Q	9 – S	14 – C	19 – H
5 – P	10 – M	15 – E	20 – G

Answers – AND THE LOSER WAS (AGAIN) . . .

1. E, I, L, O, T
2. A, D, H, R
3. B, G, J, M, P, S
4. C, K, Q
5. F, N

Answers – AND THE WINNER WAS . . . DIRECTORS

1 – L	6 – N	11 – D	16 – J
2 – M	7 – R	12 – G	17 – B
3 – H	8 – P	13 – A	18 – I
4 – S	9 – T	14 – E	19 – K
5 – O	10 – Q	15 – F	20 – C

Answers – AND THE WINNER WAS . . . (1920s)

1 – I	5 – P	10 – B or H	14 – K
2 – O	6 – E or S	11 – G	15 – C
3 – A, F or R	7 – Q	12 – D	16 – M
4 – T	8 – N	13 – J	
	9 – L		

Answers – AND THE WINNER WAS . . . (1930s)

1 – Q	6 – M	9 – S	14 – E
2 – O	7 – B and H	10 – L	15 – I
3 – P		11 – D	16 – N
4 – J	8 – F and G	12 – C	17 – K and T
5 – L		13 – R	18 – A

Answers – LOSERS AND WINNERS (1930s)

1 – K	6 – T	11 – R	16 – E and F
2 – O	7 – B	12 – I	17 – C
3 – Q	8 – L	13 – P	18 – J
4 – S	9 – D	14 – F	19 – H
5 – N	10 – A	15 – G	20 – M

Answers – AND THE LOSER WAS . . . (1930s) (1)

1 – M	6 – T	11 – S	16 – I
2 – P	7 – O	12 – J	17 – A
3 – K	8 – N	13 – E	18 – D
4 – R	9 – C	14 – F	19 – H
5 – Q	10 – L	15 – G	20 – B

Answers – AND THE LOSER WAS . . . (1930s) (2)

1 – K	6 – T	11 – N	16 – B
2 – O	7 – R	12 – A	17 – H
3 – Q	8 – D	13 – P	18 – E
4 – I	9 – C	14 – G	19 – L
5 – S	10 – F	15 – J	20 – M

Answers – AND THE WINNER WAS . . . (1940)(1)

1 – O	6 – T	11 – B	16 – D
2 – N	7 – M	12 – P	17 – G
3 – I	8 – R	13 – C	18 – H
4 – S	9 – A	14 – J	19 – F
5 – Q	10 – E and L	15 – K	

Answers – AND THE WINNER WAS . . . (1940s) (2)

1 – M	6 – L	11 – P	16 – G
2 – Q	7 – S	12 – C	17 – B
3 – O	8 – D	13 – I	18 – F
4 – J	9 – T	14 – A	19 – H
5 – N	10 – R	15 – K	20 – E

Answers – AND THE LOSER WAS . . . (1940s) (1)

1 – M	6 – Q	11 – C	16 – I
2 – R	7 – O	12 – G	17 – B
3 – S	8 – P	13 – F	18 – H
4 – J	9 – T	14 – A	19 – L
5 – K	10 – N	15 – E	20 – D

Answers – AND THE LOSER WAS . . . (1940s) (2)

1 – K	6 – J	11 – D	16 – H
2 – N	7 – L	12 – O	17 – I
3 – Q	8 – P	13 – G	18 – A
4 – T	9 – M	14 – F	19 – E
5 – S	10 – R	15 – B	20 – C

Answers – AND THE LOSER WAS . . . (1940s) (3)

1 – M	6 – R	11 – O	16 – B
2 – P	7 – N	12 – T	17 – I
3 – K	8 – L	13 – J	18 – E
4 – S	9 – A	14 – C	19 – H
5 – Q	10 – F	15 – D	20 – G

Answers – AND THE LOSER WAS . . . (1940s) (4)

1 – M	6 – N	11 – P	16 – L
2 – R	7 – T	12 – A	17 – F
3 – O	8 – C	13 – B	18 – G
4 – K	9 – H	14 – J	19 – E
5 – S	10 – Q	15 – D	20 – I

Answers – AND THE WINNER WAS . . . (1950s) (1)

1 – S	6 – O	11 – H	16 – G
2 – M	7 – D	12 – E	17 – L
3 – T	8 – I	13 – B	18 – J
4 – Q	9 – R	14 – K	19 – N
5 – P	10 – A	15 – F	20 – C

Answers – AND THE WINNER WAS . . . (1950s) (2)

1 – J	6 – Q	11 – E	16 – E
2 – Q	7 – A	12 – N	17 – I
3 – M	8 – P	13 – B	18 – K
4 – L	9 – D or H	14 – G	19 – F
5 – O	10 – C	15 – I	

Answers – AND THE LOSER WAS . . . (1950s) (1)

1 – K	6 – Q	11 – D	16 – E
2 – I	7 – S	12 – T	17 – G
3 – P	8 – R	13 – B	18 – M
4 – O	9 – C	14 – J	19 – H
5 – L	10 – N	15 – A	20 – F

Answers – AND THE LOSER WAS . . . (1950s) (2)

1 – S	6 – N	11 – B	16 – H
2 – Q	7 – M	12 – E	17 – F
3 – P	8 – D	13 – T	18 – K
4 – L	9 – C	14 – G	19 – A
5 – R	10 – O	15 – I	20 – J

Answers – AND THE LOSER WAS . . . (1950s) (3)

1 – O	6 – P	11 – T	16 – H
2 – M	7 – J	12 – G	17 – E
3 – S	8 – A	13 – F	18 – B
4 – L	9 – R	14 – D	19 – C
5 – Q	10 – N	15 – I	20 – K

Answers – AND THE LOSER WAS . . . (1950s) (4)

1 – M	6 – S	11 – T	16 – J
2 – P	7 – N	12 – G	17 – C
3 – Q	8 – E	13 – H	18 – I
4 – R	9 – B	14 – D	19 – K
5 – O	10 – L	15 – A	20 – F

Answers – AND THE WINNER WAS . . . (1960s) (1)

1 – P or R	6 – L	11 – D	16 – B
2 – S	7 – I	12 – A	17 – H
3 – J	8 – N	13 – F	18 – K
4 – Q	9 – C	14 – E	19 – G
5 – T	10 – O	15 – M	

Answers – AND THE WINNER WAS . . . (1960s) (2)

1 – R	6 – J	11 – E	15 – F
2 – P	7 – M	12 – D	16 – E
3 – S	8 – Q	& L	17 – H
4 – K	9 – N	13 – G	18 – I
5 – O	10 – B	14 – A	19 – C

Answers – AND THE LOSER WAS . . . (1960s) (1)

1 – N	6 – S	11 – T	16 – H
2 – K	7 – M	12 – G	17 – I
3 – P	8 – A	13 – D	18 – C
4 – Q	9 – O	14 – B	19 – L
5 – R	10 – E	15 – J	20 – F

Answers – WINNERS AND LOSERS (1970s) (1)

1 – L	6 – D	11 – C	16 – K
2 – R	7 – N	12 – E	17 – F
3 – S	8 – Q	13 – A	18 – G
4 – M	9 – O	14 – H	19 – B
5 – P	10 – T	15 – I	20 – J

Answers – AND THE LOSER WAS . . . (1960s) (2)

1 – S	6 – L	11 – R	16 – C
2 – P	7 – O	12 – H	17 – E
3 – M	8 – Q	13 – I	18 – B
4 – A	9 – N	14 – J	19 – D
5 – T	10 – G	15 – K	20 – F

Answers – WINNERS AND LOSERS (1970s) (2)

1 – P	6 – Q	11 – M	16 – G
2 – N	7 – F	12 – A	17 – C
3 – L	8 – J	13 – I	18 – K
4 – R	9 – S	14 – H	19 – D
5 – O	10 – E	15 – T	20 – B

Answers – AND THE LOSER WAS . . . (1960s) (3)

1 – J	6 – Q	11 – L	16 – D
2 – N	7 – P	12 – O	17 – K
3 – S	8 – E	13 – T	18 – B
4 – M	9 – G	14 – C	19 – F
5 – R	10 – A	15 – I	20 – H

Answers – WINNERS AND LOSERS (1970s) (3)

1 – I	6 – L	11 – B	16 – S
2 – Q	7 – K	12 – G	17 – D
3 – O	8 – E	13 – R	18 – J
4 – N	9 – C	14 – F	19 – M
5 – P	10 – T	15 – H	20 – A

Answers – AND THE LOSER WAS . . . (1960s) (4)

1 – M	6 – O	11 – A	16 – E
2 – P	7 – T	12 – C	17 – K
3 – L	8 – N	13 – B	18 – G
4 – S	9 – D	14 – F	19 – J
5 – R	10 – Q	15 – H	20 – I

Answers – WINNERS AND LOSERS (1970s) (4)

1 – P	6 – L	11 – R	16 – E
2 – N	7 – Q	12 – T	17 – C
3 – K	8 – S	13 – D	18 – G
4 – O	9 – B	14 – A	19 – H
5 – M	10 – F	15 – J	20 – I